PENGUIN CLASSICS

THE LAST DAYS OF SOCRATES

PLATO (c. 424–347 BCE) stands, with his teacher Socrates and his pupil Aristotle, as one of the shapers of the whole intellectual tradition of the West. He came from a family that had long played a prominent part in Athenian politics, and it would have been natural for him to follow the same course; the reason for his not doing so, according to the seventh of the collection of letters attributed to him (all of them almost certainly inauthentic), was his disillusionment with the kind of politics that could lead, among other things, to the execution – in 399 – of Socrates. Rather less plausibly, the same letter suggests that Plato's several visits to the court of Dionysius II, tyrant of Syracuse in Sicily, were motivated by a desire to put his political theories – as developed above all in the master-work, *Republic* – into practice. The reform of society, on an ethical basis, certainly remained one of his central theoretical concerns. However, the focus of his thinking was on ethics itself, combined with a distinctive metaphysics and an equally distinctive view of the nature of the physical world. In the mid-380s, in Athens, he founded the Academy, the first permanent institution devoted to philosophical research and teaching.

Plato wrote over twenty philosophical dialogues, appearing in none himself (most of them have Socrates as chief speaker). His activity as a writer seems to have lasted over half a century; few authors in any language could claim to rival his peculiar combination of brilliant artistry and intellectual power.

CHRISTOPHER ROWE was until 2009 Professor of Greek in Durham University, where he moved in 1995 from the H. O. Wills Chair of Greek in the University of Bristol. His publications include *The Cambridge History of Greek and Roman Political Thought* (edited with Malcolm Schofield, 2000), *New Perspectives on Plato, Modern and Ancient* (edited with Julia Annas, 2002), *Plato's Lysis* (with Terry Penner, 2005), and *Plato and the Art of Philosophical Writing* (2007). In Sarah Broadie and Christopher Rowe, *Aristotle, Nicomachean Ethics* (2002), Sarah Broadie's philosophical commentary is accompanied by Christopher Rowe's translation. He has also translated, and/or written commentaries on Plato's *Phaedrus* (1986), *Phaedo* (1993), *Statesman* (1995) and *Symposium* (1998); his translation of *Phaedrus* appeared in Penguin Classics in 2005. In the Queen's Birthday Honours for 2009 he was made an OBE for services to scholarship.

PLATO

The Last Days of Socrates

Euthyphro, Apology, Crito, Phaedo

Translated with Introductions and Notes by
CHRISTOPHER ROWE

PENGUIN BOOKS

PENGUIN BOOKS

Published by the Penguin Group
Penguin Books Ltd, 80 Strand, London WC2R ORL, England
Penguin Group (USA) Inc., 375 Hudson Street, New York, New York 10014, USA
Penguin Group (Canada), 90 Eglinton Avenue East, Suite 700, Toronto, Ontario,
Canada M4P 2Y3 (a division of Pearson Penguin Canada Inc.)
Penguin Ireland, 25 St Stephen's Green, Dublin 2, Ireland (a division of Penguin Books Ltd)
Penguin Group (Australia), 250 Camberwell Road, Camberwell, Victoria 3124, Australia
(a division of Pearson Australia Group Pty Ltd)
Penguin Books India Pvt Ltd, 11 Community Centre, Panchsheel Park, New Delhi – 110 017, India
Penguin Group (NZ), 67 Apollo Drive, Rosedale, North Shore 0632, New Zealand
(a division of Pearson New Zealand Ltd)
Penguin Books (South Africa) (Pty) Ltd, 24 Sturdee Avenue, Rosebank, Johannesburg 2196, South Africa

Penguin Books Ltd, Registered Offices: 80 Strand, London WC2R ORL, England

www.penguin.com

This translation first published in Penguin Classics 2010
005

Translation and editorial material copyright © Christopher Rowe, 2010
All rights reserved

The moral right of the translator has been asserted

Set in 10.25/12.25pt Postscript Adobe Sabon
Typeset by TexTech International
Printed in England by Clays Ltd, St Ives plc

ISBN: 978-0-140-45549-6

www.greenpenguin.co.uk

MIX
Paper from
responsible sources
FSC™ C018179
www.fsc.org

Penguin Books is committed to a sustainable
future for our business, our readers and our planet.
This book is made from Forest Stewardship
Council™ certified paper.

ALWAYS LEARNING   PEARSON

Contents

Chronology

We know as little about Plato's life as we do about most ancient figures. The chronology of his writings – with the exception of the *Apology*, all are in dialogue form – is particularly uncertain. Nevertheless, studies of his style have resulted in a broad division of the works into three groups, which is reflected in the (very rough) chronology below. For this division, see especially Charles Kahn, 'On Platonic Chronology', in Julia Annas and Christopher Rowe (eds.), *New Perspectives on Plato, Modern and Ancient* (Cambridge, MA, 2002), pp. 93–127. (Only certainly genuine works are listed.)

c. 424 BCE Birth of Plato, son of Ariston. The story that the name 'Plato' derived from the adjective *platus*, 'broad' (referring to the width of the great man's shoulders, to his intellectual capacity or the 'breadth' of his style) has been discredited. (The usual date given for Plato's birth is 428 or 427; I have accepted the arguments of Debra Nails for placing the birth some three or four years later: Debra Nails, *The People of Plato* (Indianapolis, IN/Cambridge, MA, 2002).)

404 The defeat of Athens in the great war against Sparta (the 'Peloponnesian' war) signals the temporary end of the democracy which had governed Athens for most of the previous hundred years. It is replaced by a junta of oligarchs, at least two of whom are members of Plato's immediate family. The Thirty Tyrants, as they become known, last only a few months before being overthrown in a civil war and replaced by a revived democracy.

399 Under the new democratic government, Socrates – Plato's
mentor and friend for up to ten years previously – is brought
to trial on charges brought by private prosecutors. The
charges are failing to recognize the gods recognized by the
city and of introducing new divinities in their place; also of
corrupting the young. Socrates' condemnation and subsequent execution by hemlock poisoning are the last straw:
Plato more or less withdraws from the world of practical
politics.

390s Plato may have spent some time out of Athens, travelling
both in Greece and around the eastern Mediterranean.
Meanwhile, he is beginning to publish, i.e., to release works
to be copied for, and read by, others.

390s–380s Plato composes a large and varied group of works,
in alphabetical order as follows: '*Apology of Socrates*' (i.e.,
Defence of Socrates), *Charmides, Cratylus, Crito, Euthydemus, Euthyphro, Gorgias, Hippias Minor, Ion, Laches,
Lysis, Menexenus, Meno, Phaedo, Protagoras, Symposium*.
The relative dating of the items in this group is controversial, though it may be that *Cratylus, Phaedo* and *Symposium*
were among the last written.

389–388 Plato visits Sicily and southern Italy and establishes
contact with Pythagoreans in the area.

c. 387 Plato founds the Academy, an institute for research and
teaching, adjacent to one of the main gymnasia of Athens,
sacred to the local hero Academus.

380s–370s Second group of dialogues: *Parmenides, Phaedrus,
Republic, Theaetetus*.

367 Plato's second visit to Sicily, at the invitation of Dion, uncle
of Dionysius II, tyrant or dictator of Syracuse. Some have
supposed that Plato had hopes of making Dionysius an ideal
ruler, a philosopher-king; if so, they were soon dashed. Plato
evidently had some difficulty getting home.

c. 365 Arrival in the Academy of its most eminent member,
Aristotle.

361 Plato visits Sicily once more, for unknown reasons; in any
case this visit too seems to have ended badly.

360s–350s Third group of dialogues: *Philebus, Sophist, Statesman, Timaeus-Critias, Laws* (known to have been Plato's last work; he may still have been working on it when he died).

c. **347** Plato dies.

Acknowledgements

I am grateful to Peter Carson for first proposing to me the project of a new version of *The Last Days of Socrates*, at a moment when the original version was past its fiftieth birthday and – despite some significant revisions and improvements – showing its age. In putting the volume together, I have enjoyed the support of a magnificent team of helpers, who have all been through the translations and notes, in some cases more than once, and saved me from a variety of infelicities and blunders. Martin Foulkes consented to read my material as someone with an educated interest in, but no great familiarity with, Plato. Debra Nails looked at earlier versions of the translations and notes especially from the point of view of someone who regularly teaches Plato to US students; I soon lost count of the places where she either helped me refine the English of the translations or saved me from embarrassment in the notes. I have gladly accepted many of her suggestions – too many to be acknowledged individually. Finally, Heather Rowe has read and reread everything, rightly insisting on the removal of the worst idiosyncrasies in my English, and generally contributing a huge amount of time and effort towards helping put the whole into publishable form. The flaws that remain are mine alone.

Christopher Rowe
June 2009

General Introduction

1. PLATO AND SOCRATES

Socrates (469–399 BCE) and Plato (c. 424–347), together with Plato's student Aristotle (384–322), are the three dominant figures in ancient Greek philosophy; everything that comes after them is partly shaped by them. Surprisingly, since he himself wrote nothing, Socrates was probably the most influential of the three, not only providing the foundations for Plato's philosophy, and thus for a whole succession of Platonist thinkers, but living on as the figurehead and inspiration of a range of schools that were founded in the fourth century BCE, the most important and long-lasting of which was that of the Stoics. In the modern period too Socrates has remained a pivotal figure, surfacing in different guises, whether as friend or enemy, in the work of Hegel, Kierkegaard and Nietzsche.

But it was Plato's writings, above all, that assured Socrates' lasting influence; and especially those describing, or rather purporting to describe, the great man's last days – *Euthyphro*, *Apology*, *Crito* and *Phaedo*, but most of all *Phaedo*, which ends with the death scene. There are few nowadays who would insist even that the *Apology of Socrates* – to give it its full title, i.e., *Socrates' Defence* – gives us what Socrates actually said at his trial. The *Phaedo*, too, while – like the *Apology* – based on real events, is mostly a fiction. All four works in the present volume, which centre on the trial and execution, are in fact as much introductions to Plato's own thinking as they are celebrations of Socrates. They are also at least partly written as introductions to philosophy itself: the *Phaedo*, in particular, has a lot to say not just about the importance of philosophy but also about how philosophy is to be done. In more than one sense, then, the title of the present volume is misleading, if harmlessly so. The four works it contains are not only not a historical account of anything, they are hardly history at all. What they represent above all is philosophy as Plato, the student of Socrates, understood and wished to promote it. Three of the four, *Euthyphro*, *Crito* and *Phaedo*, also represent philosophy in the form in which Socrates evidently understood it: that is, in the form of conversation, or dialogue. The written dialogue was the medium that – with the necessary exception of the *Apology* – Plato preferred throughout. He was not the only or even the first to use it, but ancient authorities were agreed that no one else even approached his mastery of the form.

How much of the original Socrates there is in these four works, and how much of Plato, is an impossible question to answer. In the modern period it has often been supposed that Plato's writing career began with a 'Socratic' period, in which he concentrated on a more or less faithful reproduction of his teacher's ideas and arguments, before moving on and introducing the ideas that subsequent generations have always regarded as the distinctive features of Platonic thought: above all the 'forms' or 'ideas',[1] belief in an immortal soul, and the proposal that society would be better off if run by philosophers. Now as it happens, these features are either absent from or, at least, not prominent in *Euthyphro*, *Apology* and *Crito*, whereas the *Phaedo* not only devotes most of its pages to an attempt to justify the belief in immortality, but in doing so uses arguments that heavily depend on the hypothesis of 'forms' (i.e., the hypothesis that there are such things). By the measure in question, then, the first three works will look more 'Socratic', the *Phaedo* more Platonic. However, it is unclear whether separating off the *Phaedo* in this way from the others is particularly helpful; indeed it may be positively unhelpful, if it leads us to miss the clear continuities between all four. In particular, Socrates in the *Phaedo* introduces the theme of the fate of the soul after death in a way that clearly evokes, and is clearly intended to evoke, some more fleeting hints on the same subject at the end of the *Apology*, and similarly goes out of his way to emphasize that the things he will label 'forms' are actually the sorts of things he and other members of his circle are talking about all the time when they discuss the nature of goodness, or justice, or piety, or whatever it may be[2] – piety being the very subject of the first of our group, the *Euthyphro*. Admittedly, Socrates' interlocutor in that dialogue is clearly from outside Socrates' circle, and no philosopher; and it may still be, as advocates of a 'Socratic' period in Plato will suppose, that the 'forms' of piety, or courage, or whatever it may be, as they appear in the *Phaedo*, are quite distinct from the piety, courage and so on that we see Socrates discuss in the *Euthyphro*, the *Laches* and other similar dialogues. Nevertheless, it is by no means obvious that this is so, and it is at least an interesting question how much of an innovation 'forms' as understood in the *Phaedo* actually are.

In general, there seems little to be gained by trying to distinguish the parts of Plato's Socrates that are true to the original Socrates from those that are not. The sources present us with other Socrateses too: for example there is the Socrates of the general and historian Xenophon, who wrote his own version of Socrates' defence speech. There is the Socrates of the comic poet Aristophanes, whom Plato's Socrates, in the *Apology*, blames for making all sorts of false accusations against him in his plays. Aristotle gives us yet another Socrates, with ideas sharply different from Plato's (it is Aristotle, indeed, whose evidence ultimately lies behind the idea of a distinct 'Socratic' period in Plato). But these other Socrateses, too, differ as much from each other as they do from Plato's, and many have concluded, reasonably enough, that the search for the actual, historical Socrates is in principle hopeless, as well as theoretically misconceived (after all, there can be no Socrates who isn't *someone*'s).

At the same time, there is virtual unanimity among our sources on certain things about Socrates. If they fail to agree about the detail of his ideas, there is little or no disagreement that he was shortish and ugly, with protruding eyes, menacing eyebrows, and a snub nose; that he combined eroticism with a singular restraint; that he liked nothing better than talking, especially to beautiful young men; that he was the son of a stonemason and a midwife; and that he had an extraordinarily powerful, even mesmerizing, effect on those who came close to him, though – to judge by the number of his detractors – he could evidently also arouse powerfully negative feelings towards him.[3]

Plato, it seems, was one of those who came under Socrates' spell. But about Plato, and about his life we know rather less than we do about Socrates. He is not on the cast-list for any of his dialogues – even his name is mentioned only twice in the whole corpus,[4] and the many ancient biographies, generally compiled long after his death, are neither particularly informative nor reliable. Our best source is one of a collection of thirteen letters handed down as part of the corpus: the collection is for the most part certainly spurious, but the longest, the seventh, may be genuine, and even if it was not written by Plato, its author was evidently a near-contemporary of his. What we know independently of this letter is that he came from a wealthy family with a pedigree second to none; that he wrote, and taught, in Athens for most of his life without interference from the authorities, despite the profoundly critical, even revolutionary, nature of his political writings; and that he founded his Academy, as a centre of teaching and research. One of the most useful additions the *Seventh Letter* makes to this bare picture is a description of the effect that the execution of Socrates had on the young Plato, still in his mid-twenties: that event, the letter tells us, made him finally decide against a career in politics as currently practised, reflecting that the only salvation for humankind would be to bring about the union of political power with philosophy. On this account, then, Socrates' death – the focus of the four dialogues in the present volume – represented a turning-point for Plato himself. The second important contribution made by the letter to our understanding of Plato lies in its account of a well-meaning but ultimately disastrous involvement in the politics of the Sicilian city of Syracuse. He evidently thought that he might realize, in Syracuse, the scenario outlined in both of his two political *tours de force*, *Republic* and

Laws, of a philosophically based political expert helping a young autocrat to set up the best possible kind of city and constitution; but his relationship with the young prince Dionysius did not turn out well – after Dionysius succeeded to power, things went from bad to worse, and Plato twice had serious difficulty in getting away safe from Syracuse, or at all. Evidently, then, he was prepared not just to write about the problems of existing political arrangements, of all kinds, but to try to follow up his ideas in practice. Whatever these episodes may tell us about the quality of his practical judgement, they surely testify to the strength of his commitment to radical reform.

2. 'WHAT EXACTLY IS IT THAT YOU *DO*, SOCRATES?'

The ultimate objects of Plato's critique are, however, not so much political institutions themselves as the societies they help to create and maintain. Politicians and leaders are to blame for not using their power to change society and individuals in the way they could. Plato drives home his attack on contemporary society everywhere in his writing, not merely in his overtly political works. Thus, for example, we find his Socrates, in the *Phaedo*, proposing that people fail even to understand what the core virtues of justice, courage or moderation actually are: they think they are living justly and moderately and behaving courageously, but they are actually doing nothing of the sort. In his picture of the afterlife, they – or rather their souls – will find themselves on the gloomy shores of lake Acheron, being prepared for a return to the world above in the form of bees, perhaps, or ants, or possibly human beings. The lesson is clear. Ordinary, that is, non-philosophical, people live lives that are in truth barely distinguishable from those of irrational animals, who may be capable of social living and of rubbing along with each other, but in an entirely unreflective way. The constant refrain of Plato's Socrates is that his fellow citizens fail to recognize that they know nothing. He doesn't know anything himself, he says, but at least he knows he doesn't: thus he is in a position to do something about it, and begin living a life that is truly human because it is rational, and 'examined'.

In his defence speech, in the *Apology*, Socrates imagines someone, perhaps a member of the jury, asking if he isn't ashamed to be doing something that puts him in the danger he's now in, of losing his life. This imaginary questioner clearly has no real idea what Socrates actually does. Socrates proceeds to enlighten him:

> What I *do*, as I move around among you, is just this: I try to per-
> suade you, whether younger or older, to give less priority, and
> devote less zeal, to the care of your bodies or of your money than
> to the care of your soul and trying to make it as good as it can be.
> What I say to you is: 'It's not from money that excellence comes,
> but from excellence money and the other things, all of them,
> come to be good for human beings, whether in private or in pub-
> lic life.'[5]

The form that this 'persuasion' takes is well illustrated by the *Euthyphro*, in which Socrates discusses the nature of 'piety', the very thing that his prosecutors at his trial are accusing him of lacking. But how can they do that, if they have not thought about what piety really is? Euthyphro shows that he doesn't know what it is, either. But because he still supposes that he does (as a self-proclaimed religious expert), and everyone else supposes they do, none of them has any inclination to pursue the kind of inquiry Socrates thinks necessary. In failing to do this, they fail to 'care for their souls' (as he puts it), preferring to go on exercising in the gymnasium or making money rather than making themselves, their souls, 'as good as possible'. The way to do that, as he makes clear, is precisely through asking questions, challenging themselves and others and making them-selves as *wise* as possible; and wisdom itself will bring the genu-ine virtues in its train. Wisdom it is, too, that gives everything else its value ('from excellence money and the other things . . . come to be good'). What is the point of money, or honours, or power, if you have no idea of what to use them for?

Plato's Socrates, then, and presumably Plato himself, are thoroughgoing radicals. The key to life lies not in observing conventional opinions and usage, but in questioning them, and only committing oneself to what can be rationally justified – or rather, to what so far seems better justified than the alternatives. Live any other way, and you run the risk of not living a genuinely human life: the unexamined life, declares Socrates, is unliveable for a human being.[6] But at the same time he has some fairly well-defined views about just what *can* be rationally justified. We do not improve the quality of our lives, or our 'souls', just by the act of examining, whether ourselves or others, but by altering our behaviour in the way that such examination shows to be necessary; or in other words, not merely by doing philosophy, but by applying to our practice whatever substantive lessons philosophy teaches us. The outcome, Socrates proposes, for ordinary, conventional people, would be a complete change in our priorities, a new sense of what is important in life, and new and better ways of dealing with each other.

The truly radical nature of Plato's writing is often missed by his readers, not least because it is often partly concealed by the form of that writing. After all, the character Socrates is for much of the time talking to representatives of the very people whose attitudes and opinions he is criticizing and trying to change, and therefore more often than not has to start from their assumptions rather than from his own. Indeed, on some occasions the conversation will end without his having shown his hand in any but the most sketchy and tantalizing way. So it is with what are often called the 'dialogues of definition', like the *Euthyphro*, which formally end in failure to define the target item – piety in the *Euthyphro*, courage in the *Laches*, moderation in the *Charmides* – and may leave the impression that the main aim of the exercise was to find a simple set of words to express the nature of the definiendum. In such cases the real purpose is rather to disturb the interlocutor's, and perhaps the reader's, assumptions about the subject in question, and to suggest new starting-points, which always have something to do with that connection between virtue or excellence and wisdom, or knowledge.

For Plato's Socrates, in fact, virtue *is* knowledge, of a particular sort: knowledge about good and bad, that is, what is good and bad for the agent. This identification between virtue and knowledge at first sight looks strange; it is one of the so-called 'Socratic paradoxes'. But Socrates' paradoxes are intended not merely to surprise or shock. They are rather intended as plain statements of the truth. Thus, in this case, he is seriously proposing that virtue – courage, for example, or justice – *is* a matter of knowing what is really good and what is really bad, i.e., for oneself. Behind this proposal lie two more: first, that no one actually wants to do what is bad for himself or herself; and second, that all our desires (even what Socrates calls 'desires of the body' in the *Phaedo*) are for the good; that is, for what is really good for us. In the terms of another 'Socratic paradox', 'no one goes wrong intentionally':[7] again, Socrates intends this to be taken quite literally, so ruling out even the possibility of what has traditionally come to be known as 'acratic' – i.e., un-self-controlled – behaviour, in which our desires and passions get the better of us and cause us to behave contrary to our rational judgements.[8] This is why there is so much emphasis, in the *Euthyphro*, the *Apology*, the *Phaedo* and elsewhere, on the importance of knowledge. The problem is never with our desires, always and only with our beliefs. We all want to live happy and successful lives, which for Socrates as for his contemporaries will include living justly, courageously and so on; and for that, we will all desperately be in need of knowledge. Anything less, or at least anything less than a commitment to *searching* for knowledge, will reduce us – whether we recognize it or not – to the state of animals. Which human being would wish, knowingly or unknowingly, to live the life of a bee or an ant?

'Philosophy', then, for Plato, is nothing if it is not radical. Its outcomes will tend always to be, in principle, provisional: that is one important reason for his Socrates' continuing reluctance to claim that he knows anything, or anything very much. But what he will insist on is that the way things are is actually very different from the way they appear to be, to the ordinary, non-philosophical eye. Socrates may observe conventional forms, and conventional usage, but he will always have a perspective on what he is doing that is significantly at odds with the conventional; frequently, he will interpret conventional ideas in new ways and claim that that was what they amounted to, what their originators had in mind, all along – which, in a sense, will be perfectly reasonable, provided only that his perspective is, as he claims, the true one.

3. GODS, THE AFTERLIFE, AND THE TRUE NATURE OF THE COSMOS

One subject on which Plato's Socrates is especially prone to innovate is that of the nature of the gods. In particular, he will not accept the traditional view of the gods as capricious and unpredictable individuals, exhibiting the worst as well as the best of human characteristics but on a superhuman scale, and capable of things that even human society regards as unspeakable: parricide, infanticide, incest. Quietly and consistently, Socrates substitutes a set of gods that share the same names but are also everything that he thinks human beings should be but are not; in particular, they are unfailingly rational, wise, even providential. And he does this even, indeed especially, in the context of his trial on a charge of *impiety*, in the *Euthyphro*, then in his defence in the *Apology*, and in the *Phaedo*. His references to his own personal 'divinity', and the 'divine voice' that intervenes with him directly from time to time, introduce a still further level of innovation, even as he continues to maintain that he observes an exceptional piety. Here is another particularly striking example of what we might be inclined, probably unhelpfully, to call redefinition;[9] Socrates himself would presumably say that he had just understood piety better than everyone else.

Socrates' treatment of Hades, the traditional destination of the dead, follows a similar pattern. The traditional Hades is a dreadful place, where everyone – or their insubstantial 'souls' or 'shades' ('shadows') – suffers equally, except for a few who have attracted the particular anger of the gods; a few others, privileged by their divine connections, are granted an indefinite stay elsewhere, on the Isles of the Blest. By contrast the Hades Socrates describes in the *Phaedo*, on the authority of an unnamed person or persons, is ruled over by a 'good and wise god' (Hades himself), and its geography, comprising regions above us as well as below the earth, provides for the reward of genuine goodness and wisdom as well as for the punishment of criminals, and that unhappy treatment handed out to the unfortunate unphilosophical majority. In fact the whole description bears the marks of an imaginative projection of what the world would look like, from here, if it were so designed that the good and wise prospered and the bad and ignorant suffered in proportion to the degrees of their goodness and badness. That the world is in fact so constructed is a standard claim in Plato,[10] forming part of a larger teleological view of the cosmos as a whole. The gods, it seems, look after their own – or, to put it another way, our universe is ruled by reason and justice.

4. 'FORMS'

If, as Socrates proposes, philosophers can in principle *discover* the true nature of justice, courage, piety, goodness, or whatever it may be, then it seems that these things must somehow be there, in nature, waiting to be discovered. In the *Phaedo*, he founds three major arguments on the hypothesis that there are indeed such entities, existing 'in nature'[11] – and suggests, as he does so, that the hypothesis will already be familiar to anyone who, like his two interlocutors Simmias and Cebes, has taken part in philosophical discussions with him. As we have seen in §1 above, this can be taken in one of two ways: either (1) Plato is hinting that there is something special and esoteric about the entities in question, which only his close associates will be privy to; or else (2) he is suggesting exactly the opposite, namely that they are precisely the sorts of things presupposed in other dialogues – *Euthyphro*, on piety, say, or *Laches* on courage – and so in principle available to any reader. On the whole, it seems best at least to begin by taking the second option. This is for two reasons: first, in the *Euthyphro* Socrates gives us rather few hints about what kind of thing this piety is whose 'essence' he is investigating;[12] second, in the *Phaedo* itself he shows some signs of wanting to suggest that, however important 'forms' may be, not just for his argument but for our understanding of the nature of things, they are at bottom things whose existence most of us either already to some extent accept – even if we do not fully understand what it is that we are accepting – or can readily be brought to accept.[13] The translation of the *Phaedo* offered in the present volume accordingly attempts to treat the relevant contexts in as low-key a way as possible, and to avoid any suggestion that Plato is talking over our – his readers' – heads;[14] meanwhile notes to the translation will indicate any places where such a policy may risk short-changing the reader, and make good the deficit.

The key points about 'forms' are these. Philosophers systematically talk, as ordinary people sometimes talk, about things 'in the abstract': justice, goodness, beauty, and so on.[15] Plato's philosopher, by contrast, describes such talk as being about things 'in themselves', or 'by themselves', where the phrase 'by itself',[16] in each case, serves a dual purpose. On the one hand, 'by itself' distinguishes the justice (or whatever it is) being talked about from the things – people, or actions, or whatever – that are just, or have justice 'in' them;[17] on the other, the phrase indicates completeness and perfection. Just people or just actions may simultaneously be unjust in some respect or other; justice by itself, or justice itself, will always be exactly what it is and nothing else. There may even not be any perfectly just people or just actions at all – but justice (by) itself will continue to exist, perfectly encapsulating (however it may do so) that justice, perfect and entire, to which people will aspire in their actions. Just so, it may well be that there are no genuine statesmen actually in existence, and never have been (that seems to be Plato's view),[18] but statesmanship itself, or the 'form' of statesmanship, *does* exist, always has and always will, to be investigated and imitated to the best of our ability. Outside space as well as time, 'forms' exist – if Socrates' 'hypothesis' in the *Phaedo* is correct, as he believes it is – as paradigms for human life and action. *These* are the things that – whether we know it or not – we are talking about when we discuss things, as we say, 'in the abstract'; they are anything *but* abstract. If we ask 'but what kind of thing is *that*?', the simplest answer is: the same kind of thing that numbers are for a 'platonizing' mathematician, i.e., a mathematician who believes in the substantive reality of numbers.

However there are not only forms of 'the good, the fine and the just', and of other things in the sphere of value; as we discover from the *Phaedo*, there are also forms of equality, of numbers,[19] of bigness and smallness, hotness, coldness, and so on. The role of forms as 'paradigms' is merely an aspect of their more general role in explanation: things around us are what they are – just, equal, three, big, cold ... by virtue of their relationship with the relevant forms. Quite what that relationship is, Socrates leaves an open question;[20] he also leaves open how we come to have knowledge of forms, if we come to have it at all, if they are neither part of this world nor, as such, in the things that 'share in' them.[21] He argues that our souls gain knowledge of forms at some time prior to their entry into bodies, i.e., when we are born as composites of soul and body;[22] that we forget that knowledge at birth, but with effort can recover it at least partially. But how exactly our souls gained that original knowledge, if not by the kind of painstaking philosophical work illustrated in the *Phaedo* itself,[23] he does not say.

5. PLATO'S RELATIONSHIP
WITH HIS READERS

The foregoing sections have been written on the general assumption that it is Socrates who speaks for Plato; and though many have questioned such an assumption, it still appears perfectly reasonable, certainly in the context of *Euthyphro*, *Apology*, *Crito* and *Phaedo*. The one workable alternative is to suppose that Plato's voice is to be identified with that of all his characters taken together (perhaps even including the jurors); but the dominance of the figure of Socrates is such that even this might amount to no more than a minor – if nevertheless important – corrective to a straightforward identification between Socrates and Plato.[24]

The more pressing and difficult question is about Plato's audience: what kind, or kinds, of readers did he intend to address? This is an issue that has already surfaced more than once in this Introduction, in relation to the *Phaedo*: was he writing for a specialized or a more general readership? If we look at other Platonic works, some stand out as plainly too technical and difficult for the ordinary reader; perhaps above all the *Parmenides*, but with the *Sophist*, the *Statesman*, the *Theaetetus* or the *Philebus* not far behind. The *Phaedo*, in terms of difficulty, is not in this league at all. Indeed, with the exception of some parts (and not just the ones that bring in 'forms'), the *Phaedo* is thoroughly accessible: clear, readable and attractive, with a degree of interplay between the characters, of incident, and of variations of pace and tone, that are probably unmatched except in the *Symposium*. In short, it seems likely that Plato intended the *Phaedo* for a wide audience; perhaps for any intelligent person capable of reading Greek. Similarly with the *Apology*, which after all is formally addressed to a jury of 500 (or 501) citizens; and probably the *Crito* too. Though very different from either of the other two works, the *Crito* is relatively simple in terms of its argument, addressed as it is to one of the slower members of the Socratic circle (Crito, who generally shows more concern for practical arrangements than he does taste for argument), and probably in part adapted to his needs. The *Euthyphro*, perhaps, is the odd one out among the works in the present volume, being drier and more technical, in proportion to its short length, than any of the other three.

But even here appearances may be deceptive. The *Euthyphro*, after all, finds Socrates addressing, and demolishing, someone with absolutely no experience of philosophy, or of argument, and it is not immediately clear why Plato should expect such a spectacle to attract readers who were already better qualified philosophically than Euthyphro (and might in any case be expected to be familiar with the fairly basic points that are made). By and large, the best guide to the intended readership of a Platonic work is probably the type of interlocutors chosen to take part in it. This makes the *Phaedo*, which has a double set of interlocutors, particularly interesting: see the Introduction to the *Phaedo* below.

6. A NOTE ON 'SOUL'

The 'soul' in the *Apology* is both what we improve by caring for – and doing something about acquiring – wisdom and truth,[25] and also that part or aspect of us that continues in existence after our death and relocates to Hades. In the *Crito*, it is presumably the part of us that Socrates says is improved by justice and corrupted by injustice, as the body is corrupted by what's unhealthy;[26] that he holds back from using the term 'soul' here (as we might have expected, and as the *Apology* shows he might easily have done) might simply derive from a desire to keep away, in the context of the particular argument he is conducting, from the larger issues that the term 'soul', or *psuchê*, would by itself tend to raise for a Greek of the fifth and fourth centuries BCE. For despite the fact that the term regularly occurs in medical contexts, standing for something like our 'mind' as opposed to body, one of its most immediate associations would have been with death, or, more precisely, with the *psuchê*, 'soul' or 'shade', which in Homer flits off to Hades when we die.[27] The fate of the soul, whatever sort of thing this might be, is supremely relevant to Socrates' argument in the *Apology*; to introduce it in the *Crito* would be merely distracting.

'That part of us, whatever it is, to which injustice and justice attach':[28] the nature of this mysterious entity is finally identified in the *Phaedo*, and precisely by contrast with the Homeric 'soul'.[29] 'Soul', as Plato's Socrates understands it, is on the one hand what brings life, in all its forms and aspects, to the body, and, on the other, a rational entity, somehow – in its essential nature – akin to the forms. Later, especially Christian, conceptions of 'soul' will have much in common with, and indeed derive much from, this Platonic conception, but it is important not to read history backwards in this case, and begin reading later ideas back into Plato.

7. THE DEATH OF SOCRATES

Quite why Socrates was tried and condemned to death remains a controversial question. That he could actually have been guilty as charged, of impiety and 'corrupting the young', has seemed to most people, especially those who have read the *Apology*, implausible to the highest degree; though evidently a fair sample of Athenians at the time – a majority of the huge jury – *did* think him guilty. A further question is why he should have been put on trial just then, in 399 BCE. The easiest answer to both questions is probably that a group of influential people with a grudge against him simply took the opportunity offered by a time of political instability to get rid of an old enemy, perhaps because of his radical political views; perhaps because of his – apparently quite innocent – earlier association with prominent members of the oligarchic regime; or perhaps even because he had humiliated them.[30] This is consistent both with the *Apology* itself,[31] and with the *Seventh Letter*. 'By some chance', the author of the letter writes,

> certain powerful individuals took this friend of ours, Socrates, to court, on the most shameless of charges, and one that was least appropriate to him: they prosecuted him for *impiety*, and the jury condemned him – the very person who, when they themselves were suffering the misfortune of exile, refused to take part in the unjust arrest of one of their friends.[32]

But the argument will evidently go on, for as long as we moderns continue to be captivated by the apparent enormity of the mistake the Athenians made – in Plato's view, as endorsed by the vast majority of his readers – in killing off someone who was at worst a free-thinker and who turned out, by most measures, to be *the* founding figure of Western philosophy.

NOTES

1. See §4 of this Introduction.
2. See especially *Phaedo* 75c–d. In order to refer to particular passages in Plato, this volume uses – as do all modern translations and editions – the page numbers and page sections (usually five, marked a–e) as fixed by the Stephanus edition of Plato's text, dating from the Renaissance. Thus '*Phaedo* 75c–d' means 'sections c to d of page 75 of the volume of the Stephanus edition containing the *Phaedo*', and will take the reader straight to the relevant passage in the translation below, where the markers are printed in the margin.
3. The *Apology* gives us more detail of some particular events in Socrates' life; see also Alcibiades' encomium of him at the end of the *Symposium*, which describes among other things his bravery as a soldier on campaign.
4. See *Apology* 34a, *Phaedo* 59b.
5. *Apology* 30b.
6. *Apology* 38a: 'for a human being a life without examination is actually not worth living'.
7. Often represented, misleadingly, in the form 'No one *does* wrong willingly'.
8. The special theory of human action of Socrates' that is involved here generally goes under the heading of (Socratic) 'intellectualism', because of the special role given to intellect over against the passions or desires.
9. 'Unhelpfully', because Socrates' concern is never with the mere definition of *terms*.
10. The claim is made in the *Apology* as well as in the *Phaedo*, if in a rather less elaborate form; it is also hinted at in both *Euthyphro* and *Crito*.
11. The phrase is from the *Phaedo* (103b).
12. See *Euthyphro* 11a.
13. Thus when first introducing what he will only many pages later call 'forms', at *Phaedo* 65d, he asks simply 'Do we say that there exists something that's just and nothing but just?', by which – so long as 'we' refers to people generally, not just a few experts – he

seems to have in mind no more than our ability to talk and think about *justice*, by itself (i.e., whatever kind of thing it might be).

14. On Plato's intended readership, see §5 below.

15. For Plato and his Socrates, the good, the beautiful or fine and the just are in fact *the* key subjects.

16. Or just 'itself', as in 'the good itself', etc.; 'by itself' is merely a more informative rendering of the Greek *auto*.

17. In some contexts, 'in itself' may also serve to separate off (e.g.) justice as it is 'in nature' (see *Phaedo* 103b) from the justice 'in us'; but the crucial distinction will be that between justice, itself, and particular just things.

18. The example is taken from the dialogue *Statesman*.

19. The 'platonizing' mathematician, then, is genuinely following Plato.

20. See *Phaedo* 100d.

21. 'Sharing in' is Plato's standard – metaphorical – term for the relationship between particulars and forms.

22. 'Their entry into bodies': that is, their *re*-entry, bound as they are into an unending cycle of death and rebirth.

23. That is, in some previous life, or in some dialectical encounter of souls in between lives.

24. If Euthyphro in the *Euthyphro* and Crito in the *Crito* make little or no input (still less, the jury or the prosecutors in the *Apology*), Socrates himself will fully acknowledge the contribution of Cebes and Simmias to the outcomes of the *Phaedo*.

25. *Apology* 29e, 30b.

26. *Crito* 47d.

27. See *Phaedo* 70a–b; the notes to the passage give some of the basic Homeric references.

28. *Crito* 47e–48a.

29. *Phaedo* 70a-b again, with the arguments that follow.

30. 'Political instability': the democracy had not long been restored, after a brief period of oligarchic rule (see, e.g., *Apology* 21a). For Socrates' humiliation of politicians, see *Apology* 21c.

31. See *Apology* 23e–24a.

32. *Seventh Letter* 325b–c; for the incident in question, see *Apology* 32c–d.

Select Bibliography
and Further Reading

On the Cultural and Historical Background

Walter Burkert, *Greek Religion* (Cambridge, MA, 1985).

Paul Cartledge, *Ancient Political Thought in Practice* (Cambridge, 2009). (Includes some reflections on Socrates' death.)

Kenneth Dover, *Greek Popular Morality in the Time of Plato and Aristotle* (Berkeley/Los Angeles, 1974).

Charles H. Kahn, *Pythagoras and the Pythagoreans* (Indianapolis/Cambridge, MA, 2001).

Robert Parker, *Athenian Religion: A History* (Oxford, 1998).

Christoph Riedweg, *Pythagoras: His Life, Teaching and Influence*, tr. S. Rendall (Ithaca, NY, 2002).

The Greek Text

John Burnet, *Platonis opera*, vol. I (Oxford (Oxford Classical Texts), 1903).

E. A. Duke, W. F. Hicken, W. S. M. Nicoll, D. B. Robinson, J. C. G. Strachan, *Platonis opera*, vol. I (Oxford (Oxford Classical Texts), 1995). (The 'new Oxford' text.)

A Complete English Translation of Plato

John M. Cooper (ed.), *Plato: Complete Works* (Indianapolis/Cambridge, MA, 1997).

On Plato and Socrates

Julia Annas and Christopher Rowe (eds.), *New Perspectives on Plato, Modern and Ancient* (Cambridge, MA, 2002).

Ruby Blondell, *The Play of Character in Plato's Dialogues* (Cambridge, 2002). (Thought-provoking on the general issue of the relationship between the philosophical and the literary and dramatic elements in the dialogues.)

Gail Fine (ed.), *Plato I* and *II* (Oxford, 1999). (A useful general collection of articles on Plato.)

Terence Irwin, *Plato's Ethics* (Oxford, 1995). (A standard modern treatment of its subject.)

Charles H. Kahn, *Plato and the Socratic Dialogue: The Philosophical Use of a Literary Form* (Cambridge, 1996).

Mark McPherran, *The Religion of Socrates* (University Park, PA, 1996).

Debra Nails, *The People of Plato* (Indianapolis/Cambridge, MA, 2003). (A complete prosopography of the people who figure in Plato's dialogues; indispensable.)

Andrea W. Nightingale, *Genres in Dialogue: Plato and the Construct of Philosophy* (Cambridge, 1995). (On the intersection between philosophy and literature in Plato.)

Catalin Partenie (ed.), *Plato's Myths* (Cambridge, 2009).

Terry Penner, 'Socrates and the Early Dialogues', in Richard Kraut (ed.), *The Cambridge Companion to Plato* (Cambridge, 1992), pp. 121–69. (A short account of the Socratic theory of desire and action; for a much longer and more complete account, see the following item.)

Terry Penner and Christopher Rowe, *Plato's Lysis* (Cambridge, 2005).

Gerald A. Press, *Who Speaks for Plato?* (Lanham, MD, 2000).

C(hristopher) J. Rowe, *Plato* (2nd edition, London, 2003). (A basic introduction to Plato which acknowledges that he wrote *dialogues*.)

Christopher Rowe, *Plato and the Art of Philosophical Writing* (Cambridge, 2007). (Includes detailed analysis of the *Apology* and *Phaedo*, and places them in the larger context of Plato's work.)

Gerasimos Santas, *Goodness and Justice: Plato, Aristotle and the Moderns* (Oxford, 2001).

Nicholas D. Smith and Thomas Brickhouse, *Plato's Socrates* (Oxford, 1994).

I. F. Stone, *The Trial of Socrates* (Boston, 1987).

Thomas Szlezák, *Reading Plato* (London, 1999). (A useful short introduction.)

C. C. W. Taylor, *A Very Short Introduction to Socrates* (Oxford, 2000). (Very short, but very useful.)

Gregory Vlastos, *Socrates: Ironist and Moral Philosopher* (Ithaca, 1991). (A modern classic.)

Robin Waterfield, *Why Socrates Died: Dispelling the Myths* (London, 2009).

On the *Euthyphro*

R. E. Allen, *Euthyphro and the Earlier Theory of Forms* (New York, 1970).

Peter T. Geach, 'Plato's *Euthyphro*: An Analysis and Commentary', *The Monist* 50 (1966), pp. 369–82.

On the *Apology*

Michael C. Stokes, *Plato: Apology, with Introduction, Translation and Commentary* (Warminster, 1997).

E. de Strycker and S. R. Slings, *Plato's Apology of Socrates: A Literary and Philosophical Study with a Running Commentary* (Leiden, 1994).

On the *Crito*

R. E. Allen, *Socrates and Legal Obligation* (Minneapolis, 1980).

David Bostock, 'The Interpretation of Plato's *Crito*', *Phronesis* 35 (1990), pp. 1–20.

Richard Kraut, *Socrates and the State* (Princeton, 1983).

Mitchell Miller, 'The Arguments I Seem to Hear: Argument and Irony in *Crito*', *Phronesis* 41 (1996), pp. 121–37.

Terry Penner, 'Two Notes on the *Crito*: The Impotence of the Many, and "Persuade or Obey"', *Classical Quarterly* 47 (1997), pp. 153–66.

On the *Phaedo*

George Boys-Stones, 'Phaedo of Elis and Plato on the Soul', *Phronesis* 49 (2004), pp. 1–23. (Raises the question whether Phaedo's own theory of soul, in his dialogue *Zopyrus*, may have had some part to play in Plato's construction of the *Phaedo*.)

Nicholas Denyer, 'The *Phaedo*'s Final Argument', in Dominic Scott (ed.), *Maieusis: Essays in Ancient Philosophy in Honour of Myles Burnyeat* (Oxford, 2007), pp. 87–96.

David Gallop, *Plato's Phaedo* (Oxford, 1975). (A philosophical commentary.)

Denis O'Brien, 'The Last Argument in Plato's *Phaedo*', *Classical Quarterly* 17 (1967), pp. 198–231; 18 (1968), pp. 95–106.

C(hristopher) J. Rowe, *Plato: Phaedo* (Cambridge, 1993). (A commentary with a more linguistic emphasis than Gallop.)

Dominic Scott, *Recollection and Experience: Plato's Theory of Learning and Its Successors* (Cambridge, 1995).

David Sedley, 'Teleology and Myth in Plato's *Phaedo*', *Proceedings of the Boston Area Colloquium in Ancient Philosophy* 5 (1990), pp. 359–83.

David Sedley, 'The Dramatis Personae of Plato's *Phaedo*', in Timothy Smiley (ed.), *Philosophical Dialogues: Plato, Hume, Wittgenstein* (Oxford, 1995), pp. 3–26.

David Sedley, 'Equal Sticks and Stones', in Dominic Scott (ed.), *Maieusis: Essays in Ancient Philosophy in Honour of Myles Burnyeat* (Oxford, 2007), pp. 68–86.

C. J. F. Williams, 'On Dying', *Philosophy* 44 (1969), pp. 217–30.

On the Afterlife of Socrates and Plato

Anna Baldwin and Sarah Hutton (eds.), *Platonism and the English Imagination* (Cambridge, 1994).

Sarah Kofman, *Socrates: Fictions of a Philosopher* (London, 1998).

Mario Montuori, *Socrates: Physiology of a Myth*, tr. J. M. P. and M. Langdale (Amsterdam, 1981).

Emily Wilson, *The Death of Socrates: Hero, Villain, Chatterbox, Saint* (London, 2007).

Catherine H. Zuckert, *Postmodern Platos: Nietzsche, Heidegger, Gadamer, Strauss, Derrida* (Chicago, 1996).

A Note on the Text and Translation

For the *Euthyphro*, the *Apology* and the *Crito*, the text translated is that printed in volume I of the new Oxford Plato (Oxford Classical Texts, 1995). For the *Phaedo*, I have translated what is essentially the text printed in C(hristopher) J. Rowe, *Plato: Phaedo* (Cambridge, 1993); but that text was itself put together with the generous help and advice of the team responsible for the new Oxford *Phaedo*. In the translation of all four works, the punctuation will sometimes differ from that suggested by the editors of the Greek texts followed.

Plato's text, at least as much as any other, requires interpretation. It is not the function of translators to impose any particular interpretation on readers, and indeed the ideal translation would leave readers with exactly the same range of possible choices as would be available to them if they were addressing the text in its original language. But in practice, as everyone would agree, the ideal translation is impossible, especially if accuracy needs to be combined with readability; the demand for idiomatic English will by itself sometimes necessitate the resolution of ambiguities, the substitution of the more familiar for the less familiar, and – occasionally, and quite harmlessly – a certain spelling out of what is not spelled out in the original. Where I am conscious of having made such choices, and where they may have significant consequences, I have drawn attention to the fact in the notes; the choices themselves are for the most part justified in my 1993 commentary (see above), although a further decade and a half of thinking about the *Phaedo* has caused me to change my mind on some points.

Accuracy, combined with idiomatic English, is nevertheless what the translations in the present volume aspire to. There are some passages, for example, where particularly close argument is involved, in which accuracy must take priority over readability. But such passages are relatively rare. *Euthyphro*, *Apology*, *Crito* and *Phaedo* are on anyone's account among the most accessible of all Plato's works.

THE LAST DAYS
OF SOCRATES

INTRODUCTION TO *EUTHYPHRO*

The main subject of the dialogue is 'piety': in Greek, *hosiotês*, or *eusebeia*. Many translators have prefered to translate *hosiotês* as 'holiness' rather than 'piety', perhaps because 'holy' in English can – just about – cover the idea of what we are likely to call 'moral correctness', as the Greek *hosion* (the adjective corresponding to *hosiotês*) certainly can. However, as the dialogue proceeds, it becomes clear enough that what is being discussed is not morality in general, but a particular virtue or excellence: 'piety'. The discussion starts from Euthyphro's decision to prosecute his father for unlawfully killing a man, under circumstances that could scarcely have been more complicated. But killing in any case brings pollution and requires careful handling if relations with the gods are to be kept in good order; and what Euthyphro is expressly concerned about, before anything else, is that he should be getting things right from the point of view of his understanding of correct religious observance. If the rest of his family is criticizing him for taking his father to court, that is because they understand less well than he does 'the way things are with the gods when it comes to pious and impious behaviour' (4e2–3). This response to his relatives may even amount in itself to a rejection of that broader conception of piety as 'holiness' (or 'moral correctness'), according to which piety will merely be a matter of doing what is right and impiety a matter of doing what is wrong, with the more or less vague implication that the gods approve of the former and disapprove of the latter. What Euthyphro claims to *know* is pious is his action in prosecuting his father and so cleansing both himself and his father from pollution. In short, piety in the context of the *Euthyphro* is that virtue or excellence that is exhibited in a correct relationship to the gods and 'the things to do with the gods', or the sphere of 'the divine' (*ta theia*) – thus being, as Socrates and Euthyphro will agree (11e–12e), that part of justice that has to do with gods, leaving the remaining part to cover our relationship with other human beings.

There are perhaps two turning-points in the main discussion. The first is when Socrates asks Euthyphro 'Is what is pious loved by the gods because it's pious, or is it pious because it's loved by them?' Once Euthyphro has understood the question, the two of them agree that the first option is the right one: what is pious is loved by the gods because it is pious; the piety of any action isn't brought about, or constituted, by the fact that the gods happen to love it. If they do love it, that is just a feature of piety, not its *essence*, which is what Socrates, at least, is looking for. Why he goes for this option and not the other, he does not say; but it is at any rate consistent with his expressed unwillingness to 'accept, just like that, whatever we ourselves or other people say, agreeing merely on the basis that someone's said something's so' (9e) – why should it make any difference if the 'someone' is a god? (Just so, in the *Apology*, Socrates reports how he set about inquiring into a response from Apollo's oracle, albeit reluctantly.) If someone had asked him why, then, he was happy to obey the instructions of his 'divine voice' (see General Introduction, §3), his answer might well have appealed to the greater wisdom that he tends to attribute to the gods (cf. *Apology* 28d–29a) – an appeal which in turn will ultimately derive from a commitment to the idea that actions, including 'pious' ones, should be based on *reasons*, and not mere fiat, divine or otherwise. In any case, the consequence is that piety will be something to be investigated in itself, rather than being reduced to a study of what the gods love and hate.

The second turning-point in the dialogue is one marked by Socrates himself. Near the end, he and Euthyphro have begun to identify piety as having something to do with service or slavery to the gods. Socrates asks 'what that . . . outcome is that the gods bring about through using us to serve them'; and when

Euthyphro is unable to give a satisfactory answer, Socrates accuses him of veering off 'just when you were at the point of enlightening me' (14c). If *only* he'd answered as asked, then they might have got somewhere. Given Socrates' portrayal of himself, during his defence against a charge of impiety, as the servant or slave of gods (see *Apology* 23c, 30a), it will presumably not be too wildly speculative to suppose that we are here being given the most delicate of hints that the discussion has come very close to finding out what piety really is – and that it is exemplified in the person, and activities, of Socrates himself. If so, the *Euthyphro* is not just an investigation into the nature of piety, but itself an implicit response to Socrates' accusers.

EUTHYPHRO

2a   EUTHYPHRO What's changed, Socrates, to make you abandon your usual business in the Lyceum and busy yourself here around the portico of the King Archon instead? I don't suppose for a moment that *you*'ve a lawsuit pending with the Archon, as I have.

    SOCRATES Athenians certainly don't call it a suit; they call it an indictment.

2b   EUTHYPHRO What do you mean? Someone must have indicted you – I won't accuse you of indicting anyone.

    SOCRATES I should think not.

    EUTHYPHRO Someone's indicted you?

    SOCRATES Exactly.

    EUTHYPHRO Who's that?

    SOCRATES I scarcely know the man myself, Euthyphro; it appears he's a young person no one knows, but I think they call him by the name of Meletus. The deme he belongs to is Pitthus, if you can call to mind a Meletus from Pitthus with long straight hair, not much of a beard but more of a nose.

    EUTHYPHRO That doesn't help me, Socrates. But anyway,
2c what's the indictment he's brought against you?

    SOCRATES The indictment? No trivial one, I think; it's no mean feat for a young person to have mastered something so important. What he says, at any rate, is that he knows how young people are corrupted, and who their corrupters are. And he really must be some sort of expert if he's able observe my ignorance and the way I use it to corrupt his age-group, running off to the city to tell on me as if she were their mother. Actually, he seems to me to be the only political expert around to be starting from the right place, because it *is* correct to make a priority of young people, taking care that they turn out as well as possible – just as we'd expect a good farmer to tend to his young plants first, and the others only after that. Just so, probably, Meletus is weeding us out first, as the ones who are corrupting the shoots of his young plants (so he says); next, clearly, after this, he'll take care of older age-groups, and end up bringing about the greatest and most numerous benefits to the city. At any rate, that's how it's likely to turn out, if someone's started as he has.

EUTHYPHRO I'd be delighted if that were so, Socrates, but I'm fearful that the opposite will happen: to put it simply, he seems to me to be starting out to harm the city, from its very hearth, by setting out to wrong you. Just tell me, what exactly is it he says you're doing to corrupt the young?

SOCRATES Strange things, my fine friend, at any rate by the sound of them. He says I'm a maker of gods, and it's for making new gods and not believing in the ancient ones that he's indicted me – on these very grounds, he says.

EUTHYPHRO I understand, Socrates; it's because you talk, each time it happens, about your 'divinity' having intervened.[1] So he's put together this indictment on the basis that you're innovating in theological matters, and he's going to court in order to misrepresent you, in the knowledge that things like this are easy to misrepresent to the masses. I can tell you, it's the same for me: when I say anything in the Assembly[2] about matters to do with the gods, predicting to the audience what's going to happen to them, they laugh at me and say I'm raving mad; and yet none of my predictions has turned out not to be true – even so they resent everyone like us. There's no need to worry about them; we should carry the attack to them.

SOCRATES My dear Euthyphro, being laughed at is probably nothing much. My view is that as a general rule Athenians don't care much one way or the other if they think someone clever, so long as they don't also think he's good at passing on

2d

3a

3b

3c

3d his wisdom; what makes them angry is when they find someone
producing others like himself as well – either because they
resent him,[3] as you say, or for some other reason.

EUTHYPHRO Well, I've no wish at all to test how they're
disposed towards me on that count.

SOCRATES That's probably because you appear as someone
who rarely puts himself forward, and is reluctant to teach the
wisdom he has. My case is different: I'm afraid that to them I
give the appearance of passing on whatever I have to anybody
and everybody, out of a love for humanity, quite indiscrimin-
ately, and not just without being paid for it – they think I'd
happily pay out myself to anyone willing to listen to me. Now
3e as I was just saying, if they were going to laugh at me as you
say they laugh at you, there'd be nothing too disagreeable about
their passing the time playing games and laughing in court; but
if they're going to be in earnest, then how all this will turn out
is unclear, except to you seers.

EUTHYPHRO But probably, Socrates, it will be nothing
much; you'll contest your case to your satisfaction, and I think
that's how I'll contest mine too.

SOCRATES What about this case of yours, Euthyphro? Are
you defending or prosecuting?

EUTHYPHRO I'm prosecuting.

SOCRATES Who's the defendant?

4a EUTHYPHRO Someone people call me raving mad – again –
for prosecuting.

SOCRATES Why, has he already flown the coop?[4]

EUTHYPHRO Flying is something he'd find difficult; he's not
just old, but very old.

SOCRATES Who is it?

EUTHYPHRO My father.

SOCRATES *Your father*, my fine friend?

EUTHYPHRO Exactly.

SOCRATES What's the charge, and what's the basis of the
case?

EUTHYPHRO It's for homicide, Socrates.

SOCRATES Heracles! It's certainly something most people don't
know about, Euthyphro, what's right and what's not; I don't think

acting as you are is for just anyone – it'd have to be someone 4b who's already a long way along the road to wisdom.

EUTHYPHRO Zeus! A long way indeed, Socrates.

SOCRATES Then is the man your father killed one of your family? It's clear he must be, because you wouldn't be taking out proceedings for homicide on behalf of someone who wasn't family.

EUTHYPHRO It's funny, Socrates, that you think it makes any difference at all whether the dead man is an outsider or a family member, instead of thinking the only thing to watch out for is whether the person who did the killing did so justly or not. If he did it justly, he should be left alone, but if not, you have to proceed against him, if he actually shares not just your 4c hearth but your table; because the pollution that results is the same for you as for him, if you knowingly associate with someone under these circumstances, and don't take steps to purify both yourself and him by taking him to court on the appropriate charge. In fact the dead man was a dependant of mine, and as we were farming on Naxos then, he was working for us as a day-labourer. Well, he gets violently drunk, and in a fit of rage with one of our slaves he goes and slits his throat. So my father ties him up hand and foot, throws him into some ditch, and sends a man to find out from the office of the Exegetes[5] what he should do. But while waiting for the answer he paid him little 4d thought and even less care, on the grounds that he was a murderer, and that it'd be of no consequence even if he died – which is exactly what did happen, because the man died from hunger, cold and just being tied up before the messenger arrived from the Exegete. That's why my father and the rest of my family are annoyed with me: because I'm proceeding against my father for homicide on behalf of the the man who actually murdered someone, when not only did my father not kill him – that's what they claim – but even if he really and truly killed him, the victim was a murderer anyway, and there's no need to worry about someone like that. The really impious thing, they say, is 4e for son to proceed against father for homicide; just shows how poorly *they* know the way things are with the gods when it comes to pious and impious behaviour.[6]

SOCRATES And – I ask you, Euthyphro, in Zeus' name! – do *you* think you know so precisely how things are, to do with the gods, and with what's pious and impious, that – if everything happened in the way you describe – you're not afraid of turning out to be doing something impious yourself, on your own account, by prosecuting your father?

5a EUTHYPHRO Just so. I'd be no use at all, Socrates, nor would Euthyphro have anything to make him stand out from the ordinary run of mankind, if I didn't have precise knowledge of everything like that.

SOCRATES In that case, estimable Euthyphro, is my best course to become your student? Then before the indictment I'm to defend against Meletus I could challenge him on these very grounds: I could say that even before this I myself made it a high priority to know about divine matters,[7] but now, since his claim is that I'm going wrong in such matters by speaking out of turn and innovating, I've started studying with *you*. I'd 5b say 'So, Meletus, if you agree that Euthyphro is wise in such matters, then you should suppose me too to be right-thinking, and drop your case; if you don't agree about Euthyphro, then you should take him, my teacher, to court before you take me, on the grounds that he's corrupting the older generation, not just me but his own father – by teaching me and by admonishing and proposing to punish him.' And if he doesn't do as I say, and doesn't give up his case or indict you in my place, then I could make the same claims before the judges that I was saying I could make in my challenge. Is that what's best for me?

5c EUTHYPHRO Zeus! I should say so. If he really did launch an indictment against me, I think I'd find his weak point; I'd have made sure *he* was the one being talked about in the court long before I was.

SOCRATES And it's because I recognize this, dear friend, that I so want to study with you, in the knowledge that whether it's this person Meletus or – apparently – anyone else, they don't even seem to *see* you, whereas me he spotted so sharply and easily that he's indicted me for impiety.[8] So now, in the name of Zeus, tell me what you were claiming just now to know with such clarity: what sort of thing do you say the pious is, and the

impious,[9] in relation not just to homicide but to everything   5d
else? Or isn't the pious the same in every type[10] of action, I
mean the same as itself, and isn't the impious too, while being
opposite to everything pious, itself like itself, possessing some
single character[11] in respect of its impiety, whatever it is that is
going to be impious?

EUTHYPHRO Of course, Socrates, absolutely.[12]

SOCRATES So tell me what you say the pious is, and what
the impious is.

EUTHYPHRO Then I tell you that the pious is the very thing
I'm presently doing – proceeding against the person committing
criminal acts, whether it's acts of homicide, or stealing sacred
objects, or any other crime of a similar sort,[13] whether the per-
petrator happens to be his father or his mother or anyone else   5e
whatsoever, and that it's not to proceed against them that's
impious. Just observe, Socrates, how impressive a proof I'm
going to give you that that's what the law is[14] – not to let the
person acting impiously get away with it, even if he happens to
be, well, whoever he is. It's a proof I've already given to others,
too, to show that things would be correctly done in the way I'm
proposing: don't humans themselves actually believe Zeus to
be the best and most just of the gods? And don't they also agree   6a
that he tied up his own father, because he was swallowing his
sons – unjustly[15] – and that Zeus' father too had castrated his
father, for similar reasons? Yet they react angrily against me for
proceeding against my father when *he* acts unjustly, so managing to contradict themselves by saying one thing about the gods
and another about me.[16]

SOCRATES I do wonder, Euthyphro, whether the reason why
I'm being indicted is just that it's difficult for me, somehow, to
accept it when a person says this sort of thing about the gods;
this, it seems, is why someone or other will claim that I'm in
error – and now if you, an expert in such matters, agree with   6b
them as well, then people like me had better go along with it
too. What else are we going to say for ourselves, when we ourselves admit that we know nothing about the subject? But do
tell me, in the name of friendship,[17] do you really and truly
believe that these things happened as you say?

EUTHYPHRO Yes, and still more amazing things than these, Socrates – things most people don't know about.

SOCRATES War too – is it your view that there actually is war among the gods, against each other, and that they hate each other frightfully, fight battles, and do lots of other such things; the kinds of things that are not only told us by the poets but thanks to expert painters also decorate all of our sacred objects, not least the robe at the Great Panathenaea, which is brought up to the acropolis full of such pictures? Are we to say these things are true, Euthyphro?

EUTHYPHRO Not only that, Socrates; as I was saying just now, there are a lot of other things about the divine realm that I'll explain to you if you really want to hear about them, and I've no doubt you'll be astounded when you do.

SOCRATES I wouldn't be surprised. But these are things you can explain to me at leisure on another occasion; for now, just try to give a clearer answer to the question I put to you just now. The fact is, my friend, that you didn't give me adequate instruction before when I asked you what the pious was. You told me that what's actually pious is what you're doing now in proceeding[18] against your father for homicide.

EUTHYPHRO Yes, and what I said was true.

SOCRATES Maybe. But the point is, Euthyphro, that you say there are many other things too that are pious.

EUTHYPHRO Because there are.

SOCRATES Well, do you remember? I wasn't telling you to instruct me about one or two of the many things that are pious; what I was after was that very character[19] by virtue of which all pious things are pious. Because you said, I think, that it was by virtue of a single character in each case that impious things were impious, and pious things pious. Or don't you recall?

EUTHYPHRO I do.

SOCRATES Well then, instruct me about this character of the pious – tell me what it is, so that by referring to that and using it as a benchmark[20] I'll be in a position to say that piety belongs to whatever is like this, among all the actions either you or anyone else perform, and to deny it belongs to anything not of that sort.

EUTHYPHRO Of course if that's what you want, Socrates, I'll put it that way too.

SOCRATES That's exactly what I do want.

EUTHYPHRO In that case it's what's lovable to the gods that's pious, and what's not lovable to them that's impious.   7a

SOCRATES Very fine, Euthyphro; now you've answered in just the way I was looking for you to answer. On the other hand I don't yet know whether what you've said is *true*. But evidently you'll go on yourself to teach me how what you're saying is true.

EUTHPHRO Yes; quite.

SOCRATES Come on, then, let's take a look at what we're saying: the thing or person that's god-loved is pious, and the thing or person[21] that's god-hated is impious; and the pious isn't the same as the impious, but as opposed to it as it could be. Isn't that how we're proposing to put it?

EUTHYPHRO Just so.

SOCRATES And does it appear *well* put like that?

EUTHYPHRO I think so, Socrates.   7b

SOCRATES Well, wasn't it also said that the gods fight, Euthyphro? That they dispute with one another, and that there's enmity among them towards each other? Wasn't that said too?

EUTHYPHRO It was.

SOCRATES And when enmity and anger occur, my excellent friend, what are the disputes that cause them *about*? Let's look at it like this. If you and I were having a dispute about counting, and about which of two sets of things was larger than the other, would the quarrel in this case make us enemies and angry with each other? Or would we resort to calculating and quickly resolve our dispute in such matters?   7c

EUTHYPHRO Just so.

SOCRATES So too if we were disputing what was bigger and smaller in size, we'd quickly stop our disagreement by resorting to measuring?

EUTHYPHRO True.

SOCRATES And it's by resorting to weighing, I imagine, that we'd settle questions about what was heavier and lighter?

EUTHYPHRO Of course.

SOCRATES Then what sort of thing would we dispute about without being able to arrive at a settlement, leaving ourselves enemies, and angry with one another? Probably you haven't an answer ready to hand; but see what you think if I say that what we're looking for is the just and the unjust, the fine and the shameful, the good and the bad. Aren't these the things we'd get into disputes about without being able to reach a satisfactory settlement about them, so that this rather than any other time is when we become enemies, when we do – not just you and I but all the rest of mankind?

EUTHYPHRO Yes, this is the sort of dispute in question, Socrates, and these are the things it's about.

SOCRATES And what about the gods, Euthyphro? If they really do get into disputes at all, wouldn't they do it for the very same reasons?

EUTHYPHRO Necessarily so.

SOCRATES In that case, my noble Euthyphro, among the gods too, on your account, different individuals will think different things just, and fine and ugly, and good and bad; for I imagine they wouldn't fight with each other if they didn't get into disputes about these things. Right?

EUTHYPHRO Correct.

SOCRATES Well then: what each side loves is what it thinks fine and good and just, and the opposites of these they hate?

EUTHYPHRO Quite.

SOCRATES Yes, but the same things, you yourself say, will be thought just by one side and unjust by the other – the things at issue between them in the disputes and wars they have with one another; isn't that so?

EUTHYPHRO It is.

SOCRATES In that case, it seems, the same things are both hated by the gods and loved by them, and the same things will be both god-hated and god-loved.

EUTHYPHRO It does seem so.

SOCRATES In that case the same things will be both pious and impious, Euthyphro – on this account.

EUTHYPHRO I dare say they will.

SOCRATES In that case you didn't answer the question I asked, my fine friend. I certainly wasn't asking you to tell me what was actually both pious and impious, even while being one and the same thing; anything god-loved is also god-hated, it seems. And this, Euthyphro, affects what you're now doing 8b in trying to punish your father: it'll be nothing to be astonished at if in acting like this you're doing something of the sort Zeus loves, but Cronus and Uranus are hostile to, and that Hephaestus loves but Hera doesn't – and the same will apply in the case of any other pair of gods who are at odds over this sort of thing.[22]

EUTHYPHRO But it's my opinion, Socrates, that there's something over which none of the gods will quarrel with any other: that anyone who kills someone unjustly must pay the penalty.

SOCRATES What's that? What about human beings, Euthyphro? Did you ever hear one of them disputing that the person 8c who's killed unjustly or does anything else whatever unjustly should pay the penalty?

EUTHYPHRO Indeed I have; in fact people never stop disputing this, especially in the law-courts; they behave unjustly in a thousand different ways and then do and say anything to avoid the penalty for it.

SOCRATES Do they actually admit, Euthyphro, to acting unjustly, and still claim, even while admitting it, that they shouldn't pay the penalty?

EUTHYPHRO They certainly don't do that.

SOCRATES So in fact they don't do and say *everything* to get off – I imagine they don't have the face to say that they shouldn't pay the penalty if they really are acting unjustly, or to dispute 8d the point with anyone. Instead, I imagine, their claim is that they're not acting unjustly. True?

EUTHYPHRO True.

SOCRATES So what they're arguing about is not whether the person who acts unjustly should pay the penalty. What they *are* probably arguing about is who it is that's acting unjustly, and by doing what, and when.

EUTHYPHRO True.

SOCRATES Then are the gods in this very same situation, if in fact they fight with one another about the just and the unjust in the way that you say: do some of them agree that they're treating each other unjustly, while others deny it? Because, my good man, there's surely one thing that no one, whether god or human being, has the face to say, and that's that the person who *is* acting unjustly shouldn't pay the penalty.

EUTHYPHRO Yes, that much is true, Socrates; you're getting the main point, anyway.

SOCRATES Now I imagine, Euthyphro, that it's individual actions that the disputants dispute about in each case, whether they're human beings or gods (if in fact gods do get into disputes): they quarrel about some action or other, and some of them say that it was done justly, others that it was done unjustly – isn't that how it is?

EUTHYPHRO Yes, quite.

SOCRATES Come then, Euthyphro, be my teacher, and make me a wiser person: what evidence have you that all the gods think *that* kind of person[23] is killed unjustly – a day-labourer who'd killed someone else, was tied up by the master of the victim, and died as a result of being tied up before the person who did the tying could get the answer he needed from the Exegetes as to what to do with him? What evidence do you have that it's correct, on behalf of such a person, under such circumstances, for a son to proceed against his father and denounce him for homicide? Come on, do try and give me some sort of unambiguous demonstration that all the gods more than anything think this action correct; and if you do give me an adequate proof, I'll sing your praises without end.

EUTHYPHRO It's probably no small task, Socrates, though I would be able to prove it to you quite unambiguously.

SOCRATES I understand; it's because I seem to you to be a worse pupil than the judges in court, because obviously you'll demonstrate to *them* that the sorts of things your father did are unjust and hated by all the gods.

EUTHYPHRO Quite unambiguously, Socrates, if they actually listen to what I tell them.

SOCRATES They will surely listen, provided that you seem to

be saying something worth hearing. But here's a thought I had as you were speaking just now, and I'm mulling it over: 'Let's suppose that Euthyphro managed to teach me absolutely that all the gods think this sort of killing is unjust. How will I have progressed towards learning, from Euthyphro, what the pious and the impious are? This action will, it seems, be god-hated. But that's no help, because that didn't turn out just now to be what distinguished what was pious from what was not; what was god-hated actually turned out to be god-loved as well.' So I'll let you off the task I was setting you: if you like, let's suppose that all the gods think your 9d father's action unjust and all hate it. Now let me ask you about this correction we're now making in the account of piety, to the effect that whatever all the gods hate is impious, whatever they all love is pious, and whatever some of them love and others hate is neither or both together – is that how you want things to be marked off[24] in relation to the pious and the impious?

EUTHYPHRO Yes, what's to stop us doing that, Socrates?

SOCRATES There's nothing to stop *me* from doing it, Euthyphro, but you'd better look at things from your angle, to see if setting things up like this will be the easiest way to teach me the lesson you promised.[25]

EUTHYPHRO Well, my view is just this, that the pious is 9e whatever all the gods love, and that the opposite, whatever all the gods hate, is impious.

SOCRATES Then are we to examine this too, in its turn, to see if it's well said, or are we to let it stand? Are we to accept, just like that, whatever we ourselves or other people say, agreeing merely on the basis that someone's said something's so? Or must we examine what the speaker's saying?

EUTHYPHRO We must examine it; all the same I do actually think that what we have now is well said.

SOCRATES Soon, my good friend, we'll be in a better pos- 10a ition to know. Consider this sort of question: is what is pious loved by the gods because it's pious, or is it pious because it's loved by them?

EUTHYPHRO I don't know what you're saying, Socrates.[26]

SOCRATES Well, I'll try to put it more clearly. We talk about a thing's being carried, and carrying, being led and leading, being seen and seeing; you understand that in all such cases there's a difference between the two, and how they're different?

EUTHYPHRO I do understand, I think.

SOCRATES Then there'll also be something that's loved, and the thing loving it will be different from it?

EUTHYPHRO Of course.

10b   SOCRATES So tell me, is the thing that's carried carried because it's carried, or for some other reason?

EUTHYPHRO No, for the reason you say.

SOCRATES The thing led, then, is led because it's led, and the seen thing seen because it's seen?

EUTHYPHRO Yes, quite.

SOCRATES It's not, then, because it's a seen thing that a thing is seen, but the other way round: it's because it's seen that it's a seen thing; nor is it because it's a led thing that a thing is led, but because it's led that it's a led thing; nor is a thing carried because it's a carried thing, rather it's a carried thing because

10c   it's carried.[27] Is what I want to say becoming clear, Euthyphro? What I have in mind is this: if something changes[28] or is affected in some way, it's not because it's a changing thing that it changes, nor is it affected because it's an affected thing, but rather it's a changing or affected thing because it changes or is affected – or don't you agree that this is how it is?

EUTHYPHRO I agree.

SOCRATES Well then, is the thing that's loved, too, either something that's changing or something that's being affected by something?

EUTHYPHRO Yes, it certainly is.

SOCRATES In that case it's the same in this case as in the previous ones: it's not because it's a loved thing that it's loved by those by whom it's loved, but because it's loved it's a loved thing.

EUTHYPHRO Necessarily so.

10d   SOCRATES What is it, then, that we're saying about the pious, Euthyphro? Just that it's loved by all the gods, as your account of it goes?

EUTHYPHRO Yes.

SOCRATES Because it's pious – or for some other reason?

EUTHYPHRO No: because it's pious.[29]

SOCRATES In that case it's because it's pious that it's loved by the gods; it's not pious because it's loved by them?

EUTHYPHRO It seems like it.

SOCRATES But just because it's loved by the gods, it's something loved – god-loved, in fact.

EUTHYPHRO Of course.

SOCRATES In that case the god-loved isn't pious, Euthyphro, nor is the pious god-loved, as you say it is, but the two things are different from each other.

EUTHYPHRO How so, Socrates?   10e

SOCRATES Because we're in agreement that the pious is loved for the very reason that it's pious, and that it's not pious because it's loved; right?

EUTHYPHRO Yes.

SOCRATES Whereas we're also agreed that the god-loved is so because it's loved by the gods – it's god-loved by virtue of the very fact that it's loved; it isn't loved because it's god-loved.

EUTHYPHRO What you say is true.

SOCRATES If they *were* the same thing, my dear Euthyphro, the god-loved and the pious, then for a start, if the pious were loved because it is pious, the god-loved would also be loved   11a
because it is god-loved; and then, if the god-loved were god-loved because it was loved by the gods, the pious would also be pious because it was loved; but as it is you see that the two things are the opposite way round to each other, which shows that they're completely different from one another – one is lovable because it is loved, while the other is loved because it is lovable.[30] The chances are, Euthyphro, that if asked what the pious is you don't want to reveal its essence to me, but just to tell me some feature[31] it has – that the pious is affected in a particular way, namely that it's loved by all the gods; as for   11b
what it *is* that has this feature, you haven't told me. So then, if it's all right with you, don't conceal it from me: start from the beginning again and say what the pious is that it should be loved by the gods or be affected in whatever other way you like (we shan't quarrel about that); just say, without holding back, what the pious and the impious actually are.

EUTHYPHRO The truth is, Socrates, that I'm at a loss as to how to say what I want to say; somehow or other whatever we put forward has a habit of moving around and refusing to stay wherever we try to make it stand.

11c   SOCRATES What you say, Euthyphro, seems like the work of my ancestor Daedalus.[32] Actually, if I were the one doing the talking and making the proposals, you'd probably be making fun of me for inheriting a family trait, and having my word-crafted works run away from me and refuse to stay wherever anyone put them. But as it is, the proposals we've been discussing are yours, not mine, so we'll need a different joke; they refuse to stay put for *you*, as you yourself think too.

EUTHYPHRO I actually think, Socrates, the things we're talking about require pretty much the same joke, because this ability to move around and not stay in the same place isn't

11d   something I've given them – it seems to me that Daedalus *is* you, because so far as I'm concerned they'd stay just as they are.

SOCRATES Then apparently, my friend, I've turned out a better exponent of the craft than he was, at least by one measure: he only used to make his own works move, whereas I do it not only to mine, it seems, but to others'.[33] But the subtlest aspect of this craft of mine is that I'd rather not be expert[34] in it at all; if I could have forms of words[35] that stayed put and

11e   were settled immovably, I'd rather have that than the wealth of Tantalus on top of the skill of Daedalus. Enough of that; let's move on. Since my impression is that you're slacking, I'll join forces with you to help you give me my lesson about the pious. And don't despair too soon. See if you don't think the whole of the pious necessarily *just*.

EUTHYPHRO I do think that.

SOCRATES Then do you also think the whole of the just is

12a   pious, or is the whole of the pious just, whereas the just is not all pious, but some is pious and some of it is actually something else?

EUTHYPHRO I don't follow what's being said here, Socrates.

SOCRATES But you're younger than me,[36] no less than you're wiser; as I say, you're merely slacking, as only those rich in wisdom can afford to do. I'm happy for your good fortune, but try extending yourself, because it really doesn't even take much effort to grasp what I'm saying. I'm saying the opposite of what the poet put in his poem, the one who said

> Zeus was the cause, yet not even he who
> Set things in motion assigns him the blame.
> For where there is Fear, there too there is Shame.[37]

12b

Well, this is where I quarrel with the poet – shall I tell you what my quarrel is?

EUTHYPHRO Absolutely.

SOCRATES It doesn't seem to me that 'where there's fear, there too there is shame'. Lots of people seem to me to be afraid of things like disease, poverty and so on and so forth, but their fear of them isn't accompanied by shame. Don't you agree?

EUTHYPHRO Absolutely.

SOCRATES On the other hand I do think that where there's shame, there's fear too; is there anyone who shrinks back in shame from some action or another and isn't at the same moment in a state of apprehension and fear, of appearing to behave badly?

12c

EUTHYPHRO Yes, he'll be afraid too.

SOCRATES In that case it's not correct to say 'where there's fear, there too there is shame'; it's where there's shame that there's fear too, without there being shame everywhere fear is, since I take it fear is more widespread than shame. Shame is a part of fear just as the even is of number, meaning that it's not wherever number is that there's even too, but where even is there too is number. I suppose you're following me now?

EUTHYPHRO Absolutely.

SOCRATES Well, it was that kind of thing I had in mind when I asked you about the original case: is it where the just is that the pious is too, or is it that where the pious is, there too the just is, without there being the pious everywhere the just is – because the pious is a part of the just? Is that how we're to put it, or do you take a different view?

12d

EUTHYPHRO No, the same as you. You appear to me to be putting it correctly.

SOCRATES Fine. Now look at what comes next. If the pious is a part of the just, then it seems to me we must discover exactly *which* part the pious is of the just. Well, if you were asking me about one of our recent examples, for example which part the even is of number, and what this number actually is, I'd have said that it's any number that's isosceles and not scalene;[38] don't you think so?

EUTHYPHRO I do.

12e SOCRATES So you take your turn and try to show me in the same way which part of the just is pious, so that I can tell Meletus, too,[39] not to go on treating me unjustly and indicting me for impiety, on the basis that I've already learned sufficiently well from you what's pious[40] and what isn't.

EUTHYPHRO Well, then, Socrates, the part of the just that seems to me to be pious is the part concerned with tending to the gods, while the remaining part of the just seems the one concerned with tending to human beings.

SOCRATES Yes, and what you say, Euthyphro, seems to me
13a absolutely fine; I just need one little thing more from you. I'm not yet clear about what you're calling 'tending' here. I don't suppose you have in mind, with this 'tending to the gods', the sorts of tending that go on in relation to other things. I think we talk in this sort of way – take the example of horses: not everyone, we say, knows how to tend to horses, only the horse-trainer; right?

EUTHYPHRO Absolutely.

SOCRATES Because, I imagine, horse-training is tending to horses.

EUTHYPHRO Yes.

SOCRATES And it's not everyone who knows how to tend to dogs, only the kennelman.

EUTHYPHRO Just so.

SOCRATES I imagine because kennelmanship is tending to dogs.

13b EUTHYPHRO Yes.

SOCRATES And herdsmanship is tending to cattle?

EUTHYPHRO Absolutely.

SOCRATES So then piety[41] is tending to gods? Is that what you have in mind?

EUTHYPHRO I do.

SOCRATES Well, if it's all tending, does it all have the same function? Is it something like this: is it for some good to, and benefit of, whatever's being tended to – as you can actually observe horses that are tended by horse-training being benefited and becoming better horses; don't you think so?

EUTHYPHRO I do.

SOCRATES As I think dogs become better dogs, when they're tended to by kennelmanship, and cattle by herdsmanship, and so on in every other case; or do you think people tend things to do them harm? 13c

EUTHYPHRO Zeus! I certainly don't.

SOCRATES To do them good?

EUTHYPHRO Of course.

SOCRATES Then piety too, since it's tending to gods, both benefits gods and makes the gods better? And will you agree to this in your own case – that whenever you do something pious, you're making one of the gods better?

EUTHYPHRO Zeus! I certainly won't.

SOCRATES Right, Euthyphro, nor do I suppose this is what you have in mind – far from it; indeed that's *why* I asked you what sort of 'tending to the gods' you had in mind, because I didn't think it was one like that. 13d

EUTHYPHRO Yes, quite correctly, Socrates; that's not what I have in mind.

SOCRATES Fine. So what sort of 'tending to gods' will piety be?

EUTHYPHRO The sort, Socrates, that slaves give to masters.

SOCRATES I understand: apparently it'll be some sort of expertise[42] in serving the gods.

EUTHYPHRO Absolutely.

SOCRATES Then take expert service to doctors:[43] what's the outcome it's expert at helping bring about? Would you be able to say? It's health, don't you think?

EUTHYPHRO I do.

SOCRATES What about expert service to shipwrights? What's the outcome this expertise helps bring about? 13e

EUTHYPHRO Evidently, Socrates, it's a ship.

SOCRATES And expert service to builders, presumably, helps bring about – a house.

EUTHYPHRO Yes.

SOCRATES So tell me, my excellent friend: and this expertise in serving the gods – what'll be the outcome *this* expertise helps to bring about? Clearly you're the one to know, seeing that it's exactly in things to do with the gods that you claim to be the world expert.

EUTHYPHRO Yes, and I'm telling the truth, Socrates.

SOCRATES Then I appeal to you in Zeus' name to say what that super-fine outcome is that the gods bring about through using us to serve them.

EUTHYPHRO It's many fine things, Socrates.

14a SOCRATES Yes. And the same is true of generals, my friend; all the same, you'd easily be able to say what sums up what they bring about – victory in war.

EUTHYPHRO Of course.

SOCRATES And farmers too, I think, bring about many fine things; all the same, what sums these up is nourishment from the earth.

EUTHYPHRO Absolutely.

SOCRATES So what, then, about the many fine things the gods bring about?[44] What will it be that sums these up?

EUTHYPHRO I told you before, only moments ago, Socrates, 14b that it's too great a task to learn exactly how it is with all these things. But this much I'll simply say to you: that if a person knows how to speak and to act in a way that's gratifying to the gods, whether in prayer or in sacrifice, these are the things that are pious, and these are the sorts of things that preserve both private households and the common interests of whole cities; and the things that are the opposite of gratifying are impious – the very things that overturn and destroy everything.

SOCRATES Surely, Euthyphro, you could have given me a much briefer summing up of the sort I was asking for, if you 14c wanted to; but as it is you're not eager to teach me, that's obvious. Look at what you've done, taking a side-turning just when you were at the point of enlightening me; if you'd only answered my question, by now I would have had a sufficient lesson from you about piety.[45] But as it is, because questioner must follow respondent wherever the respondent may lead,[46] tell me again what you say the pious and piety are. Isn't it a kind of expertise in[47] sacrifice and prayer?

EUTHYPHRO That's it.

SOCRATES Now sacrifice is giving to the gods, prayer asking for things from them?

EUTHYPHRO Very much so.

SOCRATES In that case, piety will be an expertise in asking 14d from and giving to the gods, if we follow this line.

EUTHYPHRO Socrates, you've grasped what I said quite perfectly.

SOCRATES That, Euthyphro, is because I lust after your wisdom and pay such attention to it that not a single word you may utter will fall uncaught to the ground. But tell me what this service to the gods is. You claim that it's asking them for things and giving to them?

EUTHYPHRO I do.

SOCRATES Then won't correct asking be a matter of asking for what we need from them?

EUTHYPHRO Of course.

SOCRATES And correct giving, in its turn, will be a matter of 14e giving to them in return the things they actually need from us? I imagine it wouldn't be expert gift-giving to give someone things he had no need of.

EUTHYPHRO True, Socrates.

SOCRATES In that case, Euthyphro, piety will be a kind of expertise in trading between gods and men.

EUTHYPHRO 'Trading', yes – if it gives you more enjoyment to call it that.

SOCRATES It gives me not the least bit more enjoyment if it isn't *true*. But tell me, what benefit, actually, to the gods is there from the gifts they receive from us? As for the things they give us, that's clear to anyone: nothing is good for us that doesn't 15a come as a gift from them.[48] But what benefit do they get from what they receive from us? Or do we enjoy so much advantage in the trading between us and them that we get all our goods from them while they get nothing from us?

EUTHYPHRO Do you really think, Socrates, that the gods get benefit from the things they receive from us?

SOCRATES If they don't, what in the world will these gifts be, Euthyphro, the ones from us to the gods?

EUTHYPHRO Esteem, honours and what I was talking about just now, gratification. What else do you think?

15b SOCRATES The pious, then, Euthyphro, is gratifying to the gods, but it's not beneficial, or what the gods love?

EUTHYPHRO As a matter of fact I think they love it more than anything in the world.

SOCRATES So *this*, it seems, is what the pious is, all over again – what the gods love.

EUTHYPHRO Yes, most certainly.

SOCRATES When you say this, will it be any wonder to you that your proposals visibly shift around and don't stay put? Will you accuse me of being the Daedalus that makes them shift, when you demonstrate a greater skill than Daedalus yourself by making them go round in a circle? Or do you not notice that our discussion has gone round and arrived back where it 15c started from? I suppose you do remember that previously we found the pious and the god-loved turning out *not* to be the same thing, but different things? Or don't you remember?

EUTHYPHRO Yes, I do.

SOCRATES Then are you now not noticing that you're claiming that what the gods love is pious? Is what the gods love going to be something other than god-loved? Or not?

EUTHYPHRO No, absolutely not.

SOCRATES Then either our earlier agreement wasn't well founded or, if it was, our present proposal isn't correct.

EUTHYPHRO It seems so.

SOCRATES In that case we need to start our investigation of what the pious is all over again from the beginning, since I for 15d one won't willingly give in until I learn what it is. Don't treat me with disrespect; use all your resources, put your mind to it as best you can and tell me, here and now, the truth of the matter; if any human being knows it, you do, and you're not to be let go until you utter, like some Proteus.[49] For if you didn't have clear knowledge of what's pious and what's impious, there's no way you would ever have undertaken, on behalf of a day-labouring man, to prosecute an old man who was your *father*,

for homicide. Not only would you have been too afraid of the gods to take the risk that you'd not be acting correctly, but you'd have been ashamed at what your fellow humans would think of you. But as it is I'm quite sure you think you have clear   15e
knowledge of what's pious and what's not; so do tell, excellent Euthyphro, and don't hide from me what you think it is.

EUTHYPHRO It'll have to be another time, Socrates; at this moment I'm in a hurry to be somewhere, and it's time for me to leave.

SOCRATES My friend, what a thing to do! Letting me down by leaving like this, when I had such high expectations of you. It'd be from you, I hoped, that I'd learn about what was pious and what was not and so be rid of Meletus and his indictment, having demonstrated to him that thanks to Euthyphro I was   16a
now an expert[50] in divine matters, no longer spoke out of turn or innovated in them, out of ignorance, and what's more would live better for the rest of my life.[51]

INTRODUCTION TO THE *APOLOGY*

Socrates was brought to court for impiety. More precisely, as Plato has him say in the *Apology*, the charge against him was of 'corrupting the young and not believing in the gods the city believes in, but in other new divinities' (24b–c). No one else, it seems, before Socrates had ever been tried for corrupting anyone; the charge, in this respect, was specifically designed for him, as the law evidently allowed. The prosecutors were private citizens, who brought the case on their own initiative and presented it, as their framing of the actual charge demonstrates, on behalf of the city. Socrates, correspondingly, spends some of his main speech ridiculing the chief prosecutor and his affidavit, but for the most part concentrates on explaining what he does, why he does it and how in fact it benefits the city as a whole. (The main speech is followed by two short ones, only one of which – the first, in which he proposes an alternative to the death penalty – would probably have been allowed by court procedure; in the second, Plato allows Socrates to reflect on what has happened with the jurors, 'just while the court authorities are busy and before I go off to the place where I'm to go and die' (39e).)

Socrates begins by suggesting that the jury will have to make allowances for his lack of skill as a speaker. In fact, his speech shows every sign of careful composition, allowing it simultaneously to fulfil the various purposes its author evidently had for it: first, of course, as a defence; then as a description of a philosophical life, which evolves into, and becomes indistinguishable from, an exhortation to others – whether jurors, or readers – to live philosophically; and finally as a kind of prospectus for

Plato's own activity of writing, insofar as the dialogues – mostly with Socrates as chief character – mimic the ideas and themes 'Socrates' lays out in his account of his life. (There are no chronological implications here; the *Apology* need not have been Plato's first work, although the signs are that it was probably written not long after Socrates' death.) But even in its first role, as a defence speech, the *Apology* is no mere improvisation. It is a systematically organized whole, with beginning, middle and end; and when Socrates declares that what the jurors hear from him 'will be in the words that come to me at the time, and as they come to me' (17c), that is itself little more than a rhetorical commonplace. What is certainly true is that Plato's Socrates does not normally make speeches, indeed has a horror of them, for the very good reason that the kind of philosophy he does is nothing without dialogue, exchange and challenge. For that, he has a brief opportunity in the *Apology*, in the shape of a brief cross-examination of Meletus, the chief prosecutor; but for the rest, he needs a speech, and a persuasive one, and Plato duly writes one for him.

The main speech is organized roughly as follows:

1. Introduction: Socrates (S) will simply tell the truth (17a–18a).
2. There are two sets of accusers – the present ones, and much older ones like Aristophanes, the comic poet; S will deal with the latter first, then the former (18a–19a).
3. S's older accusers totally misrepresent him (19a–20c).
4. S describes what he is actually like, and actually does, and explains how this has led to the present accusations against him (20c–24b).
5. S interrogates Meletus (24b–28b).
6. Objection 1: S should not have lived in a way that laid him open to the dangers he is facing now; S responds (28b–31c).
7. Objection 2: why has S spent all his time talking to people privately, rather than raising his voice publicly? S responds (31c–34b).
8. Peroration: S will not plead with the jury as others do (34b–35d).

Following this first speech, the jury votes by a majority to convict. There then follows the second speech (35e–38b), in which Socrates proposes an alternative to the death penalty – or rather two alternatives. First, he proposes the penalty he says he deserves, which is to be fed and watered at public expense; then, even while maintaining his innocence, he proposes a punishment of a kind: a small fine, which is all he says he can afford. But after an intervention from his friends, he raises this by a factor of thirty. The jury votes again, and the majority against is even larger. At this point Socrates launches into his final reflections (the third speech: 38c–42a).

THE APOLOGY
OF SOCRATES
('SOCRATES' DEFENCE')

SOCRATES

17a   I don't know what effect my accusers have had on you, men of
Athens, but I can tell you they almost made even me forget where
I was, so convincingly did they speak. But when it comes to the
truth, they've said virtually nothing. The most astounding of the
many lies they told came when they claimed that you needed to
17b   take care not to be deceived by me, because of my artfulness as
a speaker. Their lack of concern that their claim will immediately be proved false, as I display my total lack of artfulness
as a speaker, seemed to me more shameful than anything else
– unless, of course, 'artful speaker' is what these people call
someone who tells the truth; because if that's what they have in
mind, I'll admit to being an orator, and one in a different league
from them. In any case, I repeat, they've said either little or
nothing that's true, whereas you'll hear from me the whole
truth. What you won't hear from me at all, I swear to you by
17c   Zeus, men of Athens, is language like theirs, full of fine words
and phrases and arranged in due order. What you will hear will
be in the words that come to me at the time, and as they come
to me, since I'm confident that what I say is just. Let none of
you expect any more. It wouldn't be fitting in any case for
someone of my age, Athenians, to come before you and fiddle
with words like an adolescent boy. But if there is one thing I ask
of you, men of Athens, it's that if you hear me talking, in my
defence, in the same language I habitually use in the market-
place around the bankers' stalls (where many of you have heard
17d   me)[1] and elsewhere, you shouldn't be astonished or protest at

it. This is the way it is: this is the first time, in my seventy years, that I've come before a law-court, and so the way people talk here is simply alien to me. So just as, if I were actually an alien, you'd obviously be sympathetic to me if I spoke in the same kind of Greek and the same style that I'd been brought up to speak, so I ask you here and now (and it's a just request, at least as I see it) to disregard the manner of my delivery – perhaps it won't stand comparison, perhaps it will – and to consider just this, and give your minds to this alone: whether or not what I say is just. For that is what makes for excellence in a juryman, just as what makes an excellent orator is telling the truth.

18a

Well, then, the right thing for me to do first, men of Athens, is to defend myself against the first false accusations made against me, and my first accusers, leaving till after that the accusations and accusers that have come along later. The fact is that it's nothing new for you Athenians to hear accusations against me; plenty of people have made them for plenty of years now, without saying anything that's true. Those accusers are the ones I fear more than Anytus and his lot, frightening though these latter ones are; more frightening, Athenians, are the ones who've been filling the ears of most of you since you were children and trying to convince you of something that's not the slightest bit truer than the rest: that there's a Socrates around who's an expert[2] – one who dabbles in theories about the heavenly bodies, who's already searched out everything beneath the earth and who makes the weaker argument the stronger.[3] It's the people spreading accusations like these, men of Athens, that are genuinely frightening. Why? Because their audience thinks that people who conduct research into these things don't even believe in the gods. There are also a large number of these accusers, and they've been making their accusations for a long time; what's more they were already talking to you at an age when you would have most readily believed them, being children, some of you, or adolescents, and they were prosecuting a case that went by default because there was no one there to defend it. But what is most unreasonable of all is that even their names aren't available to be listed, unless, that is, one or another of them happens to be a comic writer.[4] The ones who have

18b

18c

18d

slandered me out of malice and convinced you of their slanders, and the ones who, having been convinced themselves, have gone on to convince others – all these accusers are the most difficult to deal with, because it isn't even possible to have them appear in court, or to cross-examine a single one of them; I must simply shadow-box my defence against them, as it were, and mount my cross-examination with no one there to answer me. So I ask you to accept that, as I say, my accusers are two-fold: apart from the ones who have spoken out recently, there 18e are these other, more long-standing accusers I'm talking of, and I ask you to join me in supposing that I must defend myself first against the latter sort – for you yourselves heard them making their accusations earlier, and you were exposed to them much more than to these later accusers.

So, then: defend myself I must, men of Athens, and attempt 19a to remove from your minds, in this short time allotted to me, the slander that you have been exposed to for so long. Well, that's what I would like to achieve, if it's in any way the better outcome whether for you or for me. I would like to have some sort of success[5] in my defence. But I think it's going to be hard, and I'm well aware what kind of task it is. Never mind; let it go as it pleases the god,[6] and meanwhile the law must be obeyed and a defence made.

Let's start, then, from the beginning, by asking what the 19b accusation is that lies at the root of all the slander on which I suppose Meletus must be relying in taking out the present indictment against me. Well, then: what did the slanderers actually say when they slandered me? I should read it out, as if it were the prosecutors' affidavit: 'Socrates is guilty of busying himself with research into what's beneath the earth and in the heavens 19c and making the weaker argument the stronger and teaching the same things to others.' That's the sort of thing that's in my pretend affidavit: you saw it for yourselves in Aristophanes' comedy – a 'Socrates' being whirled around above the stage, claiming he's 'walking on air' and uttering a whole lot of other nonsense about things of which, speaking for myself, I have no inkling whatsoever. Nor do I say this out of disrespect for such knowledge, if there's someone around with expertise in such matters (please let me not have to defend myself against another suit brought by Meletus!); the simple fact is, men of Athens, that I have nothing to do with these things. As witnesses, I offer you yourselves, or most of you: I ask those of you who've ever heard me in conversation[7] (and there are plenty of you who have) to tell the others, if any one of you has ever yet heard me making the smallest mention of such things, and then you'll be in a position to see that the same also holds good for all the other things that people in general say about me.[8]

In fact not only is none of these things true, but also, if you've heard from any source that I undertake to teach people and charge money for it – that's not true either, though I think it would be a fine thing if someone did turn out to be able to teach people, like Gorgias of Leontini, or Prodicus of Ceos, or Hippias of Elis.[9] Each of these individuals, Athenians, is able to go into one city after another and persuade her young men, who have the option of spending time with whichever of their own fellow citizens they wish for no charge at all, to get together with *them* instead and not only pay good money for it but be grateful to them as well. Indeed I've learned there's another expert, a Parian, who's here in Athens at the moment. As it happened, I recently went up to someone who's paid out more money to sophists than everyone else put together, Callias son of Hipponicus, and I asked him – he has two sons – 'Callias, if your two sons had been born colts or calves, we could find someone to hire to take charge of them and make them fine and good, equipped with the appropriate excellence; and this person would be an expert in horse-training or farming. But as it is, since the two of them are human beings, whom do you have in mind to put in charge of them? Who is expert in this sort of excellence – the human, citizen sort? I imagine, seeing that you've acquired sons, that you've looked into the question. Is there anyone like this,' I said, 'or not?' 'Yes, absolutely,' he said. I asked 'Who is it? Where does he come from? And how much does he charge for his teaching?' 'It's Evenus, Socrates,' he said; 'he's from Paros, and he charges five minas.'[10] My reaction was to call Evenus a fortunate man if he genuinely possessed this expertise, and teaches it at so low a price.[11] I'd certainly be

19d

19e

20a

20b

20c

preening myself and putting on all sorts of airs if I had this knowledge. But the fact is that I don't, men of Athens.

One of you will probably then interject 'But Socrates, what is it about you? Where have these slanders against you come from? So much gossip and talk can't have come about because you were up to nothing more extraordinary than anyone else; you must be doing something different from what ordinary people do. So tell us what it is, so that we don't get things wrong about you in the way others do.' Now *this* seems to me a legitimate thing to say, and I will try to show you just what it is that has brought about the false reputation that I have. So hear me out. Probably some of you will think I'm not being serious; but I can assure you that what I'm going to say will be the whole truth. I have earned my reputation, men of Athens, for no reason other than that I possess a certain sort of wisdom. What sort of wisdom could this be? Probably a wisdom of a human sort. It's likely enough that I really am wise in this way; whereas those others I mentioned just now will be wise with a sort of wisdom that's beyond the human – or if that's not so, I don't know what to say, because *I* certainly don't have their wisdom, and anyone who says I do is lying and deliberately misrepresenting me.

Now please don't protest, men of Athens, even if I may seem to you to be boasting a bit. What I say won't be coming from me; it comes from a source you'll find impeccable. As to my . . . well, as to whether it actually *is* wisdom, and what sort of wisdom it is, as witness I mean to offer you: the god at Delphi.[12] How so? I imagine you know Chaerephon. He was not only a friend of mine from my youth, but a friend of the people, who shared your recent exile and returned from exile with you.[13] You also know what kind of person Chaerephon was, and how single-minded he was about anything he undertook. This time he actually went to Delphi and had the face to ask the oracle (once again, Athenians, I ask you not to protest) – he actually asked whether anyone was wiser than I was, and the Pythia duly replied that there was no one wiser. Chaerephon's brother here will testify to all this, since the man himself is dead.

Consider why I'm telling you this: to explain to you the

"Please stop booing."

source of the slander against me. When I heard what the Pythia had said, I thought to myself 'What can the god be saying? It's a riddle: what can it mean? I've no knowledge of my being wise in any respect, great or small, so what is he saying when he claims that I'm the wisest? He certainly can't be *lying*; that's out of the question for him.' For a long time I was at a loss as to what the god was saying, but then, with great reluctance, I turned to inquiring into his response. I went about it like this: I approached one of those individuals people suppose to be wise, on the basis that here if anywhere I could challenge the 21c oracle's response by pointing out someone it had missed – 'This person here is wiser than me, and you said I was wiser than him!' Well, I examined this person – I've no need to mention his name, but the person with whom I had the sort of experience I'm about to describe, when I examined him, was one of the political experts;[14] and as I conversed with him, I formed the conclusion that, while this person seemed wise to lots of other people, and especially to himself, in reality he wasn't; upon which I made a concerted attempt to demonstrate to him that he only thought he was wise, but really wasn't. Well, that made 21d him hate me, as it did a lot of those who were present; but I reasoned to myself, as I left him, like this – 'I am actually wiser than this person; likely enough neither of us knows anything of importance, but he *thinks* he knows something when he doesn't, whereas just as I don't know anything, so I don't think I do, either. So I appear to be wiser, at least than him, in just this one small respect: that when I don't know things, I don't think that I do either.' After that I went on to someone else, supposedly wiser than him, and reached exactly the same conclusion; at that point I became an object of hate both for him 21e and for many others.

Well, after that I went on to another person, and another; distressed and fearful though I was as I perceived their hatred for me, I thought I must make my business with the god the first priority. So, as I searched for the meaning of the oracle, there was nothing for it but to approach everyone with a repu- 22a tation for knowing something. And by the Dog,[15] men of Athens, because I'm bound to tell you the truth, I swear to you that it turned out something like this: that those with the greatest reputations seemed to me, as I continued my divinely instigated search, practically the most deficient, while others who were supposedly inferior seemed better endowed when it came to good sense.

I should give you a picture of these wanderings of mine – these labours,[16] as it were, that I undertook in order to leave the oracle's response unrefuted. After the political experts I 22b went on to the poets – tragic, dithyrambic and the rest – on the basis that it was here I'd catch myself red-handed, as actually more ignorant than them. So, picking out those of their poetic compositions they seemed to me to have spent most effort on, I would ask them what they were trying to say, with a view to learning a thing or two from them as well. Well, Athenians, I blush to tell you the truth, but it has to be told: practically speaking, almost everyone present would have better things to say than they did about their own compositions. So I quickly came to the same conclusion about the poets as I 22c had about the others, that it wasn't through wisdom that they did what they did, but rather through some sort of natural talent, or because they were inspired like the seers and the soothsayers, who make many fine utterances but have no knowledge about the things they're saying. That, I thought, was clearly the case with the poets too; and I noticed that they thought their poetry-making also made them the wisest of men about everything else too, which they weren't.[17] So I left the poets thinking that I'd outdone them in the same respect that I'd outdone the political experts.[18] Finally, I went on to the craftsmen. I knew 22d that I myself had practically no knowledge, whereas I knew that I'd find them knowing lots of fine things. Nor was I mistaken about that. They did know things I didn't, and in that respect they were wiser than me.[19] But, men of Athens, the good craftsmen[20] too seemed to me to suffer from the same failing as the poets: because they were accomplished in practising their skill, each one of them claimed to be wisest about other things too, the most important ones at that – and this error of theirs 22e seemed to me to obscure the wisdom they did possess. The outcome was that I asked myself, in defence of the oracle, whether I'd prefer to be as I am, and not be either in the least bit wise with their wisdom or ignorant with their ignorance, or to have both their wisdom and their ignorance together. And the answer I gave myself, and the oracle, was that I was better off as I was.

The result of my inquiry, then, men of Athens, has been that I have become an object of hatred for many people, and hatred of a particularly intractable and intolerable kind, which has brought about numerous slanders against me and given me that reputation of being *wise*; for on every occasion the onlookers suppose that if I refute someone else I must myself be an expert in whatever the discussion is about. But the truth most likely is, Athenians, that it's the god who's really wise, and that in this utterance of the oracle he's simply saying that human wisdom is worth very little, or nothing at all. And in mentioning this 'Socrates', he appears to be using my name just to treat me as an illustration – as if he were to say 'The wisest among you, humans, is the one who like Socrates has recognized that in truth he's worth nothing when it comes to wisdom.' That's why I, for my part, still go around even now on this search of mine, instigated by the god, so that if I think anyone, whether fellow citizen or foreigner, might be wise, I'll sniff him out; and whenever I conclude that he isn't wise, I come to the aid of the god by demonstrating that he isn't. It's because of this preoccupation of mine that I've not had the leisure to make any contribution worth speaking of either to the city's affairs or to my own; instead I find myself in extreme poverty, because of my service to the god.[21]

In addition to all of this the young ones follow me around, since they have all the leisure in the world – that is, the wealthiest of them, and they do it of their own accord, because they love hearing those fellows being put to the test; often they copy me amongst themselves, and then they go on to try out their technique by examining others, and I imagine that as a result they find a great superfluity of people who think they know something but actually know little or nothing. So the next thing is that their victims get angry with me instead of with themselves, and talk about some quite abominable Socrates who corrupts

23a

23b

23c

23d

the young; and when anyone asks them what they have against
him, and what he teaches that has this effect, they have nothing
to say and simply don't know; but so as to avoid seeming to be
at a loss they produce the slogans that are ready to hand for use
against all philosophers: 'things up in the heavens and below
the earth', 'not believing in the gods', 'making the weaker argument the stronger'. They wouldn't want to admit the truth,
which is that they're shown up by their questioners as pretend-
23e   ing to know when they actually know nothing. So because of
what I take to be their desire to get ahead, their vigour, and
their sheer numbers, and because they talk so earnestly and
convincingly about me, they've managed to fill your ears from
way back with an equally vigorous slander. On the back of all
of this, Meletus has now joined in the attack on me, along with
Anytus and Lycon: Meletus out of irritation on behalf of the
poets, Anytus on behalf of the craftsmen and the political
24a   experts, and Lycon on behalf of the orators.[22] So, as I was
saying at the beginning, I'd be astonished if I turned out to be
able to remove all this slander from your minds in so short a
time, when you have been exposed to it for so long. What I'm
telling you, men of Athens, is the truth, and I address you without concealing anything, significant or not, and without dis-
simulation. But that's the reason, I'm pretty sure, that I'm so
hated; and that in itself is proof that I'm right, and that the
slanders against me and their causes are as I have described
24b   them. No matter whether you look into the matter now or
later, that's what you'll find.

Let this, then, be a sufficient defence before you in relation
to the charges made against me by my first accusers; next I shall
try to defend myself against Meletus – good, patriotic Meletus,
as he represents himself – and the other later accusers.

Let's do as we did before, then; let's read their affidavit, as if
it belonged to a different set of accusers. It's something like
this; it says that Socrates is guilty of corrupting the young and
24c   not believing in the gods the city believes in, but in other new
divinities.[23] So the charge is like that. Let's examine each aspect
of this charge, one by one.

The man says I'm guilty of corrupting the young. But I say,

men of Athens, that it's Meletus who's the guilty party, for treating serious matters as a joke – taking people to court as if it were a light matter, and pretending a serious concern for things that never meant anything to him up till now.[24] I'll try to demonstrate to you that this is so.

[*There follows a period of cross-examination.*]

Here, Meletus, and tell me this: am I right in saying it's your first priority that the younger among us should be in the best   24d possible condition?

'It is.'[25]

So come on, tell these people: who is it that makes them better? Plainly you must know, since it means so much to you. At any rate you've found the person who's corrupting them,[26] as you claim, namely me, and you're bringing him before these jurymen here and charging him; so who's the one to make them better? Come on, say who it is; reveal to them who it is. – Do you see, Meletus? You say nothing, because you've nothing *to* say. But doesn't that seem to you to be shameful, and already sufficient proof of exactly what I'm saying, that it's not a meaningful subject to you? Fine. So tell me, my good man, who makes our young ones better people?

'It's the laws.'

That wasn't what I was asking, my fine fellow; I was asking   24e you what *person* makes them better – someone who knows these very things, the laws, above anything else.

'These people here, Socrates, the members of the jury.'

What are you saying, Meletus? These people are able to teach the young, make them better?

'Certainly.'

All of them? Or just some of them, and not others?

'All of them.'

A happy answer, by Hera; you're saying there's a great superfluity of people to help them. What about the spectators over there – do they make the young better as well, or not?   25a

'They do too.'

What about the members of the Council?

'The Councillors too.'

Surely, then, Meletus, those who sit in the Assembly, the

Assemblymen – *they* don't corrupt the younger ones? All of these make them better too?

'They do too.'

In that case, Meletus, it seems that every single Athenian[27] makes them into fine and upstanding people except for me; I alone corrupt them. Is that what you're saying?

'That's what I'm saying, most emphatically.'

What great misfortune you've condemned me to! Answer me this: does it seem to you to be like this with horses too? That 25b it's all mankind that improves them, and just one person who corrupts them? Or is the situation quite the opposite of this, that there's one person or a very small number of people who can improve them, namely the horse-experts, whereas most people, if they even have anything to do with horses, or use them, actually make them worse? Isn't that how it is, Meletus, whether with horses or with any other sort of animal? Yes indeed it is, whether you and Anytus deny it or accept it; because if there's one person and only one who corrupts our young men, while everyone else benefits them, it would 25c be a great piece of good fortune in their case. But the fact is, Meletus, that your behaviour is sufficient demonstration of your total lack of concern for the young up till now; you clearly show your own negligence, and the fact that the things you're bringing me to court for aren't a meaningful subject for you[28] at all.

And answer for me this further question, for heaven's sake, Meletus: is it better to live among fellow citizens who are good or those who are vicious?[29] Sir, answer the question – it's not a difficult one. Don't vicious people do some sort of damage[30] to those closest to them, in whatever context, whereas good people correspondingly do them some sort of good?

'Yes, absolutely.'

25d   Well, is there anyone who prefers to be damaged rather than benefited by the people he has to deal with? Answer, my good man, since the law says you must. Is there anyone who wishes to be damaged?

'Certainly not.'

Come on, then: are you bringing me before the court for

corrupting the young and making them more vicious intentionally or unintentionally?

'Intentionally.'

What's this, Meletus? Are you so much wiser than me, even
though you're so young and I'm so old, that you've noticed that
the bad always do some damage to those who are nearest to   25e
them and the good benefit them, whereas I have reached such a
pitch of ignorance that I'm actually unaware of the fact that if I
make anyone among the people I associate with into a depraved[31]
person, I shall very likely be the recipient of some damage from
him? You're telling me I'm intentionally doing something *that*
bad?[32] You don't convince me that I am, and I don't think you'll
convince anyone else in the world, either.[33] Either I don't corrupt people, or, if I do, I corrupt them unintentionally, so that   26a
whichever way you take it your charge is false. And if I do corrupt people unintentionally, then the law is that for such offences
a person shouldn't be brought to court; instead he should be
taken off for private instruction and a private telling off, since
evidently, if I'm acting unintentionally, I'll stop doing it as soon
as I understand what I'm doing. But you shied away from getting
together with me to give me my lesson; you refused that option
and preferred to bring me to court, when the law says prosecu-
tion is for those needing punishment, not lecturing.

So there it is, men of Athens: what I was claiming, that   26b
Meletus has never yet concerned himself[34] in the slightest degree
with these things, is by now clear enough. But all the same tell
us *how* you say I corrupt the younger among us, Meletus. Or is
it, clearly, to go by the indictment as you've framed it, by teaching them not to believe in the gods the city believes in but to
treat new and different things as 'divine'? Isn't that what you
say I teach and so corrupt them?

'Yes, absolutely, that's what I say, emphatically.'

Well then, Meletus, by those very gods we're talking about,
make things even clearer than you have so far, both to me and
to the jurymen here. I'm unable to establish whether you're   26c
saying I teach the young to believe that there are gods of some
sort (in which case I believe there are gods myself, so that I'm
not a total atheist; I'm innocent on that score), just different

ones, not the ones the city believes in – I'm unclear whether *that*'s what you're charging me with, believing in different gods, or whether your charge is unqualified on both counts: that I don't myself believe in gods at all, and that this is what I teach others.

'This is what I'm saying, that you're a total non-believer in the gods.'

26d   Meletus, my dear man, why on earth are you saying that? Don't I suppose the sun, even, or the moon to be gods, then, like the rest of mankind?

'I swear to Zeus he doesn't, men of the jury, because he says the sun is a rock and the moon is made of earth.'

Do you suppose you're prosecuting Anaxagoras,[35] my dear Meletus? Are you so contemptuous of these people here, and think them so illiterate as not to know that these assertions are bursting out of Anaxagoras' books? Are the young really supposed to be learning things from me that sometimes they'd 26e be able to pick up from the orchestra[36] for a drachma at the very most? Wouldn't they laugh at Socrates if he should ever pretend they were his and not Anaxagoras', especially when they're so strange?[37] By Zeus, is that really how you think of me? You think I don't believe in any god at all?

'None at all, by Zeus; none whatsoever.'

You're not credible, Meletus, and in this instance I don't think you even believe yourself. Men of Athens, this person here seems to me totally insolent and unscrupulous; that's all that lies behind this indictment of his – a kind of youthful inso- 27a lence and lack of scruple. He's like someone who's putting together a riddle, to see if I'll get the point: 'Will Socrates, who's so wise, see that I'm making a joke of contradicting myself, or will I bamboozle him and the rest of those listening?' For in fact he does appear to me to be contradicting himself in the indictment: it's as if he were saying, 'Socrates is guilty of not believing in gods, but believing in gods.' Someone who says that is merely playing about and not serious.

So let me explain to you, Athenians, why I take him to be saying this. You, Meletus, answer my questions; meanwhile I 27b ask you, the jury, to remember the request I made to you at the beginning of my defence, not to protest if I express myself in my habitual style.[38]

Is there anyone on earth, Meletus, who believes in the existence of human things, but not in the existence of humans? I demand that the man answer, Athenians, instead of making one protest after another.[39] Is there anyone who doesn't believe in horses, but does believe in horsey things? Or doesn't believe pipers exist, but does believe in piperish things? There's no such person, Meletus, best of men; if you won't give the answer, I'll say it for you, and for these people here. At least answer the next question: is there anyone who believes in the existence of divine things, but not in the existence of divinities?   27c

'There's no one.'

How good of you to answer – even if you could barely get the words out, and because the jury here forced you to. Well then: you say that I both believe and teach that there are divine things, whether these are new ones or old ones – for the moment I don't mind;[40] at any rate, on your account I do believe in divine things, and you've sworn to precisely that in your indictment of me. But if I believe in divine things, then surely there's no way I can avoid believing in divinities? Isn't that so? It is; since you don't reply, I'll put you down as agreeing with me. And divinities[41] – don't we suppose these either actually to be   27d gods, or at any rate children of gods? Do you agree or not?

'Yes, absolutely.'

Fine: so if in fact I believe in divinities, as you yourself claim I do, then if divinities are some sort of gods, that'll be the riddle I'm saying you're putting together, as your way of making a joke, that while I don't believe in gods, then again I do believe in gods, given that I believe in divinities; if on the other hand these divinities are only the children of gods, whether bastards of some sort, or born from nymphs, or whoever it is they're said to be from, who on earth would believe in children of gods and not in gods? It would be just as strange as if someone were   27e to believe in the offspring of mares and donkeys, namely mules, but didn't believe there were mares or donkeys. When you composed your indictment like this, Meletus, it *must* have been to see if we'd get the joke – or else it was because you were at

a loss as to what true crime you could charge me with. If you're seriously proposing to convince anyone with even a bit of intelligence *both* that someone who believes in divine things must also believe in things to do with gods *and* that this same person
28a won't believe in divinities, or gods, or heroes – well, there's no way you can possibly convince anyone at all.

[*The cross-examination of Meletus ends.*]

So there you are, men of Athens. To show that I'm not guilty according to the terms of Meletus' indictment doesn't seem to me to require much from me; just the little I've offered is enough. But believe you me, there's no mistake about my earlier claim. I've earned myself a lot of hatred, and from a lot of people, and this is what will convict me, if that's how it turns out: not Meletus, and not Anytus either, but the malicious slan-
28b der of people in general. That's taken down many others before me, good men too,[42] and I imagine it'll take more; there's no danger it will end with me.

Well, probably someone will say to me, 'Then aren't you ashamed of yourself, Socrates, for going in for the kind of activity that puts you in the danger you're in now, of being put to death?' To this person I'll retort, and justly, 'You're wrong, my man, if you think a person who's of any use at all should take danger into account, weighing up his chances of living or dying, instead of making it the sole consideration, whenever he acts,
28c whether his actions are just or unjust, and whether they're what a good man would do or a bad one. By your reasoning all those demigods who died at Troy would be poor creatures;[43] not least the son of Thetis,[44] who was so contemptuous of danger when he compared it with incurring disgrace that when his mother, a goddess, addressed him, eager as he was to kill Hector – with words that were I imagine something like this: "Son, if you take revenge for the killing of your friend Patroclus, and kill Hector, you'll prepare your own death; for straightway," the poet[45] says, "after Hector's is your death prepared" – when he heard this, he looked down on death and danger and, having much greater
28d fear of living a coward and not avenging those he loved, the poet has him saying, "Then straightway let me die, with the guilty punished; or here shall I lie, an object of mirth beside the beaked

ships, a dead weight upon earth." Surely you don't think *he* cared about death and danger?'

That's how it is, men of Athens, in truth: wherever a person makes his stand, either because that's where he thinks it best for him to be or under orders from a superior, that, it seems to me, is where he must stay and face danger, taking nothing into account, even death, before avoiding what is shameful. I myself would have been behaving in a shocking fashion, men of Athens, if I stood firm, like everyone else, and risked death when the commanders you chose to command me gave me the order to do so, whether at Potidaea or Amphipolis or Delium,[46] but then, when the god gave me my orders, as I thought and supposed he had, to live a life of philosophy, examining myself and others, at *that* point I conceived a fear either of death or of whatever else it might be and abandoned my post. It would indeed be a shocking thing to do, and would truly give someone just cause for taking me to court for not believing in the gods; after all, there I'd be, disobeying the oracle, fearing death and thinking I was wise when I wasn't. For I tell you, Athenians, the fear of death is simply this, thinking yourself wise when you are not; it's thinking you know what you don't know. Death may even be the greatest of all good things for a human being – no one knows, yet people fear it as if they knew for sure that it's the greatest of bad things. And how is this kind of ignorance not reprehensible – thinking one knows what one doesn't? As for me, Athenians, it's just in this one respect that I probably am superior to the majority of mankind; if there's any way in which I'd claim to be wiser than the next man, it would be because, not possessing enough knowledge about the things in Hades, I actually think I don't know; whereas I do know that to be guilty of disobeying someone better than me,[47] whether god or man, is bad and shameful. So, faced as I am with bad things that I know to be bad, I'll never turn tail for fear of things that, for all I know, may even be good.[48] So now imagine you're prepared to let me go, and refuse to listen to Anytus, who said that either I shouldn't have been brought to court in the first place or, since I have been brought here, it was not an option not to apply the death penalty – because, he said, if I get off, your sons will all

28e

29a

29b

29c

set about doing what Socrates teaches and all be totally corrupted: imagine that you said to me, in response to this,
'Socrates, for the moment we're not going to listen to Anytus,
and we're prepared to let you go, but on this one condition,
that you stop spending your time in this search of yours, and
you stop doing philosophy. But if you're caught doing this in
29d   the future, we'll put you to death.' Well, my point was that, if
you let me go on these conditions, I'd say to you, 'I have the
greatest respect and love for you, men of Athens, but I shall
obey the god rather than you, and so long as I breathe and so
long as I am able I shall never stop doing philosophy, exhorting
you all the while and declaring myself[49] to whichever of you I
meet – saying the sort of things that it's my habit to say: "Best
of men, I ask you this: when you're an Athenian, and so belong
to the greatest city, the one with the highest reputation for
wisdom and strength, aren't you ashamed of caring about
29e   acquiring the greatest possible amount of money, together with
reputation and honours, while not caring about, even sparing a
thought for, wisdom and truth, and making your soul as good
as possible?" And every time one of you disputes the matter
with me and claims that he *does* care, I won't let him get away
with it and walk away. Instead I'll question and examine and
30a   challenge him, and if he doesn't seem to me to have acquired
excellence, but claims that he has, I'll rebuke him for making
things that are most valuable his lowest priority and giving
higher priority to things of lesser worth. That's what I'll do for
any one of you I meet, whether young or old, foreigner or
citizen – though I put my fellow citizens first, insofar as you are
more akin to me. This is what the god tells me to do, make no
mistake about it, and I don't think you've ever yet benefited
more from anything than you have from my service to the god.
What I *do*,[50] as I move around among you, is just this: I try to
persuade you, whether younger or older, to give less priority,
30b   and devote less zeal, to the care of your bodies or of your money
than to the care of your soul and trying to make it as good as
it can be. What I say to you is: "It's not from money that
excellence comes, but from excellence money and the other
things, all of them, come to be good for human beings, whether

in private or in public life."[51] So if it's by saying *this* that I corrupt the young, it will be this that is damaging them; and if anyone claims that I say something other than this, they're talking nonsense. So, men of Athens,' I'd say to you,[52] 'that's what you need to take into account when you make your decision either to do what Anytus says or not – either let me go or don't, knowing that I would behave no differently even if that meant I'd be put to death many times over.' 30c

Don't protest, men of Athens, but keep to the terms of my request to you, to hear me out and not protest at anything I say, because I think you'll benefit if you do listen. In any case I'm now going to say more things that probably will have you shouting out at me; just don't do it. What you should know is that if I'm the sort of person I say I am, your killing me will do me less damage than it does you; for neither will Meletus damage me, nor Anytus – nor could he, since I think it's not permitted[53] for a better man to be damaged by a worse one. He'll 30d have me killed, no doubt, or sent into exile, or stripped of my citizenship, and probably – I imagine he isn't alone in this – he thinks of these as great evils; but that's not how I think of them. I think it a much worse thing to be doing what he's now doing, trying to have a man put to death without just cause. So as a matter of fact, men of Athens, far from defending myself, as one might suppose, what I'm doing now is actually defending *you*, so that you don't make a mistake with the god's gift to you 30e by casting your votes against me. Because if you do put me to death, you won't easily find anyone else quite like me, attached by the god to the city, if it's not too comic an image, as if to a horse – a big and noble horse, but one that's rather sleepy because of its size, all the time needing to be woken up by some sort of gadfly: this is the kind of role the god gave me when he attached me to the city, and the result is that there's never a moment when I'm not waking you up and cajoling and rebuk- 31a ing you, each one of you, the whole day long, settling on you wherever you may be. Another one like me, Athenians, as I say, it won't be easy for you to find, and if you take my advice you'll spare me; but probably you'll be irritated at me, and like people who are woken up as they're nodding off you'll hit out at me,

taking Anytus' advice instead of mine, and take the easy course of putting me to death, after which you'll spend the rest of your lives asleep, unless in his care for you the god should send someone else to stop you. That I really am the sort of person to have been given by the god to the city you might infer from
31b   something about me that doesn't look quite human: that I've totally neglected my own affairs, and put up with the neglect of what belongs to me for so many years now, while always acting in your interest, approaching each of you privately as if I were a father or elder brother and trying to persuade you to care for excellence.[54] That would be a reasonable way for me to behave, if I made something out of it, and got paid for my exhortations, but as it is you can see for yourselves that, while my accusers show no sense of shame in anything else they say about me, in this one respect they weren't able to brazen it out and provide
31c   a single witness to say that I ever either received or asked for payment. I offer my poverty as witness that I'm telling the truth; that should be enough.

Now it will probably seem strange that I go about as I do, busying myself with giving advice in private but not venturing to advise the city in public, when you're gathered together in the Assembly. The cause of this is something that you yourselves have often heard me talking about,[55] all over the place, that
31d   some god or 'divinity' intervenes with me – something Meletus caricatured in his indictment. It's something that started in my boyhood, a sort of voice that comes to me and, when it comes, always discourages me from doing what I'm about to do, never encourages me. It's this that opposes my playing the statesman, and it's a fine thing that it does, it seems to me, for you can be quite sure, men of Athens, that if I'd set about a political career all those years ago, I'd long ago have come to a sticky end and
31e   would have been of no use either to you or to myself. Don't be annoyed with me for telling the truth: there isn't anyone in the world who'll survive if he genuinely opposes you or any other popular majority and tries to prevent widespread injustice and
32a   lawlessness from occurring in the city. Anyone who's really fighting for justice must live as a private citizen and not as a public figure if he's going to survive even a short time.

What I'll offer you as evidence for all this is not just words but the hard facts that you set such store by. You've heard the details of my history, which show you that fear of death will not make me give in to anything or anyone if it means going against what's just; I'll even die not giving in. What I'm going to mention to you is vulgar, the sort of thing that's typically talked about in court cases, but all the same it's true. I've never in my life held any office in the city, men of Athens, except that 32b I did serve as a member of the Council; and it happened that my tribe, Antiochis, held the presidency when you approved the proposal to put the ten generals who failed to pick up the dead from the sea-battle[56] on trial together – contrary to the law, as all of you decided later on. At the time, I alone among those presiding opposed your doing anything contrary to the laws and voted against; and when the orators were ready to move against me and have me taken away, with your loud support, I thought I should rather take my chances on the side of 32c law and justice than be on your side, out of a fear of imprisonment or death, when you were approving things that were not just. This was during the time when the city was still ruled by the democracy; when the oligarchy was instituted, the Thirty had their go at me, sending for me and four others to come to the Roundhouse,[57] and ordering us to bring Leon of Salamis from Salamis for execution; lots of other people found this sort of thing happening to them all the time, as the oligarchs gave out orders so as to spread responsibility for what was going on as widely as possible. Then it was that I showed not by mere 32d talk but by my actions that the amount I care about dying – if it's not too boorish to say so – is zero, and that all my care is devoted to doing nothing unjust, or impious. The fact is that that regime, for all its power, did not terrify me into doing something that was unjust. Instead, when we left the Round-house, the other four went off to Salamis and brought Leon in, but I went off home. I would probably have been executed for this if the regime hadn't been brought to an end shortly after-wards. You'll find plenty of witnesses for all of this. 32e

So do you think I would have survived for so many years if I had taken a public role and performed it – as any good man should – as the ally of everything just, and making this, as it must be, the highest priority? Not by a long way, men of Athens;

33a and no one else in the world would survive for long like that, either. But if I have ever performed any action in any public context, you'll find me exactly as I've described, and in private the same: someone who has never yet agreed to anything contrary to justice with anyone at all, and certainly not with any of those they slanderously call my pupils.[58] I have never, ever, been anybody's teacher; if anyone, young or old, wants to listen to me as I talk and do what I do, I've never begrudged it to any-

33b one, nor do I talk to people if I get money for it but otherwise not. Instead, I offer myself to rich and poor alike, for them to ask their questions and, if anyone wishes, to listen to whatever I have to say and answer *my* questions. Whether any one of these people turns out well or not, it wouldn't be fair for me to be held responsible for things that I never to this day promised anyone he'd learn from me, and have never taught, and if any-one says he ever learned or heard from me something in private of a sort that all the rest didn't hear as well, then you can be certain that he's not telling the truth.

33c   Why is it, then, that some people enjoy spending large amounts of time with me? You have heard my explanation, men of Athens – and it's no less than the truth of the matter: that they enjoy witnessing the examination of people who think they're wise when they're not; and it has its delights. But what I do, as I say, I do because the god has assigned it to me, whether he communicates through oracular responses, or dreams, or any other means gods use to assign whatever task it may be to human beings.[59]

And what I say, men of Athens, is both true and easily

33d checked. Just think. If I'm currently corrupting some of the young, and I have corrupted others, then surely – let's suppose that some of them are now old enough to realize that I advised them badly in their youth: surely now is the time they should be stepping up and pressing charges by way of getting their own back? Or, if they were reluctant to do it themselves, shouldn't some of their relatives be stepping in, whether fathers, brothers, or whichever? If their kinsmen were the victims of some malfeasance on my part, shouldn't they now be mindful of it and pay me back? There are more than enough of them here: I can see them with my own eyes – first of all there's Crito, my coeval and fellow demesman, who's the father of Critobulus 33e here; next there's Lysanias of Sphettus, father of Aeschines, and also Antiphon of Cephissus, Epigenes' father, both there with their sons; and then there are others whose brothers have spent their time with me, Nicostratus son of Theozotides, brother of Theodotus – admittedly, Theodotus is dead, so he couldn't have asked Nicostratus to act for him; Paralius too, son of Demodocus, whose brother was Theages; and there's Adimantus, son of 34a Ariston, whose brother is Plato there, and Aiantodorus, who's brother is Apollodorus[60] – also here. I can identify lots of others as well, one of whom Meletus should surely have offered you as a witness, preferably during his own speech; or if he forgot to do it then, let him do it now (I'll make him that concession), and let him say whether he has something like that up his sleeve. In fact you'll find it's quite the opposite. You'll find them all ready to help me, the corrupter, the one that's doing damage, or so Meletus and Anytus claim, to members of their family. It 34b might perhaps be reasonable for those who've been corrupted to come to my aid themselves; but those who weren't corrupted, and are more grown up now, the relatives of those others – what reason do they have for coming to my aid except the one that's correct and just, that they know Meletus is lying and I'm telling the truth?

So there you are, Athenians; that's pretty much all I have to say in my defence, apart from some other things probably of the same sort. Perhaps one of you will take offence when he 34c remembers how *he* behaved, if even when fighting a case less serious than the one I'm fighting he resorted to begging and supplicating the jury, in floods of tears, bringing his little children into court so that everyone should feel as sorry as anything for him, other relatives too, and lots of friends; and here I am, apparently proposing to do none of these things even when faced – so people will suppose – with the last and worst of all dangers. Perhaps these thoughts will cause one or another of you to harden his view of me; he'll get angry with me on

34d these very grounds, and cast his vote accordingly. If any one of
you is in this position – I don't think he should be, but in any
case, if he is – I think it would be a decent response to him to
say, 'Actually, best of men, even I have *relatives*, I imagine; this
is that saying of Homer's – I'm not born "from oak or from
rock", but from human beings, so that I do have relatives, and,
yes, sons too, men of Athens, three of them, one by now a lad
but the other two still small; all the same I will not bring any
one of them into court and beg you to acquit me.' So *why*
won't I do any of these things? Not out of wilfulness, men of
34e Athens, nor out of disrespect for you; whether I face death with
confidence or not is a different issue, but so far as appearances
are concerned, doing any of the things in question would seem
to me not to reflect well on me, or you, or the city as a whole,
given my age and the name that I have – whether it's true or it's
35a false, it's the established view that 'Socrates' is in some respect
superior to the common run of mankind. Well, if those among
you who are thought to excel in wisdom, or courage, or any other
kind of excellence are going to behave like that, it'd be shameful;
I've seen people doing it, when they're on trial – people who are
thought to be of some worth, but then go on to do surprising
things because they think something awful will be happening
to them if they die, as if they'll be immortal providing *you* don't
kill them off. People like that seem to me to hang a badge of
35b shame on the city, so that a visitor might even suppose that
those outstandingly excellent Athenians whom their fellow
citizens choose over themselves for public offices and other
kinds of honour are no better than women. Behaviour like that,
men of Athens, is not only something you shouldn't indulge in
yourselves, if you've any worth whatever in people's eyes, but
if I indulge in it, you shouldn't let me; you should give a clear
indication that you'll much sooner vote against someone who
makes the city a laughing-stock by bringing on these pitiful
exhibitions than against the man who keeps his peace.

But quite apart from the question of appearances, Atheni-
35c ans, it also doesn't seem to me just to *beg* a member of the jury,
or to get off by begging. The just thing is to inform and convince. A juryman doesn't sit for the purpose of giving out justice

as a favour, but to decide where justice lies; and he's sworn an oath that he won't dispense favours as he sees fit, but will make his decision according to the laws. Neither, then, should I try to get you into the habit of breaking your oath, nor should you acquire the habit, because then neither I nor you would be behaving piously. So, men of Athens, please don't expect me to behave towards you in ways that I don't think either honour- 35d able, or just, or pious, particularly and especially – Zeus! – when it's on a charge of impiety that I'm in the process of defending myself against Meletus here. Plainly, if I were to persuade you by begging, browbeating you when you're under oath, I'd turn out to be teaching *you* that the gods don't exist, and I'd literally be making it part of my defence to accuse myself of not believ- ing in them. But that's not the case at all; I do believe in the gods, men of Athens, as none of my accusers does, and I leave it in your hands and in the god's to reach whatever decision about me is going to be best both for me and for you.

[*Socrates speaks again after the voting.*]

There are many reasons, men of Athens, why I'm not upset 35e about what has occurred, and at your having voted against me, 36a but the main reason is that it was not unexpected. In fact I'm much more surprised at the numbers of votes on the two sides. I didn't think the margin would be so small; I thought it would be a big one. As it is, it seems that if a mere thirty votes had gone the other way, I would have been acquitted. So far as Meletus' contribution is concerned, I think I actually do stand acquitted, even now, and not only that, it's obvious to anyone that if Anytus hadn't come forward to accuse me, and Lycon, Meletus would have been fined a thousand drachmas for not 36b getting the required fifth of the votes.[61]

In any case, the man proposes the penalty of death. Fine: what alternative penalty shall I put to you, men of Athens? Or is it clear – the one I deserve? What, then? What do I deserve to have done to me, or what fine do I deserve to pay, for the crime of not spending my life keeping to myself? What I have done is to turn my back on the things most people care about – money-making, managing a household, generalships, popular speech-making and all the other aspects of communal life in the city, whether public offices or private clubs and factions – because

36c I concluded that I was truly too fair-minded a person to go in for this sort of thing and stay alive. So I didn't take that turning, because I knew that that way I would be no use at all either to you or to myself. Instead I headed along a different route, one that would lead, as I claim, to my doing you, privately, the greatest of good turns, as I try to persuade each one of you both to stop caring for your possessions before caring for yourself and making yourself as good and wise as possible, and to stop caring

36d for the city's possessions before caring for the city itself – and to apply the same rule in the same way in caring for everything else.[62] What, then, do I deserve to have happen to me, if that's the kind of person I am? Something good, I submit, men of Athens, if I'm to set my penalty in accordance with what I truly deserve, and not only that, the sort of good thing that would fit my case. So what does fit the case of a poor man who's your benefactor and needs free time to exhort you all? There's nothing that fits better, men of Athens, than to have such a person fed at public expense in the Prytaneum;[63] much better him than one of you who's won a horse-race at Olympia, or won with a pair or a team of four, because someone like that makes you seem happy,[64]

36e whereas because of me you *are* happy, and what's more he doesn't
37a need feeding and I do. So if I'm to make a just assessment of the penalty I deserve, this is it – free food in the Prytaneum.

Probably when I say this too I'll seem to you to be talking in the same wilful sort of way as when I talked about the practice of making pitiful appeals. But it isn't like that, men of Athens; rather it's like this – I'm convinced that I wrong no one in the world, intentionally, but I don't convince you of it, because the time we've had for conversation between us is too short. In fact, in my opinion, if the law were the same here as everywhere else, and you had to spend not just one but several days

37b judging capital cases, you would have been convinced; as it is, the slanders against me are too great to be undone in so short a time. In any case, given my conviction that I do no wrong to anyone, I'm hardly likely to go on to wrong myself by saying on my own account I deserve something bad and myself proposing that kind of penalty. Why would I do that? Out of fear? Fear of having done to me what Meletus proposes, when I say I don't know whether it's a good thing or a bad thing? Instead, then, am I to choose one of the things I know very well to be bad, proposing that as my penalty?[65] Imprisonment, perhaps? Why, I ask you, should I live in prison, as the slave of which- 37c ever collection of people happened to make up the Eleven,[66] year after year? A fine, then, and imprisonment until I pay it? It's the same answer I gave just now – I don't have any money to pay with. So what about my proposing exile – since prob- ably you'd accept that? I'd have to be possessed with a great passion for life, men of Athens, to make me so poor at adding up that I couldn't do a simple calculation: when it was even beyond you, my fellow citizens, to put up with my discourses 37d and arguments, how likely would it be that others would easily manage it? They were just too much for you, too hateful, so now you're setting out to be permanently rid of them; why should *others* put up with them? Of course I can work it out, men of Athens. A fine life it would be if I did leave Athens, a person of my age, moving on to one city after another and liv- ing the life of a fugitive. Because that's what it would be; I'm sure that wherever I go the young will listen to me talk as they do here. If I drive them away, they'll be the ones who'll per- suade their elders to drive me out; and if I don't, their fathers 37e and other relatives will drive me out on their account anyway.

Someone will probably say, 'But, Socrates, can't you live in exile without talking, just keeping your peace? Surely you can do that?' To convince some of you about this is the most difficult thing of all. If I say 'That would be to disobey the god; how *can* I keep my peace, then?', you'll not believe me 38a because you'll think I'm dissembling; if on the other hand I say that it actually is the greatest good for a human being to get into discussion, every day, about goodness and the other sub- jects you hear me talking and examining myself and others about,[67] and that for a human being a life without examination is actually not worth living – if I say that, you'll be even less convinced. But that's how I say it is, Athenians; it's just not easy to convince you.

38b   At the same time, I'm not used to thinking I deserve anything bad at all.[68] In fact if I'd had any money available, I'd
propose a fine of whatever amount I'd be in a position to pay,
since it wouldn't have done me any damage to pay it. But actually I don't have money – unless of course you're willing to set
the penalty at what I *could* pay. I imagine I'd probably be able
to find a mina of silver for you. So that's what I propose.
[*A message is passed from the audience.*]

    One moment – Plato here, men of Athens, along with Crito
and Critobulus and Apollodorus – they're telling me to propose thirty minae, with them as guarantors; so that's the amount
I propose, and as guarantors of the money these people will be
creditworthy enough.

[*The sentence of death is approved; Socrates addresses the
court for the final time.*]

38c   You'll not have bought a lot of time at this price, men of
Athens: getting the name – from anyone who wants to abuse
the city – for being the ones who killed off 'Socrates, a wise
man'. (People who want to find fault with Athens will of course
say that I'm wise even if I'm not.) At any rate if you'd waited a
little time, you'd have had the same outcome without doing
anything. You can see my age for yourselves, how far on I am
38d   in life, how near to death. I say this not to all of you, just to
those of you who've voted to put me to death. And I've got
something else to say to these people. You probably imagine,
Athenians, that I stand condemned because I lacked the sorts
of arguments with which I could have persuaded you, given
always that I supposed I should do and say everything to escape
the penalty. Far from it. If I've been condemned for the lack of
something, it's not a lack of arguments but a lack of effrontery
and shamelessness and the willingness to address you in the sorts
of ways that it'd please you most to hear – wailing and lamenting
38e   and doing and saying plenty of other things unworthy of me, as
I claim, even if they're the sorts of things you're used to hearing
from everyone else. I didn't think then that I should do anything
unworthy of a free man, despite the danger I face, nor do I now
regret having made my defence as I did. I'd far rather make that

defence and die than demean myself and live. No one, whether it's in court or in war, whether it's myself or anyone else, should try to escape death by any means he can devise. In battles the opportunity is often there to avoid death by throwing away one's arms or turning to supplicate one's pursuers, and there are other devices for avoiding death in every sort of danger, if only one has the face to do and say anything no matter what. But I hazard, Athenians, that the difficult thing is not to avoid death; more difficult is avoiding viciousness,[69] because viciousness is a faster runner than death. So now, because I'm so slow and old, I've been caught by the slower runner, but because they're so quick and clever my accusers have been caught by the quicker one; and if I'm going to leave the court condemned by you to death, *they* will leave it convicted by truth of depravity and injustice. They accept their penalty as I do mine. I suppose it's probably how it had to be, and I think it's a fair result.

The next thing I want to do is to make a prophecy to you, the ones who voted against me; I'm now at that moment when human beings are most prone to turn prophet, when they're about to die. I tell you, you Athenians who have become my killers, that just as soon as I'm dead you'll meet with a punishment that – Zeus knows – will be much harsher than the one you've meted out to me by putting me to death. You've acted as you have now because you think it'll let you off being challenged for an account of your life; in fact, I tell you, you'll find the case quite the opposite. There'll be more, not fewer, people challenging you – people that I was holding back, without your noticing it, and they'll be all the harsher because they're younger, and you'll be crosser than you are now. If you think killing people will stop anyone reproaching you for not living correctly, you're not thinking straight. Being let off like that is not only quite impossible, it's the opposite of fine; the finest and easiest kind of letting off is when, instead of trying to cut other people down to size, each of you takes the measures needed to make yourself as good as you can be. So that's the prophecy I leave behind for those who voted to condemn me.

As for those of you who voted for me, I'll be happy to talk to you about this thing that's happened to me, just while the

39a

39b

39c

39d

39e

court authorities are busy and before I go off to the place where
I'm to go and die. [*Some of the jury are making to leave.*] Do
stay, Athenians, just for those few moments, because there's
40a nothing to stop us having a good talk to each other while we
can. You're my friends, and I do want to show you what this
thing that's now happened to me actually signifies. Men of the
jury (because 'jurymen' is the correct name to give you),[70] I've
something striking to report to you. In all my time before now
that accustomed prophetic ability of mine,[71] the one I get from
my 'divinity', was always with me, intervening again and again
and opposing me in quite small matters, if ever I were to be
going to act incorrectly in some respect. And now things have
turned out for me as you yourselves observe, in a way that
40b might be thought, and people actually think, the worst that can
happen to anyone; but the god's sign failed to oppose either my
leaving my house at dawn, or my coming up here to the court,
or my saying anything I was going to say at any point in my
speech. And yet on other occasions when I've been talking it has
held me back all over the place in mid-speech; now, in relation
to this whole business it has nowhere opposed my doing or saying anything. What do I suppose to be the reason for this? I'll
tell you: it's because this thing that's happened has very likely
40c been good for me. There's no way that those of us who think
dying is a bad thing can be right; and I've had a powerful indication of that – there's no way that my accustomed sign wouldn't
have opposed me if I wasn't going to do something good.

    Let us look at things in the following way too, to see how
great a hope there is that it's a good thing. Death is one or the
other of two things: either the dead are nothing, as it were, and
have no perception of anything, or else, as some people say,
death is really a kind of change, a relocation of the soul from
its residence here to another place. Now if the dead perceive
40d nothing, but are as it were asleep, as when a sleeper sees nothing
even in dreams, death would be a striking gain; for I imagine
that if anyone had to pick out the night in which he'd slept so
soundly as not even to see a dream and compare not just all
other nights but the days of his life with that night – if he had
to say, after thinking about it, how many days and nights in his

life he'd lived through better and more pleasantly than *this*
night, I imagine that not just any private individual but the
Great King himself[72] would find these days and nights easy to   40e
count by comparison with those other, dreamless ones; so that
if death is something like that, I myself count it a gain, since
from that perspective there'll be no difference between a single
night and the whole of time. If on the other hand death is a
kind of change of residence from here to another place, and
what we're told is true, that all who have died are there, what
greater good could there be, men of the jury? For if any new   41a
arrival in Hades, who has got away from those who call themselves judges here, will find himself before the true judges who
are said to sit in judgement there, Minos, Rhadamanthus, Aeacus and Triptolemus,[73] and those other demi-gods who became
just in their own life, would that be a poor destination to move
to? And what would any of you give to get together with
Orpheus, or Musaeus, or Hesiod, or Homer?[74] I'd happily die,
myself, many times over if that's truly what awaits us, because   41b
I for one would pass the time wonderfully, when I met Palamedes, or Ajax son of Telamon,[75] or any such figure from the
past, dead because of an unjust judgement – I'd be able to compare my experiences with theirs, and I think it'd be delightful
enough; but the greatest thing is that I'd be able to spend my
time examining people there and sniffing them out as I do
people here, to see which of them is wise and which merely
thinks he is but really isn't. What would one give, men of the
jury, to examine the man who led that great army against Troy,   41c
or Odysseus, or Sisyphus,[76] or – well, one could list countless
others, women as well as men with whom it'd give immeasur-
able happiness to talk, to be with them and to examine them.[77]
People there certainly don't put one to death for it, I imagine;
they're happier than people here in every respect, and especially because for the rest of time they are deathless, if indeed
what we are told is true.

But you too, men of the jury, should be of good hope when
you think of death, keeping the truth of this one thing in mind:
that there is nothing bad that can happen to a good man   41d
whether in life or after he has died, nor are his affairs neglected

by the gods. This business of mine now hasn't come about by accident; no, it's clear to me that it was *better* for me to die now and to be rid of life's ordinary business altogether.[78] That's the reason why that sign of mine at no point turned me back, and why I'm not at all angry with those who voted against me, or with my accusers. All the same, that wasn't what was in their minds when they were voting against me and making their accusations. They did it thinking they were damaging me, and that's what they deserve to be blamed for.[79] This much I ask of them: if my sons seem to you, when they reach puberty, to be caring about money or anything else before excellence, punish them, Athenians, by making them suffer in the very same way I used to make you suffer, and if they think they're something when they're not, reproach them as I have reproached you for not caring about the things they should and thinking they're something when they're not worth anything. If you do that, then I shall have had my just deserts from you, both for myself and for my sons.

But now it is time for us to leave: for me, to go to my death, and for you to go on living. Whether it's you or I who are going to a better thing is clear to no one but the god.

INTRODUCTION TO *CRITO*

The *Crito* is one of the shortest of Plato's dialogues; strikingly, for an author centrally concerned with ethical matters, it is the only dialogue directly concerned with what we moderns would call an issue in practical ethics. (Its uniqueness in this, and in some other minor respects, has sometimes led to doubts about its authenticity, but by and large these doubts seem unnecessary.) The question is whether Socrates should remain in prison and submit to execution by the city or escape and go into exile. It seems that it would have been perfectly easy for his friends to arrange for his escape. But Socrates will not do it. The *Crito* shows Crito desperately trying to persuade him that he should, and Socrates coolly responding with his arguments for staying, and for dying, as the city has ordered.

The basis of Socrates' case is that he should not abandon long-standing positions just because he is now faced with death; if he and his friends have continued to maintain any particular view, that is because they have found no reason to give it up (and the prospect of death, given our lack of knowledge of what death will bring, is not a reason for anything). As the argument proceeds, he picks out one point in particular on which both he and Crito, and the others, have always insisted: that it is never appropriate to do anything unjust to anyone. In the central and final part of the discussion, he argues that, if he escaped from prison and death, he would in fact be doing something unjust – to the laws and to the city. He imagines the laws finding a voice, and putting their side of the argument to him just as Crito had put his side earlier on in the dialogue. 'This sound of the laws' arguments booms out in my head,' says Socrates after their speech, 'making me incapable of hearing those others' (54d), and once he has established that Crito has nothing further to say, he brings the conversation to an end.

Two aspects of the *Crito* in particular have aroused continuing debate among its readers. The first is the way Socrates seems to allow himself to be persuaded by the laws: not, at least for the most part, some impersonal Law, speaking out on behalf of laws generally, but the laws of Athens herself. Worse still, their central argument looks, on the face of it, less than compelling: injustices, surely, are done to people or groups of people, not to things like laws or a city – that is, if the 'city' is identified, as in the *Crito*, with a set of institutions rather than its citizens. In this and indeed other respects, the address by the laws has a markedly rhetorical feel to it. The second much-debated aspect of the dialogue is an apparent conflict with the *Apology*. In the *Apology*, Socrates imagines the jury saying that they will acquit him, on the sole condition that he gives up doing philosophy, to which he responds that he must politely refuse the offer: the god has ordered him to do philosophy, and he will obey the god rather than them (29c–d). Yet in the *Crito*, he has the laws claim, with no apparent dissent from his side, that once an Athenian has confirmed his citizenship by continuing to reside in the city, he has thereby contracted to do what they, the laws, tell him to do. They allow him the option of trying to persuade them that they are wrong, in which case, they claim, they would give way; but Socrates has not even tried (*Crito* 51e–52a). So the question is: are there limits to what he thinks the law can demand of him? If so, it looks as if there might be a large hole in his argument for obeying the law now, and not escaping from prison: if he can evade the laws' demands in one case, why not in another?

It may be helpful, on the first issue, to bear in mind that we do not need to imagine Socrates as supposing that he has an absolutely cast-iron justification for the action, or rather in-action, that he is proposing. All that he requires is all that he ever requires, as someone who actually *knows* little or nothing of a substantive kind: namely that the considerations in favour of that action appear to him weightier than those against. There is no reason in principle why he should not be impressed, even considerably impressed, by the perspective of the city and its institutions – not least because that perspective has at least some merit in it, at a basic level (someone who flouts the laws surely does help to damage their authority, and that will generally be a bad thing). At the same time, it will evidently do no harm to Plato's overall defence of Socrates to show him to be the loyal citizen *in principle* that he certainly was in practice.

This response to the first difficulty may also provide some help with the second. It is of course the laws' view that Socrates should do what they tell him, no matter what (if he doesn't persuade them otherwise), and this is something that he is happy to take into account. Generally, he should and will obey the laws. At the same time, there is at least one thing that is non-negotiable: he will not give up his philosophy, because that would be to disobey an authority higher than the laws (see *Apology* 28d–e) – especially when part of the mission he implicitly claims to have been given by this higher authority is to 'care for the city itself', by making it as good and wise as possible (*Apology* 36c–d). (If he does not actually say any of this in the *Crito*, that may be because it is not actually relevant to his argument there; and, given the nature of their case, the laws will hardly rush to admit that there is anything higher than them.) Given that there is no evidence of Socrates' thinking contemporary Athens to be as good and wise as it could possibly be, it might well be hard for him to find rational justification for giving up the one activity that he supposes, and supposes the god to suppose, will actually make the city better and wiser – and so, incidentally, make it less prone to killing off its benefactors.

CRITO

43a   SOCRATES Why have you come at this hour, Crito? Isn't it still early?

CRITO Yes, it is.

SOCRATES What time is it?

CRITO Still before dawn.

SOCRATES I'm surprised the prison guard was prepared to answer your knock.

CRITO He's used to me by now, Socrates, because of the number of times I've visited, and besides he owes me a favour or two.

SOCRATES Have you just arrived, or have you been here some time?

CRITO Some time – not too long.

43b   SOCRATES Then why didn't you wake me up, instead of sitting there silently beside me?

CRITO Zeus, no, Socrates! I only wish my own sleeplessness and anguish would go away. I've been struck for some time by the sight of you enjoying your sleep so much, and deliberately didn't wake you up so that you could pass the time in the most pleasant way possible.[1] I've often had cause, during your life as a whole, to think you fortunate for the way you conduct yourself, but never so much as I do now, for the easy and relaxed way you accept the misfortune now facing you.[2]

SOCRATES Actually, Crito, it would be strange to be complaining about having to die now, at my age.

CRITO Other people of your age get caught up in misfor- 43c
tunes like yours, and *they* don't let their age stop them from
complaining about what's happening to them.

SOCRATES That's true. But tell me why you've come so
early.

CRITO Bringing bad news, Socrates – not bad for you, apparently, but certainly bad for me and all your friends, and hard to
bear; I think I'll be the one taking it hardest of all.

SOCRATES What news is that? Or is it the arrival of the ship
from Delos,³ which means I have to die?   43d

CRITO It hasn't actually arrived, but I think it'll arrive today,
judging from the reports of people arriving from Sunium; they
left the ship there. Clearly, then, from what these people say, it
will arrive today, and tomorrow, Socrates, your life must come
to an end – and will.

SOCRATES Let it be for the best, Crito, if it's what pleases the
gods. But I don't think the ship will arrive today.

CRITO What's your evidence for that?   44a

SOCRATES I'll tell you. I think I've to die on the day after the
ship comes?

CRITO So it's said by the people in charge of these things.

SOCRATES Well, I don't think it'll arrive during the coming
day; it'll be the day after. I say this because of something I saw
in my sleep not long ago this very night – so it looks as if it was
just the right moment for you not to wake me up.

CRITO So what was it you saw in your sleep?

SOCRATES It seemed to me that a beautiful, shapely woman   44b
in white robes came and addressed me by name, with these
words: 'Socrates, to the fertile land of Phthia on the third day
shall you come.'⁴

CRITO What an odd dream, Socrates.

SOCRATES Clear enough, I think, Crito, in any case.

CRITO Only too clear, it seems. For goodness' sake, Socrates,
do what I say even now, and save yourself. For me, if you die,
it'll be more than just one misfortune – apart from being
deprived of a friend the like of whom I'll never, ever, find again,
many people who don't know you or me very well will think
that when I could have saved you just by being willing to spend 44c

a bit of money, I failed to look after you. And what more shameful a reputation could one have than being thought to put money above one's friends? Ordinary people won't believe that it's you yourself who refused to get away from here, when we were all for it.

SOCRATES But my dear Crito, why do we care so much what ordinary people think? The best sort of people, the ones we should pay more attention to, will think that things have happened exactly as they have.

44d   CRITO But you can see, Socrates, that we have to take into account what ordinary people think too. The present situation alone shows that the damage ordinary people can do isn't to be disregarded; in fact, once they've been taken in by slander about someone,[5] they can inflict not just the smallest but practically the greatest of evils.

SOCRATES If only, Crito, ordinary people could bring about the greatest of evils, so that then they could have brought about the greatest of goods too;[6] then all would be well. But as it is, they're not capable of either, because it's beyond their capacity to make anyone either wise or foolish. What they do to people is, well, whatever they chance to do.

44e   CRITO Fine, so be it. But tell me this, Socrates: surely you're not worried about me and your other friends, in case you get out of here and the informers make trouble for us, accusing us of stealing you away from here, and we end up having to forfeit either everything we have or at least a large sum of money, perhaps with some further penalty on top of that? If that's the

45a   sort of thing you're afraid of, think no more of it, because we're bound to take that risk to save you, and if it comes to it, even greater risks than that. Do as I say, and don't delay.

SOCRATES I *am* worried about the risks you mention, Crito, and lots of other things too.

CRITO Well, don't worry about it. I'm telling you, it isn't even a big sum people are asking for, to get you safely out of here. And don't you realize how cheap these informers are? It

45b   wouldn't take much to buy them off either. The money I have is yours to use, and I think it's enough; and even if you don't think you should spend mine, out of concern for me, there are visitors here who are ready to contribute. One of them, Simmias of Thebes, has actually brought enough funds with him for the very purpose of getting you away; Cebes[7] and a whole number of others are standing by as well. So don't let any of this make you afraid to save yourself, and don't let it bother you, as you said in court, that you wouldn't know what to do with yourself if you went abroad; there are plenty of other places where people will look after you when you arrive, and if it's Thessaly you choose, I have guest-friends[8] there who'll treat you well and give you protection, so that no one in Thessaly will give you trouble.

45c

There's another thing, Socrates. It doesn't seem to me that what you're proposing to do is even *just*, betraying yourself when you could be saved, and actively pursuing the same sort of fate for yourself that your enemies would pursue – indeed have pursued, in their desire to destroy you.[9] More than that, you seem to me to be betraying your own sons, whom you'll have gone and deserted when you could have brought them up and educated them, and so far as you're concerned the quality of their life will be, well, left to chance. But what is very likely to happen is what typically happens to fatherless orphans. Men either shouldn't have children or, if they do, they should go through all the labours of rearing and education with them; you seem to be making the laziest choice. The choice to be made is the one a good and brave man would make, at any rate if you're someone claiming to care about excellence your whole life through; which is why I'm ashamed, both on your behalf and on ours, your friends', that the course of this whole business with you will seem to have been governed by some lack of manliness on our part. First there was the way your case came to court when it needn't have done; then there was the way it was fought; and now there's this final farce, as it were, to end the whole affair – the way we'll seem to have let an opportunity slip because we're somehow just not good and manly enough, given that we haven't saved you, and you haven't saved yourself, when it was possible and could actually have been done if we were of the slightest use. So you need to watch out, Socrates, that, as well as being bad anyway, this whole situation doesn't

45d

45e

46a

bring shame on you and on us too. See what you think – or rather, it's time to *have* thought it through, not just for thinking about it; and there's only one plan, because all this has to be over and done with during the next night – if we delay, it won't be possible and we won't be able to do it. From every point of view, Socrates: do as I say, and no dilly-dallying.

46b   SOCRATES My dear Crito, your eagerness would be worth a lot if it were accompanied by a rather better sense of direction; otherwise the more eager you are, the harder it is to take. What we need to think about is whether we're to do as you say or not; because I am the same person I have always been, one who refuses to listen to anyone or anything, however close to me, except the one argument, whichever it is, that appears best by my reckoning. So I can't now just throw out the arguments I used to produce merely because I happen to have found myself
46c   in my present situation. In fact they appear to me pretty much unchanged, and I give honour and precedence to the same arguments as before; if we're not in a position to say anything better now, you can be quite sure that I won't go along with you, even if the power of the people conjures up more bogeymen to try to frighten us, as if we were children, threatening us with things like imprisonment and death and confiscation of property. How should we best consider the issues? What about if we took up first this argument of yours about what people will
46d   think? Was it or wasn't it right to say, as we've said every time in the past, that one should pay attention to some opinions and not others? Or was it the right thing to say before my death-sentence, whereas now it's become clear after all that it was said to no purpose, just for the sake of argument, and was actually a playful remark signifying nothing? I'd like to examine with you, Crito, whether what we said will appear in some respect different to me because I'm in the situation I am, or whether it'll appear the same, and whether we should wave it goodbye or stick with it. I think what always used to be said, by those who think of themselves as talking sense, is pretty much what I was saying myself just now: that of the opinions
46e   that people hold, some should be given a lot of weight, others not. For goodness' sake, Crito, doesn't this seem right to you?

You, so far as ordinary human expectations go, aren't faced with the prospect of dying tomorrow, so the present 'misfortune' won't distort your judgement; so look – does it seem to you fair enough to say that one shouldn't respect all the opinions people have, but just some of them, and not others, and not everyone's opinions, but rather some people's and not others'? 47a

CRITO Right.

SOCRATES If so, it's the right sort of opinions that are to be respected, not the wrong sort?

CRITO Yes.

SOCRATES And isn't it sensible people's opinions that are 'the right sort', foolish people's 'the wrong sort'?

CRITO Of course.

SOCRATES Come on, then, tell me what you think of this other sort of thing I used to say:[10] if a man is in training, when he's actually training does he pay attention to just anybody's opinion, whether it's praise or criticism, or only to one person's – the person who's actually a doctor or a trainer? 47b

CRITO Only the one person's.

SOCRATES So this man in training should fear the criticisms and welcome the praise that come from this one individual, not those that come from ordinary people.

CRITO Clearly so.

SOCRATES In that case he should act and train, and eat and drink, in the way the one individual thinks he should, the one in charge of him who has the specialist knowledge, rather than in the way all the others think he should.

CRITO That's so.

SOCRATES Fine. And if he disobeys the one individual and, instead of respecting his opinion and what he picks out for praise, pays respect to the praise of ordinary people, who have none of the requisite knowledge, will that not have a bad effect on him? 47c

CRITO Of course.

SOCRATES What is this bad effect, and where is it felt? In which part of the person who's disobeying?

CRITO In his body, clearly; this is what it destroys.

SOCRATES You're right. So, Crito, is it like this in other cases

too (so that we don't have to go through them all), and especially in the case of the just and the unjust, the shameful and
the fine, the good and the bad, the very things we're deliber-
47d ating about now – is it the opinion of ordinary people that we
should follow, and fear, or that of the one specialist, if anyone
with that kind of knowledge exists? Is he the one who should
make us ashamed, and the one we should fear, rather than all
the rest? Is he the one we need to follow – because if we don't,
we'll corrupt and maim the part that is improved by justice and
destroyed by injustice?[11] Or is this nonsense?

CRITO I think not, Socrates.

SOCRATES Come on, then: if we destroy what is improved
by what's healthy and corrupted by what's unhealthy through
47e listening to non-expert opinion, is life worth living when this is
corrupted? 'This', I imagine, is the body; right?

CRITO Yes.

SOCRATES So is life worth living for us with a body that's in
bad condition because it's been corrupted?

CRITO Not at all.

SOCRATES But in that case, is it really worth living if that
other part of us is corrupted – the one that injustice maims and
justice benefits? Or do we suppose that that part of us, what-
48a ever it is, to which injustice and justice attach is less valuable
than the body?

CRITO Not at all.

SOCRATES Is it more valuable?

CRITO Yes, by far.

SOCRATES In that case, my good friend, we shouldn't be
worrying at all, as we are now, about what ordinary people will
say about us; what we should be worrying about is what the
person who knows about the just and the unjust will say – the
one specialist, and the truth itself. So the first point is that your
proposal is incorrect, when you suggest we should worry about
what ordinary people think about the just, the fine and the
good, and their opposites. 'Fair enough,' someone will say, 'but
ordinary people can put us to death.'

48b   CRITO *That's* quite clear enough; yes, Socrates, someone
will say it!

SOCRATES True, but the point we've just been making, my dear friend, still seems to me the same as it did before. And see too if you think this other point still holds for us: that it's not living that should be our first priority, but living *well*.

CRITO That holds too.

SOCRATES And what about the point that living well and living finely and justly are the same thing: does that hold or not?

CRITO It does.

SOCRATES Then what we have to consider, on the basis of what's agreed between us, is whether it's just that I should attempt to get out of here without the Athenian people's releas- 48c ing me, or whether it's not just: if it's clearly just, let's make the attempt, and if it isn't, let's give up the idea. As for those points you propose for discussion, about what things will cost, and saving reputations, and bringing up children, I fear that in truth, Crito, these sorts of considerations are the mark of people who would casually send a man to his death, and bring him back to life too if they could, all without the smallest intelligent thought – these ordinary people we've been talking about.[12] As for us, given the way the argument is going, I'm afraid the only question for us is the one I was asking just now: whether we'll be acting justly in giving money, and thanks besides, to those who'll get me out of here, or whether in truth 48d we'll be acting unjustly – and by 'we', I mean not just those doing the getting out, but the ones being got out; and if we're clearly acting unjustly by behaving in this way, then I'm sorry to say there's no place for taking into account whether I'll have to die or have anything else whatsoever happen to me if I stay and do nothing. The first consideration must be 'will we be acting *unjustly*?'

CRITO What you're saying seems fine enough to me, Socrates; now please decide what we're to do.

SOCRATES Let's look at it together, my good Crito, and if you're in a position to contradict me as I develop my argument, 48e by all means contradict me, and I'll be persuaded by you; but if you're not in a position to do that, please do now stop, once and for all – there's a good man – telling me the same thing over and over again, that I must get out of here without the approval of the Athenians; because it's important to me that I do what I do after persuading *you*, not without *your* approval.

49a So see if you think the starting-point of our inquiry is well enough stated, and try to answer the questions I ask you as you think best.

CRITO I'll try.

SOCRATES Do we say that we should never intentionally do what's unjust, or that sometimes we should, sometimes not?[13] Or is acting unjustly never, by its very nature, either good or fine, as we have frequently agreed in the past? Or are all those things we previously agreed on now, in these last few days, completely cast aside, so that when we thought, Crito, all that time, that we were having adult conversations with each other,

49b we were after all chattering like children? Or is it more than anything as we used to say then: that whether ordinary people say so or not, and whether we have to put up with even harsher or gentler[14] treatment than now, injustice is nonetheless by its nature both bad and shameful for the person who does it? Do we say so or not?

CRITO We do.

SOCRATES In that case injustice should never be done.

CRITO No indeed.

SOCRATES So not even the person who's being treated unjustly should act unjustly in return, as ordinary people think – given that injustice should never be done.

49c CRITO It appears not.

SOCRATES What about the next point: should one do harm[15] to other people, Crito, or not?

CRITO Surely not, Socrates.

SOCRATES Well, then, is it just, as ordinary people claim, to do harm in return if one is being harmed oneself; or is it not just?

CRITO It's never just.[16]

SOCRATES Because, I suppose, doing harm to people is no different from treating them unjustly.[17]

CRITO True.

SOCRATES In that case neither should injustice be reciprocated nor harm done to any person whatsoever, no matter what they may be doing to you. And watch out, Crito, that by agreeing to this you don't agree to something you don't believe, because I know that there are precious few people who do or will believe it. Those who have this belief and those who don't are incapable of planning anything together; each side inevitably despises the other as it observes the nature of the other's deliberations. So you yourself must look very hard to see if you share the belief in question, and if we're to start our planning from there – that is, on the basis that it's never correct either to act unjustly, or to commit injustice in return for injustice suffered, or to defend oneself when suffering harm by doing harm in return – or whether you wish to hold back and not join me in making this the starting-point. I've held this belief for a long time, and still hold it now, but if your position is different, say so and tell me what that position is. If on the other hand you stand by what we agreed before, listen to what comes next. 49d

49e

CRITO I do stand by it, and I share the same belief as you. Go on.

SOCRATES So then I'll tell you what comes next, or rather I'll ask you about it. Should a person do whatever he's agreed to with someone as being just, or should he break his word?

CRITO He should do it.

SOCRATES Then look at what follows. By getting out of here without persuading the city that I should, am I or am I not doing harm to people, and what's more to people I should be harming least of all? And am I or am I not standing by what I agreed is just? 50a

CRITO I'm not in a position, Socrates, to respond to your question, because I don't understand it.

SOCRATES Look at it like this. Suppose that I were on the point of running away[18] from here, or whatever one should call it; and suppose that the laws, the common foundation of the city,[19] came up and confronted me with these questions: 'Tell me, Socrates: what is your intention? What else can you have in mind with this action you're embarking on, except to do what you can to destroy us, the laws and the city as a whole? Or do you suppose that a city can continue to exist and not be 50b

turned completely upside down when legal judgements that
have been passed in its courts have no force, but are overturned
by private citizens and rendered null and void?' What shall we
say, Crito, in response to such questions and others like them?
There's plenty that could be said, especially by an expert orator, to stop the undermining of the law that judgements judges
50c make are to be observed.[20] Or shall we say to the laws 'Well,
the city was treating *us* unjustly by making a wrong judgement'? Is that what we'll say, or what?

CRITO Zeus! Exactly that.

SOCRATES Then what if the laws say, 'Socrates, was that too
in the agreement between us, or did you agree that you'd abide
by whatever judgements the city makes?' If this proposal of theirs
took me aback, they'd probably say to me, 'Socrates, don't be
surprised at what we're saying. Just answer our question – since
after all you like to use question and answer yourself: what on
50d earth could your charge against us and the city be, that you try
to destroy us like this? Didn't we, first of all, actually bring you
to birth? It was through us, after all, that your father married
your mother and impregnated her with you. So tell us if you
have a complaint about the state of that particular group of us,
the laws governing marriage.' 'I've no complaint about them,'
I'd say. 'What about the laws on the upbringing and education
of children once they're born – the upbringing and education
you yourself had: any complaint there? Didn't those of us
assigned to that area give the right instructions when they told
50e your father to educate you through literature and music,[21] and
gymnastics?' 'They did,' I'd say. 'Well then: now that you've
been born and brought up and educated, could you possibly
claim, first, that you weren't both our offspring and our slave,
and not just you but your forebears as well? And if that's the
case, do you suppose that you and we have equal claims on
justice, so that whatever we take it upon ourselves to do to you,
you suppose you can justly do it back to us? Or was it perhaps
that you didn't have equal claims in relation to your father, and
wouldn't have had to your slave-master if you'd had one,
51a allowing you to do back to them what they did to you, whether
talking back when you felt the rough edge of their tongue or

hitting them back when they hit you, or retaliating in all those many other ways one could think of – whereas you *will* be able to do that to your fatherland and the laws? So if we take it upon ourselves to destroy you because we think it just to do so, *you*'ll attempt to destroy us, the laws, and your fatherland, to the best of your ability? And you'll claim, will you, that in doing this you'll be acting justly? The man who shows a true care for goodness? Or are you too wise to have seen that compared to a mother, father, all one's forebears put together, a fatherland is something more valuable, more venerable, holier 51b and more privileged, both for gods[22] and for human beings with any intelligence? – too wise to have seen that one must honour one's fatherland, giving in to it more than to a father, placating it more than a father when it's angry, and either persuading it to change its mind or doing what it says, unresistingly putting up with any instructions it gives, whether for a flogging or imprisonment, or for marching off to war to be wounded or killed – don't you see that that's what one has to do, and that's where justice lies? – that there's to be no giving way, no retreat, no abandoning one's position: that whether in war, or in the law-courts, or anywhere, one must do whatever city and fatherland order, or else persuade her of what the just thing would 51c really be? Violence to a mother or to a father isn't pious; violence to your fatherland is much less pious still.' What shall we say to all this, Crito? Shall we or shall we not say the laws are telling the truth?

CRITO It seems to me they are.

SOCRATES 'Well then, consider, Socrates,' the laws would probably say, 'whether we're telling the truth when we say what you're now attempting to do to us isn't just. After having brought you to birth, nurtured you, educated you, given you and every other citizen a share of all the fine things in our 51d power, still we make it plain, by the very fact of giving permission to any Athenian who wishes it, that when he's been enrolled as a citizen and observed the goings-on in the city as well as us, the laws, he may leave, if we're not to his liking, for whatever destination he wishes, taking his possessions with him. And none of us laws stands in the way, or forbids it, whether one of

you wishes to move to one of the colonies, if he's not happy
with us and the city, or whether he prefers to emigrate to some
other place; off he can go with his possessions, wherever he
wishes. But we claim that whoever of you stays behind, and
can see the way we judge cases in court and otherwise govern
the city, has made an agreement with us, by staying and not
leaving, that he'll do whatever we order him to do; and we
claim that anyone who doesn't obey us is guilty of injustice in
three ways: first, that he's not obeying us when we are his
progenitors; second, that he is not obeying us when we brought
him up; and third, that having made an agreement with us to
obey our instructions, he is neither obeying us, nor persuading
us if there's anything amiss in what we're doing. In all of this
we're putting forward claims, not savagely issuing a simple
command to do whatever we order to be done. We're allowing
the person in question to do one of two things – *either* to persuade us, *or* to do as we say; and he does neither. It's these
charges, Socrates, that we claim you'll be liable to yourself if
you do what you're thinking of doing; not the least liable of all
Athenians, but the most liable of all.' If I then asked 'Why so?',
the laws' riposte to me, and it would be just enough, would
probably be to say that I'd actually made that agreement with
them more definitively than any other Athenian. They'd say,
'Socrates, we've impressive proofs to hand that both we and
the city were to your liking. Your record for unbroken residence in the city exceeds that of all other Athenians; it wouldn't,
if your liking for her didn't similarly exceed theirs. You haven't
ever left her to attend a festival, apart from a single visit to the
Isthmian Games, nor have you gone off anywhere else, except
to take part in military expeditions somewhere; you haven't
taken the other sorts of trips abroad everybody else does.
You've not been overtaken by curiosity about another city, or
other laws; we and our city were enough for you. That's how
emphatic your choice of us has been, and your agreement that
you would live as a citizen in accordance with us – not just in
those other respects; you actually had three children in the city,
which shows she was to your liking. What's more, at the trial
you could have proposed exile as your penalty if you wished,

and so could have achieved then, with the city's approval, what you're now proposing to do without it. As it was, you put on a fine impression of not being upset at having to die,[23] choosing death before exile, as you said; now not only do you feel no shame about having said that, but you pay no respect to us laws, even attempting to destroy us – and you behave as the 52d meanest of slaves would behave, taking it on yourself to run away, in breach of the contracts and agreements with us that you accepted as governing your life in the city. So first of all answer us this: are we or are we not telling the truth when we assert that you have agreed, not just verbally but by your actions, to live as a citizen of Athens in accordance with us?' What am I to say to this, Crito? Can I do anything but agree?

CRITO No; you have to agree.

SOCRATES 'It's right to say, then,' the laws would say, 'that you're breaking your contracts and agreements with us when 52e you weren't forced into them, when you weren't tricked into them, and when you weren't forced to make up your mind about them in a short space of time; you actually had seventy years, at any point in which you could have left, if we weren't to your liking, and if those agreements with us seemed to you not to be just. But in fact you didn't prefer either of the places you claim – whenever you have the chance – to be well governed, Sparta or Crete,[24] or any other Greek or indeed non- 53a Greek city; instead you left Athens less often than the lame, the blind or anyone similarly disabled. That's how much your liking for the city exceeded that of other Athenians, and evidently for us laws too, for who'd be happy with a city that had no laws? And now here you are, proposing not to abide by what was agreed between us. You will abide by it, Socrates, if you listen to us, and you'll not make yourself a figure of fun by leaving now.

'Just think: if you break these agreements and go wrong in any of the ways we've been saying, what good will you do yourself or your own friends? It's pretty clear that your friends 53b will run the risk themselves of being exiled and either being deprived of their citizenship or losing their property. As for yourself, first of all if you arrive in one of the cities nearest to

Athens, Thebes, say, or Megara, since both of these are well governed,[25] it's as an enemy that you'll arrive, Socrates – an enemy to their constitutions, and all those who care for their own cities will look askance at you, regarding you as a destroyer of laws; and you'll confirm the opinion of the jurymen, making
53c them think that they passed the right judgement, since after all someone who destroys legal systems might well seem likely to have a destructive effect on people,[26] especially if they're young and thoughtless. So perhaps you'll steer clear of well-governed cities, and the sort of people who live the most orderly lives. If you do that, will your life be worth living? Or will you mix with such people and shamelessly engage them in dialogue – on what themes, Socrates? The ones you talk to people about here, about how goodness and justice are what matters most to mankind, along with lawful behaviour, and laws? Don't you think
53d that what "Socrates" stands for will appear obscene as a result? You certainly should think so. Will you perhaps take off from these parts and go to Thessaly, to Crito's guest-friends?[27] That's a good place for disorder and licence, and they'll probably be delighted to hear the comic story of how you ran away from prison by putting on some sort of disguise, animal skins or whatever else runaways generally use, and changing your appearance;[28] and will no one mention that you showed such a
53e greedy lust for life, in brazen contravention of the most important laws, when you were old and probably had only a short time left to live anyway? Perhaps not, so long as you don't upset anyone; if you do, there'll be lots of things said about you, Socrates, that are unworthy of you. You'll end up living a life of toadying and running after people of all sorts – and what will you actually do, in Thessaly, except live it up, as if you'd
54a left town for a Thessalian dinner?[29] And where will all that talk of yours be then, we should like to know, about justice and the other virtues? It's for the sake of the *children*, then, that you want to live – to bring them up and educate them? Really? Will you take them to Thessaly for the purpose, making them foreigners so that they can get the benefits of that as well? Or perhaps you won't take them to Thessaly; they'll be brought up here instead. Will they be better brought up and educated

for your being alive, when you're not actually with them? Yes, your friends will care for them. Is it that they'll care for them if you go off for Thessaly, whereas they won't if you go off to Hades?[30] Well, if the people who claim to be your friends are 54b any use at all, one would certainly imagine they will.

'Take our advice, Socrates, since we're the ones who brought you up: don't think about children, or about life, or about anything before you think about justice. Then when you arrive in Hades you'll have all of what we've been through to say in your defence before those who control things down there.[31] Doing what's proposed – running away – doesn't appear to be the better thing for you up here, or for your family and friends, or to be just or more pious; nor will it make things better when you arrive down there. As things stand, you'll depart for Hades, if you do, the victim of injustice – done, not by us, but by mere 54c human beings; but if you take off from prison and thus so shamelessly return injustice for injustice and harm for harm, breaking your own agreements and contracts made with us, and doing harm to those you should have hurt least,[32] namely yourself, your friends, your fatherland and us – if you *do* do all this, then we shall be angry with you while you're alive, and our brothers the laws in Hades will not receive you in a kindly spirit because they'll know that you've attempted to destroy us, 54d to the best of your ability. Don't let yourself be convinced by Crito more than you are by us.'

These are the things, I tell you, my dear friend Crito, that I seem to be hearing, just as the Corybants[33] seem to hear the pipes, and this sound of the laws' arguments booms out in my head, making me incapable of hearing those others. I tell you – at least so far as it seems to me now: if you try saying anything against what the laws said, you'll be wasting your breath. All the same, if you really do think you can make headway with me, speak out.[34]

CRITO No, Socrates; I've nothing to say.

SOCRATES Then let it be, Crito, and let's do as I say, since 54e that's the way the god is leading us.[35]

INTRODUCTION TO *PHAEDO*

The *Phaedo* is set outside Athens, in Phlius in the Peloponnese, where Phaedo, a native of Elis and one of Socrates' younger friends, tells the story of Socrates' last hours to Echecrates and other citizens of Phlius. The story includes a long discussion between Socrates and two Thebans, Simmias and Cebes, about what happens to the soul after death, centred on four arguments for its survival as a rational entity, the first three of which also give rise to two counter-arguments, themselves followed by attempted refutations; this whole group of arguments, meanwhile, is itself set between a description of the best kind of life, at one end, and a visionary account of the earth and its regions at the other.

So much for the basic structure of the dialogue. Within this structure, Plato locates numerous other elements: a short intellectual autobiography by Socrates, expositions on philosophical method, passing comments on the nature of pleasure and pain, or on the rights and wrongs of suicide. The whole has something of the nature of a Russian doll about it, with new parts continually discovered nesting inside others. In short, there is probably a greater wealth and variety of content in the *Phaedo* than in any other single work of Plato's. Variety of content, too, is matched by variety of tone and style: there is laughter as well as sadness; dry argument alongside purple prose; moments of quick repartee beside longer exchanges; narrative and incident. The translation attempts to achieve something of the same variety, and if, for example, the language and sentence-structure becomes noticeably more elaborate, more formal, sometimes even rhetorical, that is not because the translator has gone to sleep but because the tone of the conversation itself has changed.

The structure of the dialogue is as follows:

57a–59c: introductory conversation between Phaedo and Echecrates.

59c–61c: Phaedo begins his account. How the conversation started; on pleasure and pain; Socrates is putting Aesop into verse – why?

61c–64a: Socrates claims that the philosopher will actually welcome death,

64a–69e: Socrates defends this claim (his new 'defence'); life, for the philosopher, is a kind of training for death, in which he practises separating soul from the body, its sensations, its pleasures and its desires.

69e–70c: objection – why should we believe that the soul survives death, as a substantial and rational entity?

70c–72e: the 'cyclical' argument (as death comes from life, life comes from death; our souls will be reborn into different bodies).

72e–77d: the argument from recollection (learning is really a matter of recollecting what we learned before we were born, but forgot at birth; in that case our souls must have pre-existed our birth as a composite of body and soul).

77d–84d: the 'affinity' argument (i.e., the affinity of the soul to things unseen and unchanging, like the 'forms'; an argument that gradually slides into persuasive description, for example about the fate of non-philosophical souls, so helping to provoke the objections that follow).

84d–85e: interlude; preface to Simmias' objection.

85e–88b: Simmias presents his objection, comparing the soul to the attunement of a lyre and its strings; Cebes follows up with an objection of his own (while a soul might survive many deaths and rebirths, who knows whether it isn't gradually worn out by the process, so ultimately perishing in one of those deaths?).

88c: consternation among Socrates' immediate audience.

88c–89a: a matching reaction from Echecrates in Phlius.

89a–91c: this new interlude continues, with a warning from
  Socrates against 'misology' (coming to hate all arguments
  because some turn out to be untrustworthy).
91c–95a: Socrates replies to Simmias' objection.
95a–102a: preliminaries to the final argument, which consti-
  tutes Socrates' reply to Cebes' objection (Socrates sets out
  and justifies the hypotheses he will need, by way of his own
  intellectual history).
102a: Echecrates breaks in again.
102a–107b: the final argument (the soul is altogether imperishable).
107c–115a: Socrates relates what he has been told about the
  true nature of the earth, and its various regions, ranging from
  the underworld below to the true surface, way above the hollow where we live like frogs around a pond, and perhaps
  even beyond that . . .
115b–end: Socrates dies.

  One of the most striking features about the Socrates of the
Phaedo is the prominence he gives to a set of ideas that may
broadly be termed 'Pythagorean': most notably, the idea of the
'transmigration' of souls, after death, to other bodies, and perhaps the idea of true philosophers as living a life of the mind,
'practising for death' (which, by and large, Socrates himself
consistently attributes, somewhat mysteriously, to those who
do philosophy 'in the correct way': 64c, 67b, 67d, 67e, 69d,
80e, 82c). Since Echecrates was evidently one of a group of
Pythagoreans at Phlius, and Simmias and Cebes have listened to
Philolaus, an eminent Pythagorean scientist and astronomer
(61d), the way appears open to interpreting the *Phaedo* as
Plato's Pythagorean moment; and that, indeed, is how it has
sometimes been taken, by modern as well as ancient interpreters. However, Simmias and Cebes generally appear more as
open-minded philosophers than as adherents of any special set
of doctrines (which Pythagoreanism certainly was, if it was
anything); indeed, as an enthusiast for the soul-as-attunement
theory, Simmias evidently is no supporter of that quintessential
Pythagorean doctrine, the 'transmigration' of souls – and as it

happens, Echecrates too likes the attunement theory (88d). Simmias and Cebes have simply heard Philolaus lecture, and in general the dialogue does nothing at all to identify them (or, for that matter, Echecrates) as Pythagoreans. Plato himself, it seems, was genuinely committed to the idea of transmigration, given that he introduces it in a number of different dialogues. In that respect, and no doubt in others, he may be labelled as a Pythagorean of sorts, or at least as someone who borrowed from and adapted certain aspects of that tradition. (We are not helped by the fact that most of our evidence about Pythagoras and Pythagoreans comes from much later, and is self-evidently contaminated with 'Pythagorean' ideas as discovered, by these later sources, in Plato himself.) As for the theme that the philosopher's life is a kind of preparation for death, which Plato has his Socrates develop over about a fifth of the total length of the *Phaedo* (64a–69e, 77d–84d), that could be little more than a piece of opportunistic borrowing, on a par with similar borrowing from religious traditions such as 'Orphism', or the mysteries of Eleusis (see, e.g., *Phaedo* 69c–d, *Apology* 41a, with notes). The theme is totally absent from all of Plato's other works; it is also the part of his 'defence', as begun at 64a, that most arouses the scepticism of his two interlocutors, so precipitating the final argument, which is altogether tighter than any of the first three, more closely derived from other demonstrably Platonic ideas – and more impressive. If this interpretation is right, then Phaedo will be addressing Echecrates and his friends, as Socrates is addressing Simmias and Cebes, more as philosophers than as Pythagoreans; and Phaedo is in Phlius not because it is a Pythagorean centre (as it may well have been), but to bring the story of Socrates' last conversation, and death, to fellow philosophers and sympathizers in the world outside Athens.

PHAEDO

ECHECRATES
PHAEDO

ECHECRATES Were you there with Socrates in person, Phaedo, 57a
on the day he drank the poison in the prison, or did you hear
about it from someone else?

PHAEDO I was there in person, Echecrates.

ECHECRATES So what is it the man said before his death,
and how did he meet his end? I'd love to hear. For in fact hardly
any of my fellow citizens here in Phlius go to Athens nowadays,
and we haven't had a visitor from Athens for a long time who 57b
could give us any clear account of it all, except of course that
he'd drunk the poison and died; no one could tell us anything
about the rest of it.

PHAEDO So you didn't even hear about the way things went 58a
at the trial?

ECHECRATES Yes, someone did report that to us, and there
was something that surprised us: though the trial had taken
place some time before, Socrates evidently died only much later.
Why was that, Phaedo?

PHAEDO It was chance, Echecrates; just the day before the
trial the stern of the ship the Athenians send to Delos had been
wreathed.

ECHECRATES What ship's that?

PHAEDO It's the one – so the Athenians say – in which Theseus once took the famous 'twice seven' to Crete and managed 58b
to bring them and himself back safe.[1] The story goes that the
Athenians had made a vow to Apollo that, if they did get back

safe, they'd offer an annual mission to Delos in return, and
they've gone on sending it to the god every year since. When
the mission starts, the rule is that the city should be clean from
killing, and shouldn't execute anyone until the ship has completed its voyage to Delos and back again – which sometimes
58c   takes a bit of time, if it's caught by contrary winds. The mission
starts when the priest of Apollo wreathes the stern of the ship;
and by chance, as I say, that happened on the day before the
trial. That's the reason why Socrates had a long time in the
prison between the trial and his death.

ECHECRATES So what about the circumstances of the death
itself, Phaedo? What was said? What happened? Which of the
man's friends were there? Or would the prison authorities not
allow them to be with him, so that he met his end without
friends beside him?

58d   PHAEDO Not at all; some of them were with him, indeed
quite a lot of them.

ECHECRATES Well, do your best to give us[2] the clearest
account you can of everything, unless you're too busy.

PHAEDO No, I certainly have the time, and I'll try to set it
out for you; in fact remembering Socrates always gives *me*
more pleasure than anything, whether I'm talking about him
myself or whether I'm just listening to someone else.

ECHECRATES Your audience, Phaedo, certainly feels the
same way; so do try and describe everything as accurately as
you can.

58e   PHAEDO And so I shall. I myself was affected in an extraordinary way by what I witnessed: I didn't experience pity, in the
way you'd expect of someone witnessing the death of a dear
friend – the man rather struck me as fortunate, Echecrates, both
because of his manner and because of what he said, so fearlessly
and nobly did he meet his end; the thought occurred to me that
the gods were smiling on him even on the way to Hades, and
59a   that, when he arrived there, too, his lot if anyone's would be a
good one.[3] That's why I was hardly touched by pity in the way
you'd think, given the sad things I was witnessing; but on the
other hand neither was there the pleasure that should have
come from engaging in philosophy in our usual way – that's the

form our conversation took. I was affected instead in quite the
strangest of ways; what I felt was a peculiar mixture comprising both pleasure and pain, as I reflected that this was a man
whose life would shortly be at an end. Everyone there was in
pretty much the same state, now laughing, sometimes weeping –
one of us, Apollodorus, much more than everyone else; I think
you're familiar with him and his ways.   59b

ECHECRATES Of course.

PHAEDO Well, he certainly lived up to expectations, and I
myself was in a confused state, as were the others.

ECHECRATES And who was actually there, Phaedo?

PHAEDO Of the locals, apart from this Apollodorus, Crito-
bulus was there with his father;[4] Hermogenes too, Epigenes,
Aeschines and Antisthenes. Then there was Ctesippus, of the
Paeanian deme, Menexenus, and some other local people.
Plato, I think, was ill.

ECHECRATES Was there anyone from outside Athens?

PHAEDO Yes; Simmias was there, along with Cebes and   59c
Phaedondes, from Thebes, and from Megara Euclides and
Terpsion.

ECHECRATES What about Aristippus and Cleombrotus?
Were they there?

PHAEDO No, they weren't. They were said to be in Aegina.

ECHECRATES Was there anyone else?

PHAEDO I think that's pretty much the complete list.

ECHECRATES What then about that conversation? Tell us
about it.

PHAEDO I'll try to describe everything for you, from the
beginning.

Both I and the others had got into the regular habit of visiting   59d
Socrates even during the days before, gathering at dawn at the
court building where the trial itself had taken place, since it
was conveniently near the prison. There we would wait each
day until the prison was opened, talking among ourselves,
because the prison guard tended to take his time; but when the
door was unlocked we'd go in to Socrates, and usually spend
the day with him. On the day itself, we gathered even earlier,

59e because on the day before, as we left the prison in the evening, we'd heard that the ship had arrived from Delos.[5] So we made arrangements with each other to arrive as early as possible at the usual place. Well, we came to the prison, and the guard who usually answered our knock came out to us and told us to wait; we weren't to enter until he told us to. 'The Eleven[6] are taking off Socrates' chains,' he said, 'and their orders are for him to die today.' But in fact it wasn't long before he came and

60a told us to go in. So we went in, and as we did we found Socrates freshly unchained, and Xanthippe – you know of her – sitting beside him holding his little son. Well, when Xanthippe saw us she gave out a loud cry, and said just the sort of thing that women typically do: 'Oh, Socrates, to think that this is the last time your friends will talk to you and you to them!' At which Socrates looked towards Crito and said, 'Please let someone take her home, Crito.'

60b   Some of Crito's people then led her off, crying out in grief; as for Socrates, he sat up on the bed, drew up his leg and rubbed it with his hand. As he did so, he said, 'How strange it seems, friends, this thing people call "pleasant", and how striking a relation it has to what seems opposite to it, the "painful": the two things refuse to present themselves to a person at the same time, but if anybody pursues one of them and catches it he's practically forced always to take the other as well; it's as if they

60c were two things growing out of a single head. I think,' he said, 'that if Aesop had noticed this aspect of them he would have constructed a story about how the gods[7] wanted to put an end to the war between them, found they couldn't, and so ended up fixing their heads together; which explains why whoever gets one of them finds the other one turning up after it. Just as in fact seems to be happening to me now: when I had the "painful" in my leg from the chain, the "pleasant" seems to have come along following close behind.'

          At that point Cebes interjected 'Zeus! Socrates, you did well
60d to remind me. About those poems you've composed, putting Aesop's pieces into verse, and with that prelude to Apollo – lots of people have asked me, as indeed Evenus[8] did only the other day, what on earth you had in mind by composing them, now

that you're here in prison, when you'd done nothing of the sort before. If you care at all about my having an answer to give Evenus when he asks me again, because he surely will, please tell me what to say.'

'Well, tell him the truth, Cebes,' Socrates replied, 'which is that I didn't do my versifying out of a wish to rival his expertise, 60e or that of his poems, because I knew at once how difficult that would be. I did it rather as a way of exploring the meaning of certain dreams I have, and doing what was required of me in case, after all, it was this kind of "music"[9] they were instructing me to make. The dreams in question are like this – in fact it's the same dream that's visited me many times in my life, in different guises but always saying the same thing: "Socrates, make music; make that your business!" My reaction previously was to take this instruction as a kind of encouragement; I compared 61a the dream to spectators cheering on runners in a race, thinking it was telling me to do the very thing I was already doing, "making music", because I supposed that philosophy was the highest music, and that was what I was already doing. But now, after the trial, and when it was the festival to the god[10] that was holding up my execution, it seemed to me that, just in case the dream was after all telling me to make music of this common-or-garden variety, I shouldn't be disobedient but should get on and do it; I thought it safer not to go off[11] before I'd done what 61b was required of me, composing poems as the dream told me. So it was, then, that I came first to write a poem to the god in whose honour the current festival was; then, after the god, realizing that any poet worthy of the name has to put together stories rather than arguments, and that I was no story-teller, I just took the stories that I had to hand and actually knew, which were Aesop's, and turned into verse the first ones that happened to occur to me. So that, Cebes, is what you should tell Evenus; tell him to keep well and, if he has any sense, to come running after me as soon as he can. I'll be going off today, 61c it seems; the Athenians say so.'

Simmias said, 'What a thing to suggest to Evenus! I've met the man on many occasions, and from what I've seen there's no chance he'll be willing to take your advice.'

'What?' Socrates replied. 'Isn't Evenus a philosopher?'

'I think he is,' said Simmias.

'In that case he will want to, and so will anyone who's a philosopher worthy of the name. However, he probably won't do away with himself; people say that's not permitted.'[12] And
61d as he said this he lowered his feet to the ground, and stayed sitting like this for the rest of the conversation.[13]

Cebes then asked him, 'How can you say this, Socrates? How can it not be permitted to "do away with oneself", if it's philosophical to want to emulate the dying?'

'What's that, Cebes? Haven't you and Simmias heard about this sort of thing from your get-togethers with Philolaus?'[14]

'No, Socrates, nothing precise.'

'What I'm saying is only what I've heard myself; and there's no reason not to pass on what I happen to have heard. In fact
61e there's probably nothing more fitting for someone who's about to make the journey to Hades than to ask questions and tell stories about what kind of journey we think it will be. What else would one do in the time between now and sunset?'[15]

'So why on earth, Socrates, do they say killing oneself isn't permitted? Actually, since you asked, I did hear Philolaus ruling against suicide, when he was visiting Thebes, as indeed I've heard it from others; what I haven't heard from anybody yet is a clear account of the matter.'

62a 'Don't lose heart,' said Socrates; 'perhaps you may hear one.[16] Probably it will appear surprising to you if this alone, in human affairs, is uncomplicated, and it never turns out as in other things, that in some circumstances and for some people it's better to die than to live;[17] and for people like this – well, probably it does appear to you surprising if it's not the right thing[18] for them to do themselves a good turn, but they have to wait around for someone else to do it for them.'

Cebes chuckled and said, in his own dialect,[19] 'You better believe it!'

62b 'Yes,' said Socrates, 'it would certainly seem unreasonable, put like that; all the same there is probably a certain reasonableness about it. There's what's said about the subject in secret writings, to the effect that we human beings are prisoners in a kind of guard-house, and that no one has any business running away and trying to free himself; that seems to me a deep saying,[20] and one that's not easy to penetrate, but this much at least seems to me to be well said, Cebes, namely that it's the gods that look after us, and that we human beings count, for them, among their possessions.[21] Isn't that how it seems to you?'

'It is,' came Cebes' reply.

'Well,' said Socrates, 'wouldn't you be angry if one of your own possessions killed itself, without a signal from you that 62c
you wanted it to die, and wouldn't you punish it if there was any punishment you could apply?'

'Absolutely.'

'Then probably, from that point of view, it's not unreasonable to suppose that one shouldn't kill oneself until the gods[22] somehow make it necessary, as in the situation in which I now find myself.'[23]

'That much seems likely enough,' said Cebes; 'but I'd like to take you up on what you were claiming just now, that philosophers will accept death lightly: that, Socrates, looks odd, if in fact it's plausible to say, as we were saying just now, that it's the 62d
gods that look after us, and we're their possessions. It would be contrary to reason for the wisest people not to be upset about leaving this kind of service,[24] since it's performed for the best of all possible masters; after all, they're gods. I don't imagine a wise person will think he'd be better off getting free of them and looking after himself – a foolish one, perhaps, yes: he'll suppose that what slaves do is escape their masters, not reckon- 62e
ing that a *good* master's not for escaping from but for staying with, for as long as possible. So he'd run away, not having worked it out; but a person of intelligence, I imagine, will desire always to be in the presence of someone better than himself. And yet this way, Socrates, it's likely to be the opposite of what was being claimed just now: it's for the wise to be upset about dying, and for the stupid to be happy about it.'

When Socrates heard this, he seemed to me to be pleased by Cebes' earnest response. He looked at us, and said, 'There goes Cebes, always sniffing out some argument or other; assenting 63a
at once to what someone says – that's not his line at all.'

To which Simmias said, 'But this time, Socrates, it seems to me that Cebes has a point. Why on earth would people who were truly wise try to escape from masters better than themselves? Why would they leave them so lightly? And it seems to me that Cebes is aiming his argument at you, because *you* are treating it as so light a matter to abandon not just us but what you yourself agree are good superiors to have, the gods.'

63b   'What the two of you are saying is fair enough,' said Socrates. 'The upshot, I think, is that I must defend myself against this charge you're making, as if we were in court.'

'Quite right; you must', said Simmias.

'Well, then, let me try to make a more convincing defence to you than I did to the jurors at the trial.[25] The truth is, Simmias and Cebes, that I'd be wrong not to be upset about dying if I didn't think I was going to join the company, first, of other wise and good gods, and then, too, of dead men better than those to
63c   be found up here.[26] But as things are, I can assure you I do expect to arrive in the presence both of good men – well, I wouldn't absolutely insist on that; but be assured that I would insist, if I insist on anything of this sort,[27] that where I'll be going I'll have gods for masters that are wholly good. So that's why I'm not as upset as I might have been; I have high hopes that there is something in store for the dead, and that – so it's long been said, at any rate[28] – this something is much better for the good than for the bad.'

'Well then, Socrates,' said Simmias; 'do you mean to go off and keep this thought of yours to yourself, or will you let us
63d   share in it too? It seems to me that the benefit of it ought by rights to be ours too; and if you convince us of the truth of your claim, you'll have your defence into the bargain.'

'I'll give it a try,' Socrates said. 'But first let's find out what Crito here has apparently been wanting to say for some time.'

'And what else would I be wanting to say except what *he*'s been saying to *me* all this time – I mean the man who's going to give you the poison: that I've got to tell you to talk as little as possible, because he claims if people talk it raises their body-
63e   heat, and that sort of thing interferes with the action of the

poison. Otherwise, he says people who behave like this sometimes have to take a second or even a third dose.'

Socrates replied, 'Take no notice of him; just let him do his
job and prepare to give me a double dose, or a triple one if
necessary.'

'I was pretty sure that'd be your answer,' Crito said; 'it's just
that he's been bothering me for some time.'

'Never mind him,' said Socrates. 'As for you judges, I'm now
going to give you the argument I promised, and show you how
reasonable it appears to me to be, for someone who has genuinely passed his life in philosophy, to be confident at the prospect of death and have the highest hopes for the benefits   64a
awaiting him in that other place when he dies. Exactly how this
could be so, Simmias and Cebes, I'll try to say.

'Probably the rest of mankind is unaware of what it is that
preoccupies all those who actually practise philosophy in the
correct way: it's nothing other than dying, and being dead.
Well, if that's true, it would presumably be odd for them to
look forward to just this outcome all their lives, and then, when
it came, to be upset about it – the very thing they'd been seeking all along, and actually *doing*.'

To which Simmias said with a laugh, 'Zeus only knows, Socrates, you make me laugh, when laughing is the very last thing   64b
on my mind! If ordinary people heard you saying what you've
just said, they'd think your description was a perfect fit for
those who go in for philosophy – and our countrymen[29] would
heartily agree: philosophers really do have a death-wish, and
even if they can't see it themselves, death is just what they
deserve.'

'And actually they'd be telling the truth, Simmias – except
for the claim that they can see better than philosophers. Ordinary people can't see in what way true philosophers wish for
death, or how they deserve it, or what kind of death they   64c
deserve. So let's go through it for ourselves, and leave ordinary
people out of it. Do we think there's such a thing as death?'

'Yes, absolutely,' replied Simmias.

'And we think of it,[30] don't we, as nothing other than the
separation of the soul from the body? This is what it is to be

dead: for the body to have come to be by itself, apart from the soul and separated from it, and for the soul to be by itself, apart and separated from the body – death can't, I imagine, be anything but this?'

'No, that's what it is,' said Simmias.

'Now consider the following points, in case you think the same as I do; because it's from these, I believe, that we'll reach a greater understanding of the things we're currently thinking about. Does it appear to you to be a philosopher's business to have worked hard at the so-called pleasures like, for example, those of food and drink?'

64d

'No, certainly not, Socrates,' said Simmias.

'What about the so-called pleasures of sex?'

'Not at all.'

'And what of all the other ways there are of serving the body? Do you think such a person treats these as valuable? Things like acquiring distinctive cloaks[31] or shoes, or any other ways of beautifying the body – do you think he attaches value to these, or does he rather refuse to do so, except in so far as he absolutely can't avoid having something to do with them?'

64e

'It seems to me,' Simmias said, 'that he refuses, if he's truly a philosopher.'

'So in general,' Socrates went on, 'does such a person's business seem to you not to be with the body, from which he removes himself so far as he can, but to be directed rather towards the soul?'

'It does.'

'So the first point is, isn't it, that in such contexts the philosopher manifestly tries to free his soul, so far as he can, from its association with the body, in a way that the rest of mankind does not?'

65a

'Apparently so.'

'And it does seem, presumably, Simmias, to ordinary people that anyone who fails to find such things pleasant, and doesn't share in them, has nothing worth living for; and indeed that someone who doesn't care at all for the pleasures that owe their existence to the body comes pretty close to being dead already.'

'Absolutely true.'

'What, then, about the actual business of acquiring wisdom?[32] Does the body get in the way, or doesn't it, if one takes it on as associate in the search? This is the kind of question I have in mind: do our sight and hearing possess some sort of capacity for truth, or is it perhaps as even the poets are always repeating to us, that nothing we ever hear or see is accurate? Yet if these of all the senses relating to the body aren't accurate, or clear, the others will hardly be either, since I presume all of them are inferior to sight and hearing. Don't you think so?'

'Yes, certainly,' said Simmias,

'When is it, then,' asked Socrates, 'that the soul gets a hold on truth? Clearly, on any occasion that it tries to think about something in the company of the body, the body deceives it.'

'True.'

'Then isn't it in the process of reasoning, if anywhere, that any aspect of things[33] becomes clear to the soul?'

'Yes.'

'And I imagine that the soul reasons at its best when none of these things distracts it, whether hearing, sight, pain, or indeed any of the so-called pleasures – when it comes to be as much as possible by itself, saying goodbye to the body, and when it strives to understand what things really are[34] with no more association, or even contact, with the body than it can help.'

'That's so.'

'So in this case too the philosopher's soul sets the least value on the body, and tries to get away from it, seeking to be alone and by itself.'

'It appears so.'

'What then about the following points: do we say that there exists something that's just and nothing but just?[35] Or do we say that there's no such thing?'

'Zeus! We certainly say there is!'

'And what about fine, and good?'

'Of course.'

'Well, have you ever yet seen anything like that with your eyes?'

'Certainly not.'

65b

65c

65d

'And do you get a hold on them through any of the other senses that work through the body? I'm talking here about everything – for example about size, health, strength; in a word,
65e about the essence of these and all the other things, what each of them actually is: are they observed at their truest through the body, or is it rather like this, that whichever of us puts himself in a position to *reflect* the most, and the most accurately, on each object of investigation, by itself, he'll be the one who comes closest to an understanding of each of them?'

'Absolutely.'

'So who'll achieve this outcome in its purest form? Will it be the one who succeeds most of all in approaching each thing exclusively by thinking about it, without adducing the evidence
66a of sight in his thinking, or dragging in any other of the senses to accompany his reasoning;[36] the one who, instead, using thought unalloyed, alone and by itself, tries to track down each aspect of things,[37] alone, by itself and unalloyed, having separated himself so far as possible from eyes, ears – the whole body, practically, on the grounds that it confuses the soul and prevents it from acquiring truth and wisdom when taken on as its associate? Isn't it this person, if anyone, Simmias, who'll reach understanding of how things really are?'[38]

'A masterly statement of the truth, Socrates,' said Simmias.

66b 'Well, mustn't all these points together provoke the kind of thought, among those who are genuinely philosophers,[39] that would make them say things to each other like this: "It looks as if there's a path that'll bring us and our reasoning safely through in our search. So long as we have our bodies, and our souls have that sort of contamination to contend with, we're surely never going to succeed sufficiently in acquiring this thing that we desire; and that, we declare, is the truth. For the body pro-
66c vides us with a million distractions because of the need to supply it with food; if it gets diseased, that further impedes our hunt for reality. It fills us full of lusts, desires, fears, fantasies of all kinds – in short, a whole collection of nonsense, the result of which is that really and truly, as the saying goes, we never get a moment to ourselves, thanks to the body, even to think about anything. It's the body and its desires, nothing else, that bring

about wars, factions and fighting; because all wars come about
for the sake of acquiring money, and we're forced to acquire
money for the sake of the body because we're slaves in its ser-   66d
vice. It's the body's fault, for all these reasons, that we have no
time for philosophy. The worst of it is that when we do get a bit
of time off from serving the body, and we turn to reflecting
about something, there it'll be again, breaking in on our reflections, creating uproar and confusion everywhere, and generally
stirring things up so that just because of *it* we can't get a sight
of the truth. The fact is that all this has shown us that, if we're
ever going to have pure knowledge of anything, we've got to
separate ourselves from the body and observe things by them-   66e
selves by means of the soul by itself; and as our argument indicates, we'll only achieve that separation when we die – it's then,
it seems, that we'll have what we desire, what we say we're lovers of, namely wisdom, not while we're alive. Look at it this
way: if it's impossible to get pure knowledge of anything in the
company of the body, then one or the other of two things must
hold: either knowledge can't be acquired, anywhere, or it can
be, but only when we're dead; because that's when the soul will   67a
be alone by itself, apart from the body, and not until then. And
even while we are alive, it seems, the way we'll come closest to
knowledge will be by having as little to do with the body as
possible, doing nothing in association with it unless we simply
can't avoid it, not letting it infect us with the kind of thing it is[40]
but purifying ourselves from its influence – until such time that
the gods themselves set us free. And if we become pure in this
way, by separating ourselves from the folly of the body, then it's
likely enough that we'll be in the company of others pure like
ourselves, and we'll have knowledge through our own selves,
by themselves, of everything unalloyed;[41] and this, presumably,   67b
is the truth. For perhaps it is not permitted to the impure to
grasp the pure." These, Simmias, are the sorts of things that all
who desire understanding in the correct way will, I think, inevitably say to each other; these are the thoughts they must have.
Don't you think so?'

'Yes, Socrates, without a doubt.'

'Then,' said Socrates, 'if all that is true, my friend, there are great hopes for anyone going to the place I'm going that there, well enough, if anywhere, he'll acquire the very thing that has

67c   so preoccupied us in life past; so that the change of place that's now appointed for me brings the hope of good things with it, as it does for any man who thinks he has prepared his mind as he should, through a kind of purification.'

'Absolutely,' said Simmias.

'And "purification" turns out, doesn't it, to be the very thing we've been talking about for some time in our discussion: a matter of separating the soul so far as possible from the body, and having got it used to collecting and gathering itself together, by itself, away from every part of the body, so that it lives alone and by itself, to the limit of its capacity, both in the present and

67d   in the time to come, freeing itself from the body as if from chains?'

'Absolutely,' said Simmias.

'Then it's *this* that people are referring to when they talk about "death": a freeing and parting of soul from body?'[42]

'Yes, without doubt,' Simmias replied.

'And, as we've been saying, it's especially, or rather only, those that go in for philosophy in the correct way who are always eager to set the soul free; what philosophers practise is exactly this, the freeing and parting of soul from body. Isn't that so?'

'Apparently.'

'So, as I was saying at the beginning, it would be absurd if a

67e   man should use his life to practise being as close as possible to a state of death, and actually spend his life like that – and then be upset at the approach of the real thing?'

'Absurd, of course.'

'In that case, Simmias,' said Socrates, 'those occupied correctly in philosophy really do practise dying, and death is less frightening for them than for anyone else. Look at it from this point of view: if they are at odds with the body in every respect, and what each of them desires is to have his soul alone by itself, wouldn't it be most unreasonable if they were afraid and upset

68a   about actually getting what they desired? Shouldn't they be happy to be rid of their unwanted companion and go off to the

very destination where, so the hope is, they'll achieve what they've been lovers of all their lives, namely wisdom? The death of human darlings,[43] wives, sons has prompted many a willing volunteer to pursue them to Hades, driven on by the hope of seeing there the objects of their desire, and of being with them; are we to suppose that someone who's really in love, with wisdom, and firmly holds this same hope, that nowhere else but in Hades will he encounter his love in any way worth speaking of –   68b
are we to suppose that *this* sort of person will be upset about dying? Won't be happy to go off to that other place? One should certainly think so, if, my friend, he really is a lover of wisdom;[44] because he'll firmly hold to the view in question, that nowhere else but there will his encounter with wisdom be pure. If this is so, then, as I was saying just now, wouldn't it be most unreasonable if such a person were afraid of death?'

'Zeus! Most unreasonable!' Simmias said.

'Then if you see anyone upset at the prospect of imminent death, will you take that as sufficient proof that he wasn't a lover of wisdom after all, but a lover of the body? And I imag-   68c
ine the same person will also be a lover of money and a lover of honour[45] – one of the two, or else both.'

'Absolutely right,' said Simmias.

'Then doesn't it follow, Simmias, that what's called by the name "courage" belongs especially to those in the state we've described?'[46]

'Yes, I suppose it does,' was Simmias' reply.

'Then moderation[47] as well, what ordinary people too call by that name – not being excited about one's desires,[48] but treating them with decent contempt: doesn't this belong exclusively to the sort of people in question, who despise the body more than anything, and spend their lives loving wisdom?'[49]

'Necessarily so,' said Simmias.   68d

'Yes,' Socrates went on, 'because if you think about everybody else's "courage" and "moderation", they'll strike you as pretty odd.'

'How so, Socrates?'

'You recognize,' he replied, 'that everyone else considers death one of the great evils?'

'Very much so,' said Simmias.

'Then when people with their sort of "courage" face up to death, it'll be because of a fear of greater evils?'

'That's so.'

'In that case everyone who is courageous apart from the philosopher is so through being afraid – through fear, in fact; yet it's quite illogical that a person should be made courageous by a kind of fear and cowardice.'

68e   'Yes, certainly.'

'What about those non-philosophers who live orderly lives? Isn't it the same in their case, that they're moderate through a kind of *lack* of restraint? Even though we say it's impossible, all the same what happens to them, with this simple-minded "moderation" of theirs, actually is like this; they're afraid of being deprived of different pleasures that they also desire, and so they end up perpetually abstaining from one set of pleasures

69a   because they're under the control of another. Yet the name they give to being ruled by pleasures is actually "lack of restraint". The net result is that it's through being controlled by pleasures that they control other pleasures, which is not unlike the state I was ascribing to them just now, of being somehow made "moderate" through a kind of lack of restraint.'

'Yes, it seems so.'

'Yes, my dearest Simmias, because I don't suppose that this is the correct sort of exchange for the acquisition of virtue[50] – exchanging pleasures for pleasures, pains for pains, fear for fear, the greater ones for the lesser, as if they were a kind of currency; the only true coin, I hazard, for which all these things

69b   should be exchanged is *wisdom*. It's when everything is bought and sold for this, or rather in the company of this, that there'll truly be courage, moderation, justice, all true virtue – that is, in the company of *wisdom*, whether pleasures and fears and anything else like that are added or whether they're taken away. When they're being exchanged for each other in isolation from wisdom, well, virtue like that is surely a bit like stage-painting; it's really the sort of virtue that belongs to slaves, with nothing

69c   wholesome about it, or anything true. Really and truly, perhaps, moderation, justice and courage are a sort of purification

from all such things, and wisdom itself is what does the purifying. So I dare say we shouldn't underestimate the people who
established the rites of initiation: when they said that whoever
arrives in Hades without undergoing initiation into the rites
will lie in the slime, while whoever arrives purified and initiated
will dwell with the gods, all the time they were using riddles to
hint at the truth.[51] For as the ritual experts say, there are indeed
"many that carry the thyrsus,[52] but in truth few that are the   69d
god's": the few, as I think, are none other than those who have
practised philosophy in the correct way. In my whole life, so far
as I could, I have left nothing undone in my eagerness to become
one of these; as to whether my energy has been spent correctly,
and we've made any progress, we'll know the plain truth, god
willing, when we get to that other place – and that we will, I
think, in only a short time. This, then, Simmias and Cebes,' said
Socrates, 'is the defence I offer, to show how reasonable it is for
me not to take it hard, or to be upset, that I'm leaving you behind,   69e
along with our divine masters here, in the thought that there too,
in Hades, I'll encounter good masters, and friends, no less than
here. So, if I've defended myself any more persuasively before
you than I did before my Athenian judges, I shall be content.'

   After this speech of Socrates', it was Cebes who spoke next.
'Socrates,' he said, 'the rest of what you were saying seems to
me to be well said; but in relation to the soul, a lot of people   70a
wouldn't believe you. They're afraid that, when it's separated
from the body, there's no longer any place for it to be. On the
very day a person dies, they fear, and just as it's becoming
separated from the body, the soul is destroyed, and perishes; as
it emerges, it flies off in different directions, dispersed like
breath or smoke,[53] and it no longer subsists anywhere at all. If
it were gathered together somewhere, alone by itself and rid
once and for all of the evils you described just now, then it   70b
would be a good and fine thing to hope that what you say is
true; but that soul exists after a man is dead, and that it has
some capacity for wisdom,[54] is probably something that requires
no small process of reassurance and proof.'

   'What you say is true, Cebes,' said Socrates. 'What then
should we do? Do you want us to talk these things through,[55]

to see whether they're likely to be as I say or whether they're
not?'

'I for one,' replied Cebes, 'would be delighted to hear your
thinking on the matter.'

70c   'I certainly don't think,' said Socrates, 'that anyone who
heard me now, even if he were a comic poet, would accuse me
of idle chatter, and of talking about things that don't concern
me.[56] So if you agree, we should look into the question.

'Let's look at it in this sort of way: let's ask whether, in fact,
when people are dead, their souls are there in Hades, or whether
they're not. Well, there's an ancient doctrine, I recall, to the
effect that the souls of the dead are indeed there, having trav-
elled there from here, and moreover that they travel *back* here
through being born again, out of the dead.[57] If that's how it is,
with the living being born again out of the dead, mustn't our
70d   souls indeed be there in Hades? I imagine they'd hardly be born
again if they didn't exist at all. So it'll be sufficient proof that
they do, if in fact we could show that the living are born from
the dead and only from the dead; if that's not so, then we'll
need a different argument.'

'Yes, quite,' said Cebes.

'Well then,' replied Socrates, 'if you want to see more readily
what's at stake, think about this not just in relation to human
beings, but to animals generally, plants too, and in fact to every-
70e   thing that admits of changing and coming-into-being. Let's see
whether *everything* comes to be in the following way, namely
through opposite things coming to be from no other source
than their own opposites – everything, that is, that actually has
some opposite, as for example the beautiful is presumably
opposite to the ugly, the just to the unjust, and so on in countless other cases. So the question for us is this, whether anything
that has an opposite must always come from what is opposite
to it. For example, when something comes to be bigger, I imagine
it must be from being smaller before, that it then comes to be
bigger?'

'Yes.'

'Then if a thing becomes smaller, too, it'll be from being
71a   bigger before, that it comes to be smaller later?'

'That's so,' said Cebes.

'And again, the weaker will come to be from the stronger, the quicker from the slower?'

'Yes, absolutely.'

'What about if something becomes worse? Won't it come to be worse from being better? And if more just, from more unjust?'

'Of course.'

'So we've a sufficient grasp on this point, have we: that everything comes to be in this way – things opposite to other things come from those opposites?'

'Yes, absolutely,'

'What about this next question: is there also the following sort of feature in all cases, namely that between the two members of every pair of opposites there are also two processes of coming-into-being; the first from one opposite to the other, the 71b second in the reverse direction, from the latter to the former? After all, in between a bigger thing and a smaller one there's increase and also decrease in size, and we accordingly call the one process "increasing in size", the other "decreasing in size".'

'Yes,' said Cebes.

'Then too we recognize separating and combining, and cooling and heating up, and so on and so forth – even if we don't always have names for them,[58] still in actual fact it has to be like this in all cases: opposites come to be from each other, and there is a corresponding process of coming-into-being of either opposite into its pair.'

'Yes, certainly,' Cebes replied.

'What do you say to my next question: does *being alive* have 71c an opposite, as being awake has being asleep?'

'Yes, absolutely,' said Cebes.

'What is it?'

'Being dead,' said Cebes.

'So do these come to be from each other, given that they're opposites; and are the processes between them also two, since there are two of them?'

'Yes, of course.'

'So I'll give you one of the pairs I mentioned just now,' Socrates said, 'that is, both the pair itself and the processes involved; and you go ahead and tell me what the second one is. My contribution is: there's being asleep and there's being awake; being awake comes from being asleep, being asleep comes from being awake; the two processes involved are, first, going to sleep, and second, waking up. Are you happy with that or not?'

71d

'Yes, absolutely.'

'Well, now it's your turn,' Socrates said; 'do the same for me with life and death. Don't you claim that being dead is opposite to being alive?'

'I do.'

'And that they come from each other?'

'Yes.'

'So what is it that comes from the living?'

'The dead.'

'And what', asked Socrates, 'comes from the dead?'

'There's nothing for it,' said Cebes; 'I'll have to agree it's the living.'

'Is it from the dead, then, Cebes, that living things, living people, come to be?'

71e

'It appears so,' Cebes said.

'In that case,' said Socrates, 'our souls *are* there in Hades.'

'It seems so.'

'Then is one of the two processes involved with this pair actually obvious? It's dying, presumably – isn't it?'

'Yes, certainly it is,' Cebes said.

'So what will be our next move?' asked Socrates. 'Shall we not supply the opposite process to balance this first one? Are we going to leave nature like this, hopping along on one leg? Or must we balance dying with some opposite process?'

'Absolutely, yes,' said Cebes.

'What process?'

'Coming to life again.'

'Well then,' said Socrates, 'if that really is the process in question, coming to life again, won't that be a matter of coming to be from dead to living people?'

72a

'Yes, absolutely.'

'It counts as agreed between us, then, in this way too, that the living have come from the dead no less than the dead from the living; and I think it seemed to us that if this were the case, it would be sufficient proof that the souls of the dead must be somewhere – from where they were to be born again.'

'It seems to me, Socrates,' said Cebes, 'from what we've agreed, that it must indeed be like that.'[59]

'Well, look at it in the following way, Cebes,' he said, 'and you'll see that we weren't wrong to have agreed as we did, either, or so it seems to me. If one set of opposites didn't always come into being to balance the ones corresponding to it, going round as if in a circle, and instead the process were to be in a straight line, from one opposite to the one facing it, with no turning back or bending round to the other, do you realize that everything would end up having the same character and being in one continuous state, simply ceasing to come to be anything else?'

72b

'What do you mean?' asked Cebes.

'It's not at all difficult to grasp what I'm saying,' said Socrates; 'for example, if there was such a thing as going to sleep, but no waking up from sleeping was taking place to balance it, you'll recognize that in the end the state of things would make the case of Endymion[60] seem a mere trifle; no one would notice him, because everything else too would be in the same state as he was – asleep. Again, if everything were combined without being separated out again, soon what Anaxagoras describes would be a reality: "All things together."[61] In the same way, my dear Cebes, if, everything that partakes in life were to die, and after things died they stayed like that, wouldn't it inevitably end up with everything dead and nothing alive? After all, if living things came to be from non-living ones, and the living ones died off, what would there be to prevent everything whatever from being finally used up in the process from living to dead?'

72c

72d

'Nothing whatever that I can think of, Socrates,' said Cebes; 'what you say seems to me to be quite incontrovertible.'

'Yes, Cebes; this seems to me just how things are, and in my view we're not being deceived when we agree to the points in question: these are real facts – things do come back to life; the living do come from the dead; and the souls of the dead do exist.'

72e   'And again,' responded Cebes, 'this is also in accordance with the idea you're habitually repeating to us, Socrates, if it's true, to the effect that what we're doing when we're "learning" is actually recollecting;[62] if we follow this line too, well, I imagine it follows that we must have learned in some previous time the

73a   things we're now recollecting. That'd be impossible if we weren't to suppose that the soul existed somewhere before it came to be in this human shape of ours. So if we look at it in this way too the soul seems to be something deathless.'[63]

'But Cebes,' Simmias said at this point, 'what sort of proofs are there for this? Remind me, because I don't presently have much of a memory of them.'

'There's one quite beautiful argument for it,' replied Cebes; 'it's that when people are questioned, provided someone puts the questions well, they'll give the right answers, for themselves, on everything. And they wouldn't be able to do this if they didn't actually have knowledge in them, and a correct account.

73b   So, if one points them to diagrams and things of that sort, we have here a quite clear proof that this is how things are.'[64]

'If that's not enough to convince you, Simmias,' said Socrates, 'see if you'll come to share our view by looking at things in the following sort of way. What you're doubtful about is how what's called learning can be recollection – right?'

'No,' said Simmias, 'I'm not doubting you; what I need is the very thing we're talking about – to recollect the argument. In fact I almost remember already, from the explanation Cebes tried to give, and I'm convinced; but just the same I'd like to hear how *you* tried to explain it.'

73c   'Here it is,' said Socrates. 'I imagine we agree that, if anyone's going to recollect something, he must have had knowledge of that thing at some previous time?'

'Yes, certainly,' replied Simmias.

'So do we agree about this point too, namely that recollection is when knowledge comes to one in the following sort of way? Like this: if, on seeing something, or hearing it, or perceiving it with one of the other senses a person not only recognizes that thing but also comes to have in mind a second thing too, the knowledge of which isn't the same as that of the other, aren't we right in saying that he *recollected* this second thing that he came to have in mind?'[65]   73d

'How do you mean?'

'Take this sort of case: I imagine that knowing a person is one thing, knowing a lyre another.'

'Of course.'

'Well then, you're aware that, when lovers see a lyre their beloved is always playing, or a cloak he wears, or anything like that, they're affected in this way – not only do they recognize the lyre, there also comes to mind the shape of the boy the lyre belongs to. That's recollection; just as someone on seeing Simmias will often recollect Cebes – and there must be countless other cases of a similar sort.'

'Zeus! Yes, countless,' said Simmias.

'My next question is whether cases of this kind represent a   73e
sort of recollection; what counts most of all as recollection is when someone has this sort of experience in relation to things he's actually forgotten, because time has passed and he's not been thinking of them?'

'Yes, certainly,' said Simmias.

'What about the next point: is it possible to see a painting of a horse, or a painting of a lyre, and recollect a person? And to see a painting of Simmias, and recollect – Cebes?'

'Yes, absolutely.'

'Then what about seeing a painting of Simmias and recollecting Simmias himself?'

'That's certainly possible,' said Simmias.   74a

'Then doesn't it turn out that there's recollection that starts from things that are *like* the recollected item, and also recollection that starts from things *unlike* it?'

'It does.'

'But whenever someone recollects something from things that are like it, mustn't he always have this additional experience, of having in mind whether or not this thing he's starting from is deficient at all in respect of its likeness to the thing he's recollected?'[66]

'He must,' said Simmias.

'Well, then,' said Socrates, 'see what you think of the follow-ing. We say, I suppose, that there's something that's equal – I don't mean a stick that's equal to a stick, or a stone that's equal to a stone, or anything like that, but some further thing over and above all of these, that is, the equal itself: *are* we to say that something of the sort exists,[67] or not?'

74b 'Zeus! Yes,' said Simmias; 'indeed we are, most emphatic-ally!'

'And do we also know what it is?'

'Yes, definitely,' said Simmias.

'And where have we got our knowledge of it from? Isn't it from the things we were mentioning just now, that is, through seeing equal sticks or equal stones, or whatever else it may be – isn't it from these that we come to have that other equal in mind, even while it's distinct from them? Or perhaps you don't think it's distinct from them? Here's another consideration for you: even while being the same stones and sticks, aren't equal stones and equal sticks sometimes clearly equal to one stick or stone but not equal to another?'

'Yes, certainly.'

74c 'Well, did the equals by themselves[68] ever appear clearly unequal to you, or equality inequality?'

'Not so far, Socrates.'

'In that case,' Socrates said, 'those other equals[69] and the equal itself are not the same thing.'

'It doesn't appear so at all, to me, Socrates.'

'And yet it's from these equals', said Socrates, 'even while they're distinct from that other one, that you've nevertheless come to have in mind, and gained, your knowledge of it?'

'Very true,' said Simmias.

'Then you've got that knowledge of it from them – whether it was like them or whether it was unlike them?'

'Yes, absolutely.'

'In any case it makes no difference. So long as, on seeing one 74d thing, you come to have something else in mind, like or unlike, *from* seeing the first one,' Socrates said, 'what occurs must be recollection.'

'Yes, definitely.'

'Now do we have the following sort of experience in relation to what we perceive in the case of the sticks, and in general with all those pairs of equal things we were talking about just now: do they appear to us to be equal in the way that what's equal by itself is equal, or do they fall a bit short of that, in respect of being the kind of thing *the* equal is? Or are they entirely up to the mark?'

'They fall short by a long way,' replied Simmias.

'Well, do we agree that, when a person looks at something and thinks to himself, "This thing that I'm now seeing means to be the sort of thing that something else in the world actually   74e
is, but it's falling short, and is in fact incapable of being the kind of thing the other is; it's just not up to it" – someone who's thinking that must, I imagine, inevitably have had actual knowledge beforehand of the thing he's claiming that this other thing, the one in front of him, resembles but falls rather short of?'

'He must.'

'Well, then, is it or isn't it this sort of experience that we ourselves have in relation to those equal pairs and the equal itself?'

'It is, absolutely.'

'In that case we must have known the equal before the time   75a
when we first saw those equal pairs and thought to ourselves, "All these equals strive to be the sort of thing the equal is, but they fall rather short of it."'

'That's so.'

'But we're also in agreement that we haven't got this thought, and couldn't have got it, from anywhere except from seeing, touching or one of the other kinds of perceiving; I'm counting all of them as the same in this case.'

'Yes, they are the same, Socrates, in relation to what the argument means to show.'

'But then it's precisely from our acts of perceiving that we must get the thought that all the equal things we perceive in   75b
those acts strive after what's equal by itself and fall rather short of it – or is this what we're saying?'

'Yes, it is.'

'In that case it must have been before we began seeing and hearing and using our other senses that we actually gained knowledge of what the equal by itself is, if we were to be in a position to refer to it the equals from our acts of perceiving, and to have the thought that all such equals are eager enough to be the sort of thing *the* equal is, but are just inferior to it.'

'That must follow from what we've previously said, Socrates.'

'Well, then, it was as soon as we were born, wasn't it, that we were seeing, hearing and in possession of our other senses?'

'Yes, certainly.'

75c   'And – this is what we're saying – we must have got our knowledge of the equal before we got these?'

'Yes.'

'Then we must have got that knowledge, it seems, before we were born.'

'It seems so.'

'Now if, having got it before we were born, we were born with it, here's a question for you: did we know, both before we were born and as soon as we were born, not just the equal, the larger and the smaller, but also absolutely all such things? For our present discussion isn't restricted to the equal; it's just as 75d   much about the beautiful itself, and the good itself, the just, the pious, and, as I say, *everything* of this sort – all the things to which we attach this label of ours, "what *is*",[70] both in our questions, when we ask them, and in our answers when we're in the role of respondents. So we must have got our knowledge of each one of these before we were born?'

'That's so.'

'Necessarily, too, if having got our knowledge in each case we don't forget it, we must be born knowing each of the things in question, and we must know them our whole lives through – because that's what knowing is, to possess knowledge of something after having got it, and not to have lost it; that's what we call forgetting, isn't it, Simmias, the loss of knowledge?'

75e   'Absolutely, yes, Socrates,' said Simmias.

'Whereas if we get our knowledge before we are born but lose it on being born, and then later through the use of our perceptions we get back those pieces of knowledge[71] that we had at some previous time, what we call learning would be a matter of getting back knowledge that was ours anyway; and we'd surely be correct if we called that recollection?'

'Yes, certainly.'

'Yes, because it seemed to us perfectly possible for a person   76a
to perceive something – whether he's seen it, or heard it, or whatever – and from this come to have something else in mind that he'd forgotten, which the first thing was unlike or like but was anyway close to. The outcome is that, as I say, one of two things must be the case: either we were born knowing these things, and we all know them our whole lives through, or else the people we say are "learning" are actually *recollecting* their knowledge after their birth, and "learning" will be – recollection.'

'That's how it is, Socrates, very much so.'

'So which of the two alternatives do you choose, Simmias? That we were born with the knowledge in question, or that we   76b
recollect things later on that we'd got to know before?'

'At this moment, Socrates, I'm not able to make my choice.'

'Well, are you able to choose in the following case – see what you think about it: will a man with knowledge be able to give a reasoned account in relation to the things he knows?'

'He certainly must know how to do that, Socrates.'

'And do you think everyone's able to give such an account in relation to the things we were talking about just now?'

'I wish that were true,' said Simmias; 'but I fear it's much more likely that this time tomorrow there'll no longer be anyone in the world able to do so in the manner those subjects deserve.'

'So, Simmias,' said Socrates, 'you don't think everyone does   76c
have knowledge of them?'

'Certainly not.'

'They're recollecting, then, what they learned at some point in the past?'

'That must be so.'

'So when was it that our souls got their knowledge of those things? Certainly not since we were born as human beings.'

'No, quite.'

'Then before that.'

'Yes.'

'In that case, Simmias, our souls existed even before they were contained within this human shape, existing without bodies; and they had intelligence.'

'Unless after all, Socrates, we get these pieces of knowledge at the very time we're being born; we haven't yet ruled out that it was then that we got it.'

76d 'Very well, my friend, but what other sort of time is there for us to *lose* them? We're not born with them in our possession, as we've just agreed; or is it that we lose them at the same time that we're getting them? Or do you have some other time for it up your sleeve?'

'Certainly not, Socrates; I didn't notice I was talking nonsense.'

'So is this where we end up, Simmias: if the things we're always talking about really exist – something that's beautiful by itself, something that's good by itself, in short all the things of that kind that there are;[72] if we refer their counterparts, from

76e our acts of perceiving, to them, rediscovering a knowledge that was there before and so was ours already; and if we really do compare the things we perceive to those others, then it must follow that just as the beautiful, the good, and so on exist, so does our soul, even before we've been born, and if they don't exist, all of this argument of ours will have been in vain? *Is* that how it is, namely that an equal degree of necessity attaches to the two claims – both that those other things exist, and that our souls do, before our birth as well as after it? Are we saying that, if the other things don't exist, the rest won't hold either?'[73]

'I'm emphatically in agreement, Socrates,' said Simmias, 'that an equal degree of necessity attaches to both, and it's a

77a fine thing indeed that the argument should resort to saying that our soul exists before we're born just as surely as do all those other things that you're now talking about. Speaking for myself, nothing is as evident as this, that all such things exist as certainly as anything could – a beautiful, a good and all the other things you were referring to just now; and my own view is that our proof is good enough.'[74]

'And how does it seem to Cebes?' asked Socrates. 'We must convince Cebes too.'

'He's with me,' said Simmias, 'or so I think; and yet he's the most obstinate person in the world when it comes to distrusting arguments. Still, I think he's been fully persuaded of this much, that our soul existed before we were born. On the other   77b
hand, whether it will also go on existing after we die is something that even I don't think has been shown; there's still that fear blocking the way, the one that Cebes was attributing to ordinary people, that even as a person is dying his soul is scattered into pieces and that this, for it, is the end. Why shouldn't it come into existence by being put together from some other source, so that it exists before it gets into a human body, but when it's got there it lasts only until it's separated from the body again, when it too comes to an end and is destroyed?'

'A good point, Simmias,' said Cebes; 'it looks as if only half   77c
of what's required has been shown, namely that our soul existed before our birth. What needs to be shown over and above this, if the proof is to be complete, is that the soul will exist no less after our death than before our birth.'

'Actually, Simmias and Cebes,' said Socrates, 'it's been shown even now, if you're prepared to put the present argument together with the one we agreed on before, to the effect that everything living comes from the dead. If the soul pre-   77d
exists, and if its coming into life and being born can't occur from any other source except death and being dead, how can it not exist after it dies,[75] as well, given that it's got to be born again? So actually we've already shown what you're asking for. All the same, I think you and Simmias would like to give this point more attention even now; I do believe you've the fear that children have, that the wind will literally blow the soul apart as   77e
it emerges from the body and scatter it into pieces, especially if its owner happens to die in a gale instead of calm weather.'

Cebes laughed and said, 'Well, Socrates, suppose we do have this childish fear, and try to persuade us otherwise – or rather, don't suppose *we* have it; perhaps there's a child in us, all the same, that has fears like that.[76] So go on, try to stop this infant being afraid of death like the bogeyman.'

'Yes,' said Socrates, 'but what he'll need is to be sung to each and every day, until you succeed in charming it out of him.'[77]

78a   'So where do you suppose, Socrates,' said Cebes, 'that we're going to find an expert in such spells, since you are abandoning us?'

'Greece is a big place, Cebes,' said Socrates, 'and I imagine it must have good men in it, not to mention those from non-Greek races; you'll need to hunt them all down in search of the enchanter you need, whatever the cost in money or effort, because there's nothing you could better spend your money on.[78] But you must search yourselves too, in concert with each other; for it may well not be easy to find others more able than yourselves to do what's needed.'[79]

78b   'Consider it done,' replied Cebes; 'now let's go back to where we left the argument behind, if you're happy to do that.'

'Of course I'm happy with that; why wouldn't I be?'

'You're right,' said Cebes.

'Well,' said Socrates, 'I suggest we should ask ourselves the following sort of question: what kind of thing is it that's liable to get "scattered into pieces"? What kinds of things should we and shouldn't we be afraid it'll happen to? After we've answered that, the next step will be to ask whether soul is of the first sort or of the second; that will tell us whether to be confident or fearful on behalf of *our* souls.'

'True,' said Cebes.

78c   'So will it be what's been compounded, and is composite in nature, that's liable to suffer this fate, and be pulled apart just as it was put together; whereas if there's something that's actually incomposite, it's this alone, if anything, that's liable not to have such a thing happen to it?'

'That's what I think,' said Cebes.

'Well, then: it's things that are always in exactly the same state, isn't it, that are most likely to be the ones that are incomposite, with the ones most likely to be composite being those that are always changing and never the same?'

'It seems so to me.'

'Then let's go back,' said Socrates, 'to the very same things we resorted to in our previous argument. Take by itself that set   78d
of things of whose essence we try to give an account as we question each other and offer our answers:[80] are they always in exactly the same state, or are they now like this, now like that? The equal by itself, the beautiful by itself, each "what is" by itself, which just is whatever it is:[81] can *these* ever undergo change of any kind at all? Or is each "what is" among them always, being uniform in and by itself, in exactly the same state, never allowing of any variation whatever of whatever kind?'

'They must always be in exactly the same state, Socrates,' said Cebes.

'And what about ordinary beautiful things, like people, or horses, or cloaks, or anything else of that sort, or ordinary   78e
equal things – all the ordinary things that share the same names as those other, special things? Do they stay in the same state, or is it the complete opposite with them, so that they are practically never the same at all in relation either to themselves or to each other?'

'I agree with your description of these too,' said Cebes; 'they're never the same.'

'And these you can actually touch, see and grasp with the   79a
other senses; whereas the things that stay in the same state you can't get hold of except with the mind's reasoning. Such things are unseen and not accessible to the eyes.'

'Absolutely true,' said Cebes.

'So are you happy for us to assume two kinds of existent things, one visible, the other unseen?'

'Let's do that,' said Cebes.

'And the unseen is something that's always in the same state, while the visible is never so?'

'Let's assume that too,' said Cebes.

'Now here's a question for you,' said Socrates: 'isn't it the   79b
case that part of us is body, part soul?'

'It is,' said Cebes.

'So to which of the two kinds of things do we say that the body will be more similar, more akin?'

'That's obvious to anyone,' said Cebes: 'the visible kind.'

'What about the soul? Is it something visible, or something unseen?'

'Not visible to human eyes, at any rate, Socrates,' said Cebes.

'But our question was surely just about what was visible and what was not visible with reference to human nature; or do you suppose we had some other nature in mind?'

'No, human nature.'

'So what do we say about soul? That it's something visible or invisible?'

'Not visible.'

'Unseen, then?'

'Yes.'

'In that case soul is more like what's unseen than the body is, while body is more like the visible.'

79c 'That there's no denying, Socrates.'

'Here's another point. Weren't we also saying a while ago that, when the soul brings in the body for the purpose of looking into anything, whether it's through seeing, or hearing, or some other act of perceiving (because that's what looking into something through the body is – looking into it by using our senses), then it gets dragged by the body into things that never stay the same, and itself starts wandering about in confusion, dizzy as a drunk, just because it's in contact with things like that?'

'Yes, quite.'

79d 'But when the soul does its investigation alone and by itself, it takes itself off to what's unalloyed, eternal, deathless and unchanging, and insofar as it's akin to that, it's always to be found in its company, whenever it gets the opportunity to spend time on its own; it stops wandering about, and in its relation to those other things it stays in exactly the same state, because it's in contact with things that are themselves unchanging;[82] and the name we give to what the soul experiences in this case is "wisdom" – right?'

'Quite beautifully said, Socrates,' said Cebes, 'and true.'

'So once again I ask you: both from what we were saying before, and from what we're now saying, to which of the two 79e kinds of things does it seem to you the soul is more similar, more akin?'

'It seems to me, Socrates,' said Cebes, 'that from this line of inquiry even the slowest person would agree that soul is completely and absolutely something more similar to what is always in the same state rather than to what isn't.'

'What about the body?'

'More like the latter.'

'Now look at the matter in this way too. When soul and body are together, nature lays down that the latter should be 80a ruled as a slave, while the former rules as its master: from this perspective too, which of them do you think resembles the divine,[83] and which the mortal? Or doesn't the divine seem to you the kind of thing that naturally rules and leads, and the mortal the sort of thing that is naturally subject and slave?'[84]

'It does.'

'So which does the soul resemble?'

'It's obvious, Socrates, that the soul resembles the divine, the body the mortal.'

'Then consider, Cebes,' said Socrates, 'whether from all that's been said we reach the following results: that soul is 80b something that's very like what's divine, deathless, the object of intellect, uniform, undissolved, and always in exactly the same state as it ever was; while body in its turn is something very like what's human, mortal, mindless,[85] multiform, tending to dissolution, and never the same as it was before. Have we anything to say against these results, my dear Cebes, to show that this isn't the way things are?'

'No, nothing.'

'Well then, given all this, wouldn't it be fitting for the body to be quickly dissolved, but for the soul, by contrast, to be absolutely indissoluble, or something close to that?'

'Of course.'   80c

'You're aware, then, that when a person dies, the part of him that's visible, the body, the part that's situated in the visible sphere – what we call a corpse, which it'd be fitting to find being dissolved, shrinking, being blown apart, well, in fact it doesn't have any of these things happen to it immediately; it stays around for a reasonably long time, and especially so if someone dies with his body in an attractive condition and at the sort of age that implies.[86] In fact when the body has shrunk and been embalmed, as with those who've been embalmed in Egypt, it remains practically whole for an extraordinarily long time, and some parts of the body – bones, muscle tissue, things like that – even if they do decay are still virtually immortal. Isn't that so?'

80d

'Yes.'

'Whereas the soul, the unseen part of us, the part that takes itself off to a second place of the same sort, noble, unalloyed, unseen, that is, to the true place of Hades,[87] to the presence of the good and wise god – which is where, god willing, my soul too must go even now: are we to suppose that *this*, this soul of ours, being such as it is and possessed of the nature we've described, is blown into pieces and perishes immediately on its separation from the body, in the way that ordinary people claim? Far from it, my dear Cebes and Simmias. It's much rather like this: if a soul gets away in a purified state, dragging along nothing of the body with it, because it wasn't its willing partner in anything, but rather shunned it, and now makes good its escape gathered up together into itself, because this was what it was perpetually practising – which is nothing other, is it, than doing philosophy in the correct way and in truth practising dying without complaint? *Won't* this be practising for death?'

80e

81a

'Yes, absolutely.'

'Being in this state, then, it's to its like, the unseen, that it departs, to what is divine, deathless and wise, where it is able to achieve the happy state it desired, now that it is rid of wandering, of mindlessness, fears, savage lusts and the other evils that beset us humans, and will in truth, as is said of the initiated, spend the rest of its time with the gods. Is that what we're to claim, Cebes, or something else?'

'Zeus! Just that,' said Cebes.

'But I imagine that if it's separated from the body in a pol-   81b
luted and unpurified state, because it was constantly with the
body, paying court to it, in love with it, under its spell and that
of its desires and pleasures to such a degree that it thinks nothing real unless it comes in bodily form, and something it can get
hold of, see, drink, eat or have sex with; while at the same time
it's acquired the habit of hating and fearing and trying to run
away from what is obscure to the eyes and unseen, but open to
intellect and graspable by philosophy – do you suppose that a   81c
soul in *that* sort of state will get away just by itself, unalloyed?'

'There's no way it will.'

'Rather, I imagine that when it goes off it will in fact be
interspersed with elements of the bodily, grown into it through
its close relationship with the body, and because of the long
practice it's had of continual intimacy with it.'

'Yes, quite.'

'And, my dear Simmias, this must be a weight to carry:
heavy, earthy, visible; because of it, that sort of soul must be
weighed down, dragged back into the sphere of the visible, out
of fear of Hades and the unseen,[88] roaming around tombs and   81d
memorials to the dead, as in the stories. There certain shadow-
like phantasms of souls have actually been seen, wraiths of the
kind afforded by the souls I'm now describing; the ones that
have not made a clean break with the body, but that remain
partly visible – and are duly seen.'

'Likely so, Socrates.'

'Likely indeed, Cebes; likely, too, that these are not at all the
souls of the good but those of inferior people, which are forced
to wander in such places as a penalty for the kind of life they
previously lived, because it was a bad one. They continue their
wandering until such time that the desire for the bodily that
shadows them finally causes them to be imprisoned again in a   81e
body; and as you might expect, the prison that houses them
will be marked by the very sorts of traits that they actually
practised to acquire in their previous life.'

'What sorts of traits do you have in mind, Socrates?'

'For example, it's likely that those who've practised ravening

gluttony or excessive fondness for wine, and weren't on their
82a guard, pass into the kinds represented by asses and wild animals of a similar sort.'[89]

'What you say is absolutely likely.'

'Yes, and those who've put a premium on injustice in the
form of tyranny and pillage will pass into those of wolves,
hawks or kites; where else would we say such souls would
go?'

'Without a doubt into kinds like that,' said Cebes.

'So it's clear, is it,' asked Socrates, 'where every other type of
soul will go, too, according to what it's trained itself to
resemble?'[90]

'It's clear,' said Cebes, 'of course.'

'Then happiest even of these souls, and the ones who go to
the best place, are the people who have practised the common,
82b civic virtue,[91] the sort that they call moderation, or justice, and
that has come about from habit and practice and in the absence
of philosophy and intelligence.'

'How are these the happiest?'

'Because the likelihood is that they arrive back in some other
civic-minded and gentle kind of creature, bees, perhaps, or
wasps, or ants, or actually back again into the very same kind,
the human one, and decent men are born from them.'[92]

'That's the likely thing.'

'But to the kind that *gods* belong to – for anyone to arrive at
82c that destination,[93] if he has not practised philosophy, and isn't
going off in a wholly purified state, is not permitted;[94] only the
lover of learning can go there. It's for that reason, Simmias and
Cebes, my friends, that those who practise philosophy in the
correct way resolutely keep clear of all the bodily desires instead
of surrendering themselves to them, and aren't the slightest bit
afraid of losing their property and falling into poverty, as ordinary people are because of their love of money; nor do they steer
clear of such desires just because they're afraid of the loss of
esteem and repute that comes from depravity, like those who
love power and honour.'

'No, Socrates,' said Cebes, 'that wouldn't be appropriate for
them.'

'Zeus! No indeed it would not,' said Socrates. 'That is why, 82d Cebes, those who care at all about their own soul, and don't live their lives moulding their bodies into shape, wave goodbye to all those other types, refusing to follow the same path as people who have no idea where they're going. Thinking themselves that they should not do things that are opposed to philosophy, and the release and purification it offers, they take the turning along which philosophy leads.'

'How so, Socrates?'

'I'll tell you,' Socrates replied. 'These lovers of learning recognize that before philosophy takes their soul in hand, it is 82e simply bound fast within the body, and glued to it, so that it's forced to investigate things[95] as if through prison bars and never by itself, through its own resources; the outcome is that it rolls around in total ignorance. Philosophy observes the ingenious way in which this prison is devised, and the way in which it relies on the prisoner's own desire, so that he'll collaborate enthusiastically in his own imprisonment. Well, as I was saying, the lovers of learning recognize that, when philoso- 83a phy takes their soul in hand in this condition, it speaks gently and soothingly to it and attempts to set it free, demonstrating that using our eyes to investigate things mostly deceives us, as does using our ears or any of the sense-organs, and trying to convince the soul to draw back from these to the extent that it doesn't have to use them, all the time urging it to collect and gather itself into itself and put its trust in nothing other than itself, as it apprehends, alone and by itself, what each thing, 83b alone and by itself, is.[96] It is not to consider as true anything that it investigates through other means and in other things, because that will itself be something other than what is true; that sort of thing is an object of perception, and visible, while what the soul sees by itself is an object of intellect, and unseen.[97] It's because it thinks it shouldn't oppose this kind of liberation that the soul of the truly philosophical person keeps clear so far as it can of pleasures, desires, pains and fears, making the calculation that, when someone experiences extremes of pleasure or pain, fear or desire, the harm he's suffered from the sources one might suppose – for example, because he's fallen ill, or 83c spent a bit to satisfy his desires – isn't so great at all; what he does suffer is the greatest and last of all evils, and it doesn't even enter his calculations.'

'What's that, Socrates?' asked Cebes.

'That every person's soul is forced to think, even as something causes it extreme pleasure or pain, that whatever it is that most causes this is also most dependable and true, when it is neither; and these are, especially, visible things. Isn't that so?'

'Yes, certainly.'

83d   'Then it's when this is happening to it that soul is especially the prisoner of the body?'

'How's that?'

'Because each pleasure and pain fastens it to the body as if with a nail, and causes it to be of the same kind as the body,[98] insofar as it too comes to believe to be true whatever the body says is so. For I imagine that as a result of sharing the same beliefs as the body, and finding pleasure in the same things, it is forced to take on the same traits and live the same kind of life, so becoming the kind of soul that would never arrive in Hades in a pure state, but is always filled full with the body even after

83e   leaving it; and so it quickly falls back again into another body, and grows in it like a seed, thus missing out on being with the divine, the pure, and the uniform.'[99]

'What you say is very true, Socrates.'

'So it's for these reasons, Cebes, that those justly called lovers of learning are orderly and courageous, not for the reasons ordinary people are;[100] or do you think ordinary people have got it right?'

84a   'I certainly don't.'

'No indeed. The soul of a philosophical person would reason in the way we've said, and wouldn't suppose, on the one hand, that it should be set free by philosophy, but on the other, even as philosophy was working its release, that it really should surrender itself to pleasures and pains, to bind it back into the body again, so bringing about the unending task of a Penelope[101] by setting about undoing what philosophy had woven. Instead it contrives for the storm of pleasures and pains to be stilled, following the lead of the reasoning that always preoccupies it,

and having its gaze fixed on what is true, divine, and not merely
the subject of belief,[102] is nourished by that; it thinks it should   84b
live like this, for as long as it does live, and that when it dies
and has arrived at what is akin to it, and at what is such as it is
itself, it's been released from human ills. Having been brought
up like that, Simmias and Cebes, there's no danger that this sort
of soul will be afraid – and when it's put the things I've said into
practice – that it'll be torn apart on its separation from the body,
blown apart by the winds, flying in different directions, and so
exiting and being no longer anywhere at all.'

When Socrates had finished speaking, there was an extended   84c
silence, and even Socrates, by the looks of it, was absorbed in
the argument he'd just proposed, as were most of us; but Cebes
and Simmias were talking to each other in a low voice. Socrates
saw them, and asked, 'What? Surely you don't think there was
anything incomplete about what we said?[103] There certainly are
still many ways in which it leaves room for misgivings, and for
counter-attacks, at any rate for someone who's going to go into
the matter properly. Well, it may be that you're thinking about
something else, in which case I'm talking to no purpose, but if
there's something about what we've been saying that the two of
you are unhappy with, don't hesitate to raise it and explain   84d
what it is for yourselves, if it seems to you that it would have
been better put in some other way; and don't hesitate to call me
in to help as well, if you think you'll be any better off with me
along.'

At this, Simmias said, 'Well, then, Socrates, to tell you the
truth, each of us has for some time now been egging the other
on, pushing each other to ask about what's bothering us,
because even as we're anxious to hear your answer, at the same
time we're reluctant to make trouble, in case it causes you distress in your present misfortune.'

On hearing this, Socrates gave a gentle laugh and said, 'Dear
me, Simmias! If I can't even convince you two that I don't think   84e
my present fate a misfortune, I'd certainly find it difficult to
convince the rest of mankind! You're afraid that I'm in a bit
more of a peevish frame of mind now than I used to be in my

previous life; it seems I look to you less of an expert seer than
85a   the swans, who on sensing the approach of death outdo even
their previous performances, singing more insistently and more
loudly[104] than ever because of their delight at the prospect of
going off to join the god whose servants they are. Because of
their own fear of death human beings lie about swans too,
claiming that it's distress that makes them sing their last song,
in grief at their death; they don't take into account the fact that
no bird sings when it's suffering from hunger or cold or any
other sort of distress – not even the nightingale itself, the swallow and the hoopoe,[105] the paradigm cases, people claim, of
birds' singing from grief. In fact neither these nor the swans
85b   appear to me to sing out of distress; I think it's because they
belong to Apollo and so have the power of prophecy, which
gives them foreknowledge of the benefits of being in Hades and
makes them happier on the day they die than they've ever been
before. And I regard myself, too, as a fellow slave with the
swans, sacred to the same god,[106] no worse than they are at
using the gift of prophecy we have from our master, and leaving life in no worse humour than they do. No, so far as all that
goes, you should speak out, and ask whatever you want for as
long as eleven Athenian men[107] allow it.'

'Well said,' replied Simmias; 'and I'll tell you what's worry-
85c   ing me, as Cebes here too will say why he doesn't accept what's
been said so far. In relation to subjects like the present one,
Socrates, it seems to me much as I imagine it does to you, that
to know the plain truth is either impossible or something very
difficult, but on the other hand I think it's only the most feeble
sort of person who'd not want to test what's being said in every
way possible, not giving up until he'd exhausted himself from
investigating every angle. The thought will be that the outcome
must be one or the other of the following: either one will learn
the truth of things from someone else, or one will discover it
for oneself – or else, if neither of these turns out to be possible,
one must at least get hold of the best account of things that
85d   human beings have come up with, the hardest to refute, and
sail through life using this like a raft to ride on, taking one's
courage in one's hands; unless one could find a more stable

craft to make one's way through more safely and with less risk – perhaps some divine utterance. And so now I'll not be ashamed of myself for putting my question, since you agree that I shouldn't, and I won't have cause for blaming myself later, either, for not having said what I think. The fact is, Socrates, that when I reflect either privately by myself or with Cebes on what's been said, it doesn't strike me as being quite sufficient.'

'Yes, and perhaps your view is correct, my friend,' said Socrates. 'Tell me in what way it wasn't sufficient.'   85e

'In this way, it seems to me –' said Simmias, 'in that one could claim the same about an attunement and a lyre and its strings: that the attunement is something invisible, incorporeal, altogether beautiful, even divine, in the tuned lyre, while the   86a
lyre and its strings are bodies, that is, bodily things, composite, earthy, akin to the mortal. So when the lyre gets smashed, or the strings are cut through or snap, someone could use the same argument as you do, to the effect that the attunement must still be in existence and hadn't perished at all – after all, the argument would go, there'd be no way that the lyre could continue to exist as it does, with the strings broken, or that the strings could, given that they're of a mortal sort, while the attunement, which   86b
is of the same nature and the same kin as the divine and death-less, had already perished, before the mortal. The attunement itself, this person would say, *must* still be somewhere, and the wooden bits and the strings would rot before anything happened to it. In point of fact, Socrates, I think you yourself have noticed that we[108] suppose the soul to be precisely something of this sort: given that our body is in tension, as it were, and held together by hot and cold and dry and wet and things like that,   86c
our idea is that our soul is a blending or attunement of these very things, that is, when they're blended well with each other and in due proportion. Well, if the soul actually is a kind of attunement, clearly when our soul is unduly slackened or stretched by diseases or other sorts of damage, it must follow that the soul has perished in the very process, even though it's the most divine element in us – just like other attunements, whether in the sphere of actual sound or wherever they're found in the products

of craftsmen, while the bodily remains in each case stick around
86d for a long time, until they're burned or they rot down. So see
what our response will be to this proposal: what if someone
does claim that because it's actually a blending of the constituents of the body the soul will be the first to have perished in
what we call death?'[109]

At this, with a smile, and eyes opened wide – that stare he so
often used to use, Socrates said, 'Simmias has a point. If any of
you is better equipped to respond to him than I am, why don't
they do just that? He really does look as if he's got a hold on
my argument, and not one to be brushed off. But I think before
86e Simmias gets his answer we should listen to Cebes too, see what
charge *he*'ll bring against the argument, and so give ourselves
time to decide what we're going to say. Then, when we've heard
them both, we can either go along with them, if they seem to
have hit the right note in any respect; if they don't, then it'll be
the time to put the case for my side. So come on, Cebes,' said
Socrates, 'and tell us: what was it that was troubling *you*?'

'I'll tell you,' said Cebes. 'The argument as a whole seems to
87a me to be just where it was before, and to be liable to the same
charge that we made against it earlier. I don't retract my admis-
sion that it's been quite delightfully and, if I may say so without
offence, quite "sufficiently" shown that our soul existed even
before entering this human shape of ours; but that it's also still
somewhere after we've died, this I don't think has been shown.
As for the claim that soul isn't a stronger and more long-lasting
thing than the body, here I don't agree with Simmias' objection;
in all such respects it seems to me very much superior. "Then
why," your argument will ask, "are you still not convinced,
when you can see what is actually the weaker part continuing
87b to exist when the person has died? Don't you think the longer-
lasting part must still be preserved during this time?" My reply
to which is the following – just look and see if I'm making any
sense; like Simmias, I need to use an analogy. It seems to me
what you're saying could equally be said about an elderly
weaver who's now dead: one could claim that the person hasn't
actually perished but exists intact somewhere,[110] producing in
evidence the fact that this is true of the cloak he was wearing,

the one he'd woven for his own use – *it*'s intact, and hasn't perished. If someone raised doubts about this, the next move would be to ask which of the two kinds of thing is the more long-lasting, a person or a cloak that's been used by a wearer; when the answer came back that it was the former kind, by far, one would conclude, using the model of your own argument, that the case was now proven – in that case, nothing's so certain as that the person is intact, given that the less long-lasting thing hasn't perished. But I imagine that in fact it's not like that – Simmias, I need your view on what I'm saying, too. The whole world would suppose anyone proposing such a thing a simpleton; after all, this weaver will have worn out many identical cloaks, weaving a new one each time, so that he will have perished after all the many worn-out ones, and presumably before only one of them, namely the last, which is hardly enough to make a person something lowlier or less robust than a cloak.[111] The same analogy, I think, could be applied to the relationship between soul and body: someone might reasonably say the very same things about soul and body as about the weaver and his cloak, that the soul is something long-lived, while the body is a weaker and shorter-lived thing, but all the same, he'd say, every single soul wears out many bodies, especially if it has a long life – for if the body is in flux, and is perishing even while the person is alive, still the soul always weaves again what's being worn out; even so, when the soul perishes it must do so actually still clothed in the final garment it's woven, so that it perishes before this one, but only this one, and with the perishing of the soul the body finally demonstrates its own true weakness by quickly rotting and departing the scene. So there's no justification yet for relying on this argument of yours, and it gives us no reassurance that when we die our soul still exists somewhere. Even if we conceded still more than this to a person putting forward the case you're proposing,[112] and granted him not only that our souls existed in the time before we were even born, but that there was nothing to prevent its being the case that when we die the souls of some of us still exist, will exist and will be born and die again many times over – because soul has the inherent strength to tolerate repeated births; if we granted all

of that, but stopped short of conceding that there were no ill effects on it at all from those many births, so that there might
88b be one of its deaths in which it perished altogether, and no one – our respondent would have to agree – would know which death this was, which separation from the body, that was bringing final destruction to the soul, since it'd be impossible for any one of us to see it coming: if all this is so, then anyone who's confident about death can't be said to have more than a mindless confidence, if he's not able to show that soul is completely deathless and imperishable. Otherwise, and again our respondent would have to agree, the person who's about to die must always fear for his soul, in case it completely perishes in *this* separation of it from the body.'

88c Well, when we'd heard what the two of them had to say, we all found ourselves in a disagreeable state of mind, as we told each other later on. We'd been decidedly convinced by the previous argument, and now here they were apparently throwing us into confusion again, and reducing us to distrust not only of the preceding arguments but of anything that might follow them; either we must be good for nothing as critics, or there was something inherently untrustworthy about the very matters we were discussing.

ECHECRATES Goodness me, Phaedo, I have every sympathy
88d for you. Having listened to you, I find myself, too, wanting to ask just this sort of question: what argument *should* we trust in after this? How very convincing the argument was that Socrates produced, and yet now it has been discredited. Because actually I'm extraordinarily taken, now as much as ever, with this proposal that our soul is a kind of attunement, and having it spelled out reminded me, so to speak, that that was already my own view. I really need another argument, starting again from first principles, as it were, to convince me that the soul of the dead person doesn't die with him. So tell me – Zeus help me! – how did Socrates pur-
88e sue the discussion? And did he too become visibly upset at all, as you say you all did, or did he gently try to come to the aid of his argument? And was his defence of it sufficient, or did it fail? Describe it all for us as faithfully as you can.

PHAEDO That I shall do. Echecrates, I'd often had cause to wonder at Socrates before, but never more than for what I observed in him on this occasion. That Socrates should have 89a had something to say in response to Cebes and Simmias is presumably not so surprising; what I wondered at particularly about him was first of all the pleasant, kindly and respectful way he received what these young men had to say; secondly how sharply he observed the effect on us of the exchanges; and finally how effectively he soothed us, rallying us as if we were a defeated army in retreat and urging us to keep up and continue examining his case with him.

ECHECRATES How did he manage to do that?

PHAEDO I'll tell you. As it happened, I was sitting to the right of him on a stool beside his bed, and he was much higher 89b up than I was. Stretching down with his hand he stroked my head, squeezed together the hair on my neck – he had a habit, now and then, of playing with my hair – and said, 'Tomorrow, I suppose, Phaedo, you'll be cutting off this beautiful hair of yours.'[113]

'It seems so, Socrates,' I said.

'Not if you take my advice.'

'What then?' I asked.

'Today's the day,' he replied, 'that you and I both should be cutting off our hair, at any rate if our argument dies and we can't bring it back to life. And for my part, if I were you, and 89c my argument did get away from me, I'd swear an oath like the Argives,[114] not to let my hair grow back until I'd defeated Simmias' and Cebes' objections.

'But they say not even Heracles could fight alone against two,' I said.

'Call me in as your Iolaus,' said Socrates, 'so long as the light lasts.'[115]

'So I'm calling you in,' I said, 'but I'm not the Heracles; with us it's Iolaus calling on Heracles.'

'It'll make no difference,' he said. 'But a warning first: there's one state of mind we must guard against.'

'What's that?' I asked.

'What we must beware of,' he said, 'is becoming "misologists", 89d

hating arguments in the way "misanthropists" hate their fellow men; because' he declared 'there's nothing worse that can happen to anyone than coming to hate arguments. Actually, misology and misanthropy come about in the same way. Misanthropy creeps in as a result of placing too much trust in someone without having the knowledge required: we suppose the person to be completely genuine, sound and trustworthy, only to find a bit later that he's bad and untrustworthy, and then it happens again with someone else; when we've experienced the same thing many times over, and especially when it's with those we'd
89e have supposed our nearest and dearest, we get fed up with making so many mistakes and so end up hating everyone and supposing no one to be sound in any respect. Haven't you seen this happening?'

'Yes, certainly,' I said.

'Not a pretty thing, then,' said Socrates; 'and clearly someone like that will have been trying to handle human relationships without the knowledge he needs, of what humans are like; for I imagine that if he'd been doing it on the basis of a proper understanding, he would have supposed things to be as
90a they really are, with the very good and the very bad forming a small minority, and the majority in the middle between good and bad.'

'What do you mean?' I asked.

'It's the same as with very small and very large objects,' he said; 'can you think of anything rarer than to find an extremely large or extremely small man, or dog, or anything else? Or try it with quick, slow, ugly, beautiful, pale, dark: haven't you noticed that examples at the extreme points in all such cases are rare and in the minority, while examples in between are plentiful and in the majority?'

'Yes, certainly,' I said.

90b 'Then it's your view', said Socrates, 'that if a competition for badness were proposed those out in front would be quite few in number?'

'That's likely,' I replied.

'Yes indeed,' said Socrates, 'though in fact arguments aren't like human beings in that respect;[116] I was merely following

your lead just now. The similarity is just that when someone
trusts in the truth of an argument without having the necessary
expertise, in arguments, and a bit later on it looks false to him
(sometimes it is, sometimes it isn't); then the same thing happens with another, and another – well, as you'll know, especially if it's a question of someone who's spent all his time on   90c
constructing opposing arguments,[117] he'll end up thinking he's
become very wise, because unlike anyone else he's understood
that there is nothing whatever that's sound, or stable, in things,
and nothing that's sound or stable in arguments either. Everything there is in the world is simply moving this way and that,
up and down like the currents in the Euripus, and doesn't stop
still anywhere for any period of time.'[118]

'You're absolutely right,' I said.

'Well, then, Phaedo,' said Socrates, 'wouldn't it be a quite
pitiable thing if there really were some true and stable argument that one could get hold of, and yet because a person   90d
mixed with the sorts of arguments that now seem true, now
false, he failed to blame himself, and his own lack of expertise,
and instead eased his distress by happily shifting the blame
from himself to arguments, thus living out the rest of his life
not only hating and abusing arguments but deprived of the
truth of things and of knowledge about them?'

'Zeus! It would indeed be a pitiable thing,' I said.

'Then our first priority,' Socrates said, 'must be to beware of
allowing the thought to creep into our soul that there's prob-   90e
ably nothing sound in any argument; we must much rather
suppose that it's ourselves that are not yet in a sound condition,
and that we must soldier on, eager to be sound – you, Phaedo,
and the others here, for the sake of the rest of your lives as well
as for the present moment, and I for the sake of my impending   91a
death itself, insofar as I'm presently in danger of wanting to
win the argument, like people of no education, instead of showing a properly philosophical attitude towards it.[119] Whenever
they're disputing on some subject or other, the concern of these
individuals is only that the theses they themselves have proposed should seem good to their audience; they don't care how
the things they're talking about actually are. I think the only

difference, at the present moment, between me and them is that it's not my concern, except incidentally, whether what I'm saying should seem true to my audience, but rather that it should as much as possible seem so to *me*. My reasoning is this, my dear friend (see how determined I am to get the advantage!):[120] if what I'm saying is actually true, then it's a fine thing to be convinced about it, and if there's nothing, after all, for the person who's died, then at any rate for just this short time before my own death I'll spare my audience the unpleasantness of hearing me moan about it, and this silliness of mine won't persist with me, which would be a bad thing, but will shortly perish with me. So much, then, Simmias and Cebes,' said Socrates, 'for my preparations for advancing against your argument; as for you, if you'll take my advice, you'll pay little attention to Socrates and much more to the truth: if I do seem to be saying anything that's true, agree with me, but if not resist me with all the arguments at your disposal. Take care that in my enthusiasm I don't deceive both myself and you, and that I don't go off like a bee leaving my sting behind.

'So now let's get going. Start by reminding me of what you were saying, if at any point I'm clearly not remembering. Simmias here, I think, is doubtful because he's afraid that, despite being something both more divine and more beautiful than the body, the soul may still perish before it, being the same kind of thing as an attunement; whereas Cebes, despite seeming to agree with me that soul was something longer-lasting than body, thought no one could be sure that the soul wouldn't wear out many bodies, many times over, and then perish itself, leaving behind its last body – so that death itself would be just this perishing of the soul, in so far as the body is anyway subject to constant and repeated perishing. These are the objections, Simmias and Cebes, aren't they, that we need to look at?'

The pair of them agreed.

'So', asked Socrates, 'are you refusing to accept all the previous arguments, or do you accept some and not others?'

'We accept some,' they said, 'but not others.'

'What, then,' Socrates said, 'do you say about the argument in which we claimed that learning was recollection, and that it

must necessarily follow from this that the soul exists, somewhere
else, before we do, that is, before being imprisoned in the body?'   92a

'I for one,' said Cebes, 'was wonderfully convinced by the
argument at the time, and I stick by it now as I do no other.'

'Yes,' said Simmias, 'that's my position too, and I'd be quite
amazed if I ever changed my mind about this one.'

Socrates replied, 'But you'll have to change your mind about
it, my Theban friend, if you're going to go on supposing that an
attunement is a composite thing, and that soul is a kind of
attunement, composed from the constituents of the body in
tension; I don't suppose you'll accept it from yourself to say   92b
that a harmony could be there, already put together, before the
very things it had to be put together from – or will you?'

'Not at all, Socrates,' said Simmias.

'Well,' said Socrates, 'do you see that that's just what you
will be saying, when you assert that the soul exists even before
it enters the shape of a human, and a body, and at the same
time that it exists itself by being composed out of things that
don't yet exist? An attunement certainly isn't the sort of thing
you're comparing it to, because the lyre and its strings, and the
sounds they make, come into being beforehand, still without   92c
any tuning, and the attunement is the last thing to be put
together and indeed the first thing to perish. So how will this
theory of yours be in tune with the other one?'

'It won't be,' said Simmias.

'Yet if there's any theory at all that ought to be in tune,' Socrates replied, 'it's one about attunement.'

'Yes, it ought,' said Simmias.

'Well, this one of yours is out of tune,' Socrates said. 'See
which of the two positions you prefer: that learning is recollection, or that soul is attunement?'

'The first, by far, Socrates,' said Simmias. 'The second one   92d
came to me without proof, on the basis of a certain likelihood
and plausibility, which is why ordinary people too believe in it;
but I'm aware that theories which rely for their proofs on mere
likelihoods are impostors, and that, if you're not thoroughly
on your guard against them, they'll deceive you, whether in
geometry or anywhere else. The theory about recollection and

learning was different; that was put forward on the basis of a hypothesis worthy of acceptance – I think we said that it was equally the case that our soul exists before coming into a body and that the set of things[121] that bears the name "what is" exists by itself. *That* hypothesis,[122] I persuade myself, I've accepted with sufficient reason, and correctly. In which case it seems I mustn't put up with either myself or anyone else saying that soul is an attunement.'

'And what about this consideration, Simmias?' asked Socrates. 'Do you think an attunement or any other composite object has the capacity to be in a different state from that of the elements it's composed from?'

'Not at all.'

'Nor again can it act, or be acted upon, in any way that's different from the way its elements are acting or being acted upon.'

Simmias agreed.

'In that case an attunement certainly isn't the sort of thing that has the capacity to *direct* the things it's put together from; it will follow them.'

Simmias assented.

'In that case there's no chance that an attunement will move in an opposite direction or sound or do anything else that's opposed to its own elements?'

'No chance.'

'Another thing: isn't it in the nature of any attunement to be an attunement in just the way it's been tuned?'

'I don't follow you.'

'Well,' said Socrates, 'isn't it the case that if it's been tuned more and to a greater extent, if that's actually possible, it'll be more of an attunement and a greater attunement, and if it's been tuned less and to a lesser extent, it'll be less of an attunement and a lesser one?'[123]

'Yes, certainly.'

'Well, then: is this the case with the soul, so that one soul can be even the slightest bit more this very thing, soul, than another, and to a greater extent soul – or less and to a lesser extent?'

'There's no way that could be.'

'Come on, then, for goodness' sake! One soul is said to have intelligence and virtue, and to be good, another to lack intelligence and virtue and be bad? And these things are not only what people say but actually true?'   93c

'Yes, true.'

'Then if we go back to those who put forward the hypothesis of soul as attunement, what will any of them say these things are that are found in souls – goodness and badness? That they're in turn some further attunement and lack of attunement? Will they say that the good one has been tuned, and has within itself, namely in the attunement it is, another attunement, while the other is itself untuned and doesn't have another attunement in itself?'

'I can't say myself,' said Simmias; 'but clearly the person who proposed the hypothesis would say something like that.'

'But it's already agreed', said Socrates, 'that one soul can't in   93d
any way be more, or less, of a soul than another, and this means we've agreed that one attunement can't in any way be more of or to a greater extent or less of or to a lesser extent an attunement than another. Isn't that so?'

'Yes, certainly.'

'But we've also agreed that what isn't in any way more of an attunement or less of one isn't either more tuned or less tuned; right?'

'Right.'

'And an attunement that's neither more nor less tuned – can this have more or less of a share in attunement, or will its share be equal?'

'Equal.'

'Then, given that no one soul is in any way more or less this very thing, soul, than any other, then it hasn't been tuned more   93e
or tuned less either.'

'That's so.'

'But if that's how soul is, it wouldn't have any greater share in lack of tuning or attunement?'

'No indeed.'

'And again, if that's how soul is, would any one soul have any greater share in badness or goodness than any another, given that badness is lack of tuning, goodness a matter of attunement?'

'No soul would have any greater share.'

94a   'Or rather, Simmias, I think, if we reason it out correctly, no soul will share in badness at all, if in fact soul is attunement: attunement, presumably being entirely this very thing, attunement, would never have any share in lack of tuning.'

'No indeed.'

'So neither, presumably, will soul share in badness, being entirely soul.'

'How could it, given what we've already said?'

'The result we get from this line of argument, then, is that all souls, of all living creatures, are similarly good, if in fact it's the nature of souls to be similarly this very thing, souls.'

'It seems so to me, Socrates,' said Simmias.

'And do you think this is an *acceptable* result?' asked Socra-
94b   tes. 'Do you think the argument would have ended up like this if the hypothesis that soul is attunement were correct?'

'Not at all,' said Simmias.

'And here's another question,' said Socrates: 'of all the aspects of a human being, do you say that any has a directive role except soul, especially if it's a wise soul?'

'I do not.'

'Do you say it directs in agreement with bodily events,[124] or also in opposition to them? What I'm asking, for example, is this – when there's heat present in the body, and thirst, can the soul pull in the opposite direction, towards not drinking instead of drinking, and towards not eating when hunger is present? I
94c   imagine there are countless other cases where the soul opposes bodily tendencies; isn't that so?'

'Yes, quite certainly.'

'Well, again, didn't we agree in the course of our discussion that, if soul were attunement, it would never sing tunes that were opposed to the tightenings, relaxations, pluckings, or whatever other affections it might be of the very things out of which it was composed; rather it would follow them, and never try to lead them?'

'That's what we agreed,' said Simmias, 'of course.'

'And in point of fact don't we observe it working to exactly the opposite effect? It acts as leader to all those things that it's alleged to be made up from, opposes them in practically every- 94d thing throughout life and dominates them in all the ways it can, punishing some of them more harshly, making them suffer through physical exercise or medical intervention, while treat- ing others more gently, sometimes using threats, sometimes remonstrations, talking things over with desires, fits of anger or fears as one separate thing addressing another? It's a bit like that scene in Homer's *Odyssey*, where he says of Odysseus that

> He struck his chest, and his heart he scolded thus:
> "Bear up, my heart! Much worse you have endured."[125]   94e

Do you think Homer composed these lines in the belief that the soul was an attunement, and the sort of thing to be driven by bodily events, or rather because he believed it to be the sort of thing to drive and dominate these, being much too divine a thing to be compared with an attunement?'

'Zeus, Socrates! That's certainly how it seems to me.'

'In that case, best of men, there's nothing to recommend our saying that soul is a kind of attunement; if we do that, it seems, 95a we wouldn't be in agreement either with the divine poet Homer or with ourselves.'[126]

'That's so,' said Simmias.

'So far so good,' Socrates went on. 'The matter of the The- ban Harmonia could be said, perhaps, to have turned out in a moderately propitious way for us; what, then' – here Socrates turned to Cebes – 'about the matter of Cadmus?[127] How shall we make that similarly propitious to us? What argument shall we use?'

'It seems to me,' said Cebes, 'that you'll find one, to judge by this wonderfully unexpected argument you've produced against attunement. As Simmias was expressing his worries, I was myself very much wondering whether anyone would be able at 95b all to handle his argument; so it seemed to me quite extraordin- ary that it didn't manage to withstand even the first onset of your own argument. So I wouldn't be surprised if the argument of Cadmus didn't meet with exactly the same fate.'

'Mind what you're saying,' said Socrates, 'there's a good man, in case some malign presence upsets the argument that's coming. Well, that's for the god to decide; as for us, let's come to close quarters in true Homeric fashion and test whether there really is something in what you say. I think the nub of what you're looking for is this: you think our soul needs to be
95c proved to be imperishable and immortal, or else the confident belief of a certain philosophical person who's about to die, that he'll fare better in Hades than if he were ending a different kind of life, will be just mindless and foolish. You're saying that it doesn't help to show that the soul is something strong and god-like, which existed even before we were born as human beings; all that might be so, but it could still indicate, not that the soul is immortal, but rather that it's something long-lasting, which perhaps pre-existed for goodness knows how long and so used
95d to know and do all sorts of things – even so, none of that would make it any more *immortal*. As a matter of fact, its entry into a human body is – you said – the starting-point of its own perish-ing, like the onset of a disease, after which it labours its way[128] through this life, finally perishing in what we call death. Your claim is that it makes no difference whether a soul enters a body just once or many times over, so far at least as our indi-vidual fears are concerned; the person who doesn't know, and can't even provide an argument for supposing, that the soul is
95e something immortal, *ought* to be afraid, if he has a mind at all. I think that's the sort of thing you're saying, Cebes; I'm delib-erately rehearsing it more than once in case there's anything we might miss, and in case there's anything you want to add or take away.'

Cebes replied, 'No, there's nothing I need either to take away or add at present; my objection is as you state it.'

At this juncture Socrates paused for a considerable time to think something through in his mind; after which he said, 'Cebes, this is no mean thing you're asking; it means an inves-
96a tigation of the reason behind coming-into-being and perishing in general.[129] In this connection, I'll describe my own history

for you, if you're willing for me to do that; the next step will be for you to use it, if it contains anything you can use, to help you convince us about your own position.'[130]

'Yes,' said Cebes, 'indeed I am willing.'

'Then here's my story for you. In my youth, Cebes,' Socrates began, 'I conceived an extraordinary passion for that sort of wisdom they call "inquiry into nature": it seemed to me a staggering achievement, to know the reasons for each thing – why it comes into being, why it perishes, why it exists. I used constantly to shift back and forth, starting with questions like these: "Is it when the hot and the cold are affected by a sort of putrefaction, as some people used to say,[131] that living creatures develop and grow? Is it blood that we think with, or air, or fire?[132] Or is it none of these, but rather the brain that provides us with the sensations of hearing and seeing and smelling, as a source for memory and judgement, and is it then from memory and judgement, when the latter has settled down, that knowledge comes about?"[133] And again, when I thought about the ways these things perish, and about what happens in the heavens or on the earth, I finally concluded that there was no creature less naturally gifted for this sort of investigation than I was. To give you an indication, I and everybody else used to think there were things I knew perfectly well, but this new method of inquiry so blinded me that on a whole range of subjects I unlearned even things that I thought before that I knew. So with the question why a human being gets bigger: I used to think anyone knew it was because it eats and drinks – whenever flesh was added to flesh out of the food, bone to bone, and similarly everything else had added to it what belonged to it, then what was small in bulk came to be large, and thus a small human being became a big one.[134] That was what I thought before, and quite reasonably, don't you think?'

'Yes, I do,' said Cebes.

'Well, think about these further examples. I used to think it was enough to take the view that someone was bigger if a big person stood next to a small one and looked bigger just by virtue of his head, and similarly with two horses; even more clearly, it seemed to me that ten was more numerous than eight

96b

96c

96d

96e

because two were there in the ten in addition to the eight, and two cubits bigger than one because they exceeded it by half.'

'So what do you think about such cases now?' asked Cebes.

'That I'm a long way, Zeus knows,' said Socrates, 'from supposing that in these things I know the reason for anything, seeing that I won't accept it from myself even that when someone adds one to one, either the one to which the second was added has become two, or the one that was added, or that the one that was added *and* the one it was added to become two because of their addition to each other; I'm amazed at the idea that when each of them was apart from the other, each was actually one, and they weren't then two, but when they're juxtaposed, they do then become two, just for the reason that they've been put close to each other and married up. Nor, if someone divides one, am I any longer able to believe that *that* has now become the reason for two's coming into being, namely division, because then the reason for two's coming to be turns out to be opposite to the previous one: in that case it was because the ones were brought close together and added to each other, and now it's because they're being drawn apart and separated from one another. Equally, I can't persuade myself any longer that I know why one comes into being – or, in short, why anything comes into being, or perishes, or exists, if I employ this kind of inquiry. Instead I make up some other confused jumble of a method of my own, and I have no inclination at all towards this other one.

'However there was a day when I heard someone reading from a book he said was by Anaxagoras, and proclaiming that it was actually mind that ordered things and was the reason for everything. Now *that* was the kind of reason I was happy to have; it seemed to me it was a good thing, somehow or other, that mind should be the reason for all things, and I supposed that, if this was so, mind would be ordering everything, as mind would, by disposing it in the way that was best – so that then, if anyone wanted to discover the reason for any particular thing and how it comes into being or perishes or exists, what he would have to do would be to discover one thing about it, namely how it's best for it either to be or to do or to have done

to it anything else whatsoever. I imagined, following this train
of thought, that the only line of inquiry a human investigator
would need to follow, whether about this very subject, human
beings, or about anything else, would be to ask what was best
for the thing in question – its highest good; although I also
thought such an investigator would have to know what was
worse than the best, too, since both were subjects of one and
the same knowledge.[135] Well, given that I was reasoning this
way, I was delighted to suppose I'd found someone to teach me
about the reason for things who was of a mind with myself:
Anaxagoras. I happily supposed that he'd begin by informing
me whether the earth was flat or rounded, and that when he'd   97e
done that he'd go on to expound the reason why it had to be
like that, giving it as what was *better* for it: it was just better
that it should be like that. Then again, if he declared the earth
to be in the middle of the universe, I imagined he'd similarly go
on to expound on how it was better for it to be in the middle;   98a
and, if he'd show me this, I was prepared to give up hankering
after any other kind of reason. And what's more I was prepared
to discover the same about the sun, the moon, and the other
stars,[136] about their relative speeds, their turnings, and everything else that happens to them, and how it was better that
each of them does and has done to it whatever it may be. I
never for a moment supposed, seeing that he was claiming that
these things were ordered by mind, that he'd bring in any other
sort of reason for them except that it was best for them to be as
they are; and so I thought that as he assigned the reason both   98b
to each thing separately and to everything together he would
explain not just the best for each but the common good for all.
I wouldn't have abandoned my hopes even for a tidy sum; my
commitment was total – grabbing the books, I read them as
quickly as I could, so that I'd lose no time in being enlightened
about what was best and what was worse.[137]

'It was from extraordinarily high hopes, then, my friend,
that I went hurtling down. As I continue my reading, I behold
a man who makes no use of his mind, and doesn't charge it
with any part in the ordering of things, citing air and ether and   98c
water and a whole collection of other equally bizarre things

instead.[138] It seemed to me that his position was very much as
if someone started by saying "Everything Socrates does, he
does mindfully", and then, when he set out to give the reasons
for all the various things I do, he said first of all that the reason
I'm sitting here now is that my body is composed of bones and
sinews, and that the bones are hard and separated from each

98d other by joints, while the sinews – along with the fleshy parts,
and the skin that holds everything together – cover the bones,
and have the capacity to tighten and slacken; so, with the bones
suspended in their sockets, the sinews slacken and tighten and
somehow make me able to bend my legs as I'm doing now –
and *that*'s the reason why I'm sitting here with my legs bent as
they are. The reasons he'd give in explaining my conversation
with you would be more of the same, putting it down to things
like articulate sound, air, hearing, and countless more of them,

98e all the time omitting to mention the true reasons, namely that,
since the Athenians decided it was better to condemn me, for
that very reason *I*'ve decided that it's the better thing for me to
sit here, and more just for me to stay and submit to whatever
penalty they impose on me; since I swear to you by the Dog

99a these sinews and bones of mine would long since have been –
well, I think they would – in the vicinity of Megara or Boeotia,
carried along by what appeared best to them,[139] if I didn't think
it more just, and finer, to submit to the city and whatever penalty she imposes than to escape and become a fugitive. It's just
too bizarre to call such things "reasons". True, unless I had
such things – bones, sinews, and all the other bits of me – I
wouldn't be able to do the things I decide to do; but to say that
I do what I do because of these things, and mindfully at that,

99b and not by my choice of what is best, would be an extremely
lazy way to talk. How absurd, not to be able to tell the two
things apart: the real reason for something, and that without
which the reason wouldn't ever be able to operate as a reason at
all! It's the second thing ordinary people appear to me to be
latching on to as they grope around in the dark,[140] calling it a
"reason" when the name actually belongs to something else.
That's why one person puts a whirl round the earth and makes
it stay in place under the influence of the heavens, while someone

else puts air under it as a base, treating it like some kind of flat
kneading-trough; as for the capacity of earth or anything else to   99c
be placed here and now in the best possible way for it to be
placed, *that* they don't look for, and neither do they think it has
any special power – instead, they suppose that some day they'll
discover an Atlas superior to this one, stronger, more divine and
more able to hold everything together.[141] That what truly binds
and holds things together is the good and the binding, that they
don't believe at all. So if there's anyone who can teach me exactly
how it is with *my* sort of reason, I'd be overjoyed to become his
pupil. But since, as things are, that wasn't offered to me,[142] and I
haven't either been able to discover it for myself or learn about it
from anybody else – well,' Socrates concluded, 'would you like   99d
me to give you a display of how I've engaged in my "second
sailing"[143] in search of the reason for things, Cebes?'

'Yes,' replied Cebes, 'I'd like that enormously.'

'Well,' said Socrates, 'after this it seemed to me that, since
I'd failed in my inquiry into things, I should beware of having
happen to me what happens to people who try to observe
the sun in eclipse directly – I believe they ruin their eyes, some
of them, if they do that rather than examining its image in   99e
water or some similar medium. That was the kind of thing I
had in mind; I feared my soul could be completely blinded[144]
by my looking directly at things with my eyes, or trying to
grasp them with any of my other senses. What I decided was
that I must resort to *reasoned accounts*, and look into the truth
of things in the world in them.[145] Perhaps the analogy is in one   100a
respect misleading: in fact I don't at all concede that someone
who examines things in the medium I'm proposing is any more
examining them in images than someone who examines them
as they actually are in front of us.[146] But in any case this was
my starting-point: hypothesizing on each occasion whatever
account I judge to have the most explanatory power, I posit as
true whatever seems to me to be in tune with this, whether
about the reasons for things or about anything else, and as
untrue whatever is not in tune with it.[147] But I'd like to put
what I have in mind more clearly – I think at the moment you're
not getting the point.'

'Zeus! No,' said Cebes, 'not really.'

100b 'Actually, the way I'm talking now is nothing new; it's the same old things that I'm always talking about, whenever I get the chance, and that I've not stopped talking about in the preceding discussion.[148] My aim is to try to show you the kind of reasons that engage me, and for that purpose I'm going to go back to those much-talked-about entities of ours – starting from them, and hypothesizing that there's something that's beautiful and nothing but beautiful, in and by itself, and similarly with good, big, and all the rest. If you grant me these, and agree that they exist, my hope is, starting from them, to show you the reason for things and establish that the soul is something immortal.'[149]

100c 'Well,' said Cebes, 'I certainly do grant you them, so I don't mind how quickly you show me.'

'Then,' said Socrates, 'see whether you agree with me about what comes next. It appears to me that, if there is anything that's beautiful besides the beautiful itself, it's not beautiful because of anything except the fact that it shares in that other beautiful thing; and I give a similar account in every case. Do you go along with reasons of that kind?'

'Yes, I do,' said Cebes.

'Well then,' replied Socrates, 'if we're agreed about that, I no longer understand, nor am I able to recognize, these other wise
100d "reasons": if anyone tries to tell me why something is beautiful, no matter what, by saying it's because it has a bright colour, or a particular shape, or anything of that kind, I wave goodbye to everything else – because all those other "reasons" confuse me – and I hold this one thought to myself, in my plain, artless and probably simple-minded way, that nothing else at all makes the something in question beautiful except that other beautiful thing, whether by its presence in it, or by its association with it, or in whatever way or manner it has come to be added to it;[150] which of these it is I don't insist on, but I do insist that all beautiful things are beautiful *by virtue of the beautiful*. This seems to me the safest answer to give, whether
100e to myself or anyone else, and as I cling to this I think to myself, "This way I'll never fall; it's a safe answer, to give both to myself

and to anyone else, that beautiful things come to be beautiful by virtue of the beautiful." Don't you think so too?'

'I do.'

'In that case big things too are big and bigger things bigger by virtue of bigness, smaller things smaller by virtue of small-ness?'

'Yes.'

'You wouldn't accept it yourself, then, if someone were to say that one person was bigger than another by virtue of his head,[151] and the smaller one smaller by this same thing; rather, you'd solemnly protest that whatever anyone else says, *you*'re not saying anything except that everything bigger than some-thing is bigger by virtue of bigness, and not anything else, and that it's because of this that it's bigger, namely bigness, while the smaller thing is smaller by virtue of smallness and nothing else, and it's because of this, smallness, that it's smaller. I imagine you'd be afraid, if you said people were bigger or smaller "by a head", that you'd encounter some opposing argument – first of all, the bigger would be bigger and the smaller smaller by virtue of the same thing, and then the bigger person would be bigger by virtue of something – the head – which was actually small; and wouldn't that be unnatural, if someone was big by virtue of something small? Wouldn't that sort of thing frighten you?'

Cebes laughed and said 'Yes, it would!'[152]

'Then', said Socrates, 'you'd be afraid to say that ten was more numerous than eight by virtue of two, and that that was the reason for its being more, rather than by virtue of numer-ousness, and because of numerousness? And that two cubits were bigger than one by virtue of a half rather than by virtue of bigness? I imagine there'd be the same fear.'

'Yes, certainly,' said Cebes.

'What about saying that addition was the reason for two's coming into being, when one was added to one, or division when it was divided? You'd be wary of saying that too, wouldn't you, and you'd shout out loud that you know of no other way in which anything comes into being except by having come to share in the appropriate essence of whatever it is that each does come to share in.[153] As for the present cases, you'd say you have

101A
101B
101C

no other reason to offer for two's coming into being except its sharing in twoness, that things that are going to be two must come to share in this, that anything that's going to be one must share in oneness – and you'll wave goodbye to those divisions and additions and other such subtleties, leaving them as answers

101d to be given by people wiser than yourself. As for you, fearful of your own shadow, as they say, and of your lack of experience, you'd hold on to the safety that's to be found in the hypothesis and answer accordingly.[154] Then, if someone held on to the hypothesis itself, you'd dismiss him and refuse to answer until you'd examined its consequences to see if they were in tune with each other, or out of tune; and when you had to give a reasoned account of the hypothesis itself, you'd do it in the same way, that is, by positing another hypothesis, whichever appeared best of those above the first one, until you arrived at

101e something sufficient for the purpose. Right? And you wouldn't muddle everything up together as the antilogicians do, by talking about your starting-point and its consequences as if there were no difference between them – that is, if you wanted to find the truth about anything. That sort probably don't give a moment's thought to finding things out, or care about it; their wisdom allows them to stir everything together and still be pleased with themselves; but you, I think, if you're of a philo-

102a sophical sort, will approach things in the way I describe.'[155]

'Absolutely true,' said Simmias and Cebes in unison.

ECHECRATES By Zeus, Phaedo! They'd every reason to say so. It seems to me there was an extraordinary clarity[156] about what the man said; even someone of little brain would have to agree.

PHAEDO Yes, absolutely, Echecrates; it seemed like that to everybody who was there, too.

ECHECRATES And to all of us who weren't there but are hearing it now. But how did the discussion go after that?

PHAEDO I think, when there was assent to those last points,

102b and it was agreed both that each of the forms exists,[157] and that other things share in them and get their names from them, Socrates next asked, 'Well, if you say this is how things are, when you assert that Simmias is bigger than Socrates, but smaller than Phaedo, you'll be saying, won't you, that at that moment both things are in Simmias – both bigness and smallness?'

'That's right.'

'But now do you agree,' said Socrates, 'that when we say "Simmias overtops Socrates", we aren't quite expressing things as they actually are? Because I don't imagine you think that it belongs to Simmias' nature to overtop Socrates, that is, that he does so by virtue of being Simmias – it's rather by virtue of the bigness that he happens to have; nor again are you supposing that he overtops Socrates because Socrates is Socrates, but because Socrates has smallness as against Simmias' bigness?'

'True.'

'Nor, again, that Simmias is overtopped by Phaedo by virtue of the fact that Phaedo is Phaedo, but because Phaedo has bigness as against Simmias' smallness?'

'That's so.'

'This, then, is how Simmias gets to be called both small and big, namely because he's in the middle between the other two, submitting his smallness to be overtopped by the bigness of the one and offering his bigness to overtop the smallness of the other.' At that point he smiled: 'It looks as if I'm going to be talking like a handbook.[158] Still, at least it is as I say, I think.'

Simmias agreed.

'The reason I'm saying all this is because I want you to share my view of the matter: it appears to me that it's not just bigness itself that won't consent ever to be both big and small; the bigness in us won't ever let in the small either, and it won't consent to be overtopped. Rather, I think, one of two things must happen: either it retreats and gets out of the way when its opposite, the small, advances on it, or else when the enemy has completed its advance, the bigness will already have perished – it won't consent to put up with smallness, and let smallness in, because that would mean its being other than it was. Think of my case: I've put up with smallness and let it in, and I'm still who I am, this same person, only small; but it's too much for bigness, being what it is,[159] big, to be small. In the same way the small in us won't consent ever to become, or to be, big, and neither, if they're still to be what they were, will any other of

103a the opposites consent to becoming and being their opposites, at the same time as being themselves. No, at the advance of their opposites, either they go off or they perish.'

'That's exactly how it appears to me,' said Cebes.

When he heard Cebes, one of those present – I don't exactly remember who it was – interjected: 'Wait a minute! Earlier on in the discussion, weren't you agreeing exactly the opposite of what you're now saying, namely that the bigger comes from the smaller and the smaller from the bigger, and indeed that coming-to-be, for opposites, was simply this, from opposites? And now the claim seems to me to be that this couldn't ever happen.'

Socrates turned his head towards the speaker and heard him
103b out. 'Manfully recalled,' he said, 'but you're not seeing the difference between what we're now saying and what we were saying then. What we were saying then was that opposite things came to be from their opposites, whereas we're saying now just that the opposite itself couldn't ever become opposite *to* itself, whether it's that opposite in us or its counterpart in nature.[160] To put it another way, my friend, then we were talking about things characterized by the opposites, and attaching to them the names belonging to those opposites, but now we're talking about the opposites themselves, by virtue of whose presence in
103c them the other things get their names; it's those opposites themselves that we're saying wouldn't ever consent to coming to be each other.' Socrates then looked at Cebes: 'I don't suppose any of what he said troubled you too?'

'No,' said Cebes, 'I'm not making any objections this time, though I'm not denying that there are lots of things that are troubling me.'

'We're in agreement, in that case,' Socrates went on, 'about this much, without any ifs and buts: an opposite will never be opposite to itself.'

'Completely in agreement,' said Cebes.

'Then see if you'll agree with me about this further point,' said Socrates. 'Do you recognize something you call hot, and something you call cold?'

'I do.'

'Are they what you call snow and fire?'

'Zeus! No, certainly not.'   103d

'The hot is something different from fire, the cold something different from snow?'

'Yes.'

'But this much I think you do accept, because it's the kind of thing we were saying before: snow, being snow, after having let in the hot, will never be any longer what it was, namely snow, and also something hot; when the hot advances on it, it'll either get out of the way or perish.'

'Yes, certainly.'

'And likewise you accept that when cold advances, fire will either get away or perish; it'll be too much for it ever to let in coldness and still be what it was, fire, and cold as well.'

'True,' said Cebes.   103e

'So the position with respect to some things like this is such that not only is the form itself entitled to its name for all time, but so too, for as long as it exists, is something else – something which, while not being the form, always has the character of the form. Here's an example that will probably make what I'm saying a bit clearer: the odd must, I imagine, always enjoy this name that we're now giving it – right?'

'Yes, certainly.'

'Is it the only thing there is that we call the odd – this is my question – or is there something else as well, which isn't what   104a the odd is, but which all the same, in addition to its own name, has also to be called odd, on a permanent basis, because it's by nature such as never to be separated from the odd? What I'm talking about is the sort of thing that happens to *three*,[161] to take just one example among many. Think about three: it's the case, isn't it, that it always has to have both its own name attached to it and that of the odd, even though the odd isn't what three is? Despite that, not just three but five and half of the whole series of numbers naturally have this feature, that   104b even while they're not what the odd is, each of them is always odd; and similarly two, four and the whole other half of the number series is always even despite not being what the even is. Do you go along with that or not?'

'Of course,' said Cebes.

'See here, then, what I'm trying to show you,' said Socrates. 'The point is this: it's not just the opposites that clearly don't let one another into themselves; there's also another set of things – things that aren't themselves opposites but always have the opposites – that don't look as if they'll let in whichever form it is[162] that's opposite to the one in them, instead either perishing or getting out of the way as it advances. Or shall we not say that three will die or suffer any fate rather than putting up with becoming even while still being three?'

'Yes, indeed we shall,' said Cebes.

'Nor again', said Socrates, 'is two opposite to three.'

'No indeed.'

'So it isn't just the opposite forms[163] that don't withstand each other's advance, but there are certain other things that won't withstand the advance of opposites.'

'Very true,' said Cebes.

'So', asked Socrates, 'are you happy for us to try, if we can, to determine what sorts of things these are?'

'Yes, certainly.'

'Might they be things that are compelled by whatever occupies them[164] not only to have its own character, by itself, but always to have that of some opposite?'

'What do you mean?'

'What we were saying just now. I imagine you recognize that whatever the character of three occupies must not only be three but odd as well.'[165]

'Yes, certainly.'

'Well, then, we're saying, the character opposite to the one that has this effect will never come to belong to the sort of thing in question.'[166]

'No, never.'

'And what had this effect was the character of the odd?'

'Yes.'

'And the character of the even is the opposite of this?'

'Yes.'

'In that case the character of the even will never come to belong to the three.'[167]

'No, it won't.'

'The three, then, has no share in the even.'

'None.'

'In that case the three is un-even.'

'Yes.'

'So what I said we needed to identify, namely what sorts of things they are that, while not actually being opposite to some opposite, will nevertheless not let in that opposite – just as now the three, while not being opposite to the even, will no less for that refuse to let it in, because three always brings with it the opposite of even, as the two does the opposite of the odd, fire the opposite of the cold, and so on and so forth – well, see if you'll identify what we want by saying that not only does opposite not let in opposite, but neither will what brings with it some opposite to the thing that it, itself, comes to belong to; that is, the thing bringing the opposite with it will itself never let in the opposite of the opposite it's bringing with it. Let me run through it again, because it'll be no bad thing to hear it more than once: five won't let in the character of the even, nor ten, its double, that of the odd. Of course the double has its own opposite, too, but even so it won't let in the character of the odd, any more than the half-as-much-again, and the whole series of the halves, or for that matter the series of the thirds, and so on, will let in the character of the whole[168] – if you're following me, and if you agree.'

'I'm quite emphatically in agreement,' said Cebes, 'and I am following.'

'Then go over it for me once more from the beginning,' said Socrates; 'and don't answer me by giving me back whatever it is I'm asking you about,[169] but rather by following the sort of example I've just been giving you. What I'm talking about is another kind of answer besides the one I was talking about before, and calling "safe", because I now espy another sort of "safety" as a result of what we were saying just now. Suppose you were to ask me what it is in the presence of which in the body a thing is hot: I won't give you the safe but ignorant answer "it's the presence of heat", but a cleverer answer[170] of the sort that has emerged from our present discussion, "it's the presence of *fire*"; if you ask me what it is in the presence of which in the body something will be sick, I won't say "sick-ness", but rather "fever"; if you ask in the presence of what, in a number, will that number be odd, I'll not say "oddness", but "oneness";[171] and similarly in every other case. See if you've now got a firm enough hold on what I'm trying to say.'

'Quite firm enough,' said Cebes.

'Then answer me this,' said Socrates: 'what is it in the pres-ence of which, in a body, that body will be alive?'

'A body that has soul in it,' said Cebes.

105d   'So is that always the case?'

'Of course,' said Cebes.

'In that case, whatever body soul itself occupies, it always comes bringing aliveness to that body?'

'It does indeed,' said Cebes.

'And is there something that's opposite to aliveness, or does it have no opposite?'

'It has one,' said Cebes.

'What is it?'

'Deadness.'

'Well then, given what's agreed between us from before, soul will never, ever, let in to itself what's opposite to the opposite that it, itself, always brings with it?'

'Most emphatically so,' said Cebes.

'So now tell me, what was the name we were giving just now to whatever won't let in the character of the even?'

'Un-even,' said Cebes.

'And what will we call what won't let the just in, or what won't let in the musical?'

105e   'The second, unmusical,' said Cebes; 'the other, unjust.'

'Fine; and what shall we call whatever doesn't let dead-ness in?'

'Deathless,'[172] said Cebes.

'Well, soul doesn't let in deadness?'

'No.'

'In that case soul is something deathless – immortal.'

'Yes, immortal.'

'Fine,' said Socrates; 'so are we to declare that that much is now proved? What do you think?'

'Yes, Socrates, quite sufficiently proved.'

'So what about the following question, Cebes?' asked Socrates. 'If the un-even were necessarily imperishable, wouldn't   106a
the three be imperishable?'

'Of course.'

'So if the un-heatable, too, were necessarily imperishable, whenever someone brought hot to snow the snow would get out of the way still intact and unmelted, wouldn't it? It clearly couldn't have perished, and neither would it stay behind and let in the hotness.'

'True,' said Cebes.

'And similarly, I imagine, if the un-coolable were imperishable, whenever something cold advanced on fire the fire wouldn't ever be put out, or perish, but would be off and away, intact.'

'That must be so.'

'So mustn't we say the same about the immortal too? If the   106b
immortal is also imperishable,[173] it's impossible for the soul to perish when death advances on it; because from what we've said before, it certainly won't let death in,[174] or be dead, any more than the three, as we said, or indeed the odd, will be even, or fire or the hotness in the fire will be cold. "But," someone might object, "even if we suppose, as we've agreed, that at the onset of the even[175] the odd doesn't *become* even, what's to pre-   106c
vent its perishing all the same, itself, and the even's coming to be in its place?" In response to such an objection, we wouldn't be in any position to insist that the odd doesn't perish; but then the un-even isn't actually imperishable. Because of course if we'd agreed that it was, it would be quite easy for us to insist that, yes, with the onset of the even the odd and the three are off and away; and we'd be similarly insistent if we'd agreed about the imperishability of fire and the hot and all our other examples. Right?'

'Yes, certainly.'

'So now with the immortal too – if we're agreeing that the immortal is imperishable as well as immortal, soul will be imperishable, too, in addition to being immortal; if we're not in   106d
agreement about that, then we'll need another argument.'

'No need,' said Cebes, 'at any rate so far as that goes; if the

immortal, which is after all eternal, lets destruction in, anything else would be hard put not to.'

'Yes, and the gods,[176] I imagine,' said Socrates, 'and the form
of aliveness, itself, together with anything else there may be
that's immortal, would be agreed by everyone to be permanently immune to perishing.'

'Zeus! Yes, surely, by every human being, and still more, I
imagine, by every god.'

106e 'Given, then, that the immortal is also indestructible, won't
soul also be imperishable, if it actually is immortal?'[177]

'Very much so; it must be.'

'When death advances on a man, then, it appears that the
mortal part of him dies, but his immortal part is off and away,
intact and indestructible, evading death's advance.'

'Evidently so.'

'There's nothing clearer, then, Cebes,' said Socrates, 'than
107a that soul is something immortal and imperishable, and that
really and truly *our* souls will be there in Hades after all.'[178]

'Well, Socrates,' said Cebes, '*I* don't have anything else to
add, nor do I have any grounds for not trusting in the arguments put forward. But if Simmias here or anyone else has anything to say, I advise them not to keep quiet about it; I don't
know what other opportunity they'd be reserving it for, if not
the present one, given what the subject is – whether they want
to say something themselves or just to listen.'

'No, certainly,' said Simmias; 'I don't any longer have
grounds myself, either, for not trusting the conclusion, given
107b what's now transpired; but the size of the subjects we're talking
about, together with my poor opinion of human weakness,
does still force me to maintain a certain distrust in my own
mind in relation to what's been said.'

'Right, Simmias,' said Socrates, 'not only that – that's well
said – but our initial hypotheses really must be examined more
clearly, even if the two of you do find them trustworthy. If you
analyse them[179] well enough, or so I think, you'll be following
the argument to the furthest point possible for human beings;
if you do find the necessary clarity, you'll look for nothing
beyond that.'

'True,' said Simmias.

'But this much it's right to have in mind, in any case: that if   107c
the soul really is immortal, then it needs caring for not just for
the sake of the time in which we do what we call "living", but
for the sake of all time, and from that perspective what anyone
risks by not caring for his soul really would appear to be terri-
fying. For if death meant being separated from everything, it
would be a godsend for the bad to die and be separated at once
from the body *and* from their own badness, along with the
soul; but as things are, given that the soul is evidently immortal, there'd be no way for it to escape from evils, no way of   107d
saving itself, except by becoming as good and wise as possible.[180] For a soul goes to Hades taking nothing with it except
its education and nurture, which are in fact the very things that
are said to do the greatest benefit or harm to the person who
has died,[181] from the very beginning of his journey to that other
place. What they say is that in fact each person's own divinity,
the one to whom he has been allotted in life, tries to bring him,
after his death, to a certain place where the assembled company must submit themselves for trial before journeying to   107e
Hades with the guide whose job it is to lead them on their journey from here to there;[182] there, having met with what fate they
must, and stayed for what time they must, another guide con-
veys them back here again, after many long cycles of time. The
journey is evidently not as Aeschylus' hero Telephus[183] describes
it: he says there's a simple road to Hades,[184] but actually it   108a
appears to me to be neither simple nor a single one. If that were
so, there would be no need of guides;[185] I don't suppose anyone
would miss the path at any point, if there were only one. As
things are, to go by the sacrifices and rites that there are at such
places on roads up here, there seem to be many places where it
divides and forks. Well, the orderly and wise soul follows the
guide and doesn't fail to recognize what is happening to it; but
the one that's in a state of desire for the body, something I
talked about before, finds itself for a long time all of a flutter   108b
about the body, and about the visible sphere in general, and its
appointed divinity has to bring it forcibly to leave, which it
does reluctantly and after many struggles and sufferings. When

it has arrived at the common destination for all souls, if it is unpurified and guilty of something like having engaged in unjust killings, or performed other such acts that are in fact akin to these and belong to kindred souls, everyone avoids it and turns aside from it;[186] no one wants to be its fellow travel-ler or guide, and it wanders by itself in total helplessness until certain appointed periods of time have come and gone, when it is borne by necessity to the residence appropriate to it. Con-trast the fate of the soul that has gone through its life in purity and observing due measure – such souls find gods for fellow travellers and guides, and each moves to take up its residence in the place appropriate to it. The earth has many amazing places, I tell you, and neither its nature nor its size are as they are believed to be by those who like to talk about it; or so someone has managed to convince me.'

108c

'What do you mean by this, Socrates?' asked Simmias. 'I can tell you I've heard a lot of talk about the earth myself, but not what persuades you. So please do tell.'

108d

'Well, yes, Simmias, I will, because just describing them doesn't need the skill of a Glaucus;[187] however, to show that they're *true* appears to me even beyond Glaucus' expertise – and not only that, I'd probably be incapable of it. Anyway even if I did know how to do it, the life I still have left to me, Simmias, doesn't seem to me equal to the length of the argument required. Still, there's nothing to stop me describing what I've been con-vinced is the general character of the earth and its different regions.'

108e

'Just that will suffice,' said Simmias.

'Well,' said Socrates, 'what I'm convinced of is first of all that if it's in the middle of the heavens, and spherical, it doesn't need either air or any other such physical necessity to stop it from falling;[188] the complete uniformity, everywhere, of the heavens themselves and the equilibrium of the earth itself are sufficient to hold it up, because an object in equilibrium placed in the centre of a uniform container cannot incline any more or any less in any direction, and because it is in a uniform state it will stay where it is.[189] So that', said Socrates, 'is the first thing I've been convinced of.'

109a

'And quite rightly,' said Simmias.

'Well, then, the next thing',[190] said Socrates, 'is that it's something of vast size, and we – those living between the Phasis river 109b
and the Pillars of Heracles[191] – inhabit only a small part of it,
living around our sea like ants or frogs around a pond; many
others live in many other similar regions. You see, there are
many hollows, all over the earth, and of all different shapes
and sizes, into which the water, mist and air have collected,
while the earth itself lies pure below the purity of the starry sky,
which is what most of those who like to talk about such things 109c
call the "ether"; those other things[192] are the sky's sediment,
which is always flowing down together into the earth's hollows. As for us, we're quite unaware that we're living in these
hollows, and suppose that we're living up on the surface of the
earth. It's as if someone lived in the middle of the bottom of the
ocean and thought he lived on the surface, so that when he saw
the sun and the other stars through the water he supposed the
sea was the sky; being too slow and weak, he'd never got as far 109d
as the highest points; never emerged, poked his head up into
the region above, and seen how much purer and more beautiful
it really was than the one he lived in; never even heard about it
from anyone who had seen it. The same thing has happened to
us: we live in a hollow of the earth, thinking that we live on its
surface, and calling our air "sky", as if this were the sky and
the stars moved through it. But actually it's the same thing, that
we're too weak and slow to make our way through to the fur- 109e
thest point of our air – because, if anyone did reach its furthest
limits, or grew wings and flew up there, then he'd be able to
poke his head up and see what lay beyond, just like fish who
poke their heads up out of the sea and see things in our world;
and if he had sufficient natural capacity to hold up under the
sight of what was up there, he'd recognize that *that* after all
was the true sky, the true light, and the true earth. For this 110a
"earth" of ours, its stones,[193] this whole region here is corrupted and eaten away, just as things in the sea are eaten away
by the brine, so that nothing worth speaking of grows in the
sea at all; there's practically nothing that's properly formed,
with even the earth in it reduced to mere pebbles, sand, endless

mud and varieties of slime, things that bear no comparison
with the beauties in our world. The things in the region above
us, in their turn, will surpass things here by a much greater
110b degree still, as I'll tell you; if it's right to tell stories too, this
one, Simmias, is worth hearing, about what the things on the
earth under the heavens are actually like.'

'Well, Socrates,' said Simmias, 'we'd certainly be delighted
to hear the story.'

'Then, my friend, here it is,' said Socrates. 'It's said first of all
that if you looked at the earth itself from above, it would
resemble one of those balls sewn together out of twelve pieces
of leather, variegated, picked out in different colours, of which
our colours here, they say, resemble nothing more than sam-
110c ples, like the ones that painters use. The whole earth above is
composed of such colours, and ones still brighter and purer
than these: one part of it is of a purple of astonishing beauty,
another the colour of gold, the white whiter than chalk or
snow; all the colours that compose it similarly surpass ours,
and they are more in number, too, and more beautiful, than
those that we have seen. The very hollows in this true earth,
110d full to the brim as they are of water and air, give the look of a
colour as they glitter among the variegated colours around
them, so that the general appearance is of one continuous, variegated whole. The things that grow from an earth like this,
whether trees or flowers or fruit, are proportionately more
beautiful than ours, and the mountains too, in the same proportion, the stones in them smoother, more transparent, their
colours more beautiful – of which in fact our little stones here,
carnelians, jaspers, emeralds, and all the rest, are the prized
110e fragments; but there, there is nothing that isn't like that, and
still more beautiful than these stonelets of ours. The reason is
that stones there are in a pure state, not eaten up and corrupted
as ours are by mildew and brine because of the things that have
settled here, bringing degradation and disease to stones, earth
and animals and plants besides; the actual earth is still further
111a adorned, with gold, silver, everything else of that sort. All of
these things, many in number and great in size, are in plain
view everywhere on that earth: happy the spectators who see

such a spectacle! Among the many living creatures there are humans, some of them living inland, others around the air as we live around the sea, others still on islands, close to the mainland,[194] around which the air flows; and in a word, what water and the sea are to us in relation to our needs, that air is   111b
to them, and what air is to us, ether is to them. Their seasons are of a blend[195] that enables them to stay free of sickness, and not only to live much longer lives than people here but to see better than us, hear better, be wiser and everything like that, by the same margin that air surpasses water in purity and ether surpasses air.[196] Moreover they have groves and sanctuaries of gods in which gods are actually resident, so that they receive utterances and prophecies from them in person, see and hear them, meet them face to face, just as they also see   111c
sun, moon and stars for what they are;[197] and their happiness in other respects too follows on from these aspects of their lives.

'So much for what they say about the nature of the earth as a whole and its surroundings. But we're told there are also many places situated in its hollows all around the whole, some of them deeper and wider than the one in which we live, others deeper but with a narrower opening than ours, others still that   111d
are shallower and broader. All of these are connected to each other by numerous passages under the earth, both narrower and broader, and have ways through between them, along which from one region to another and back again, as if into mixing-bowls, there pour great quantities of water, and ever-flowing subterranean rivers of unimaginable size, both of hot waters and of cold, and great quantities of fire too, great rivers of fire, and many of liquid mud, whether purer or of a slimier   111e
sort, like the rivers of mud that run in Sicily before the lava-flow, and the lava-flow itself. The places within the hollows, it's said, are filled by the flows, as these arrive in each at the appropriate moment in the cycle. What moves all of this, up and down, is a kind of oscillation within the earth, and this oscillation occurs, it seems, because of a natural phenomenon of the following kind.[198] One of the passages in the earth is actually on a larger scale than the others, especially in so far as it is   112a

bored right through the whole earth – Homer referred to it, saying of it that it was

Far, far away, a pit that lies deepest under the earth;[199]

it's what elsewhere both he and many other poets have named Tartarus. What happens is that all the subterranean rivers flow together into this passage and then flow back out of it again, and each river[200] takes on the character of the earth through which it passes. The reason why all the streams flow out of and into Tartarus in this way is that all this liquid lacks a bottom, and has no place to stand, so that it oscillates and surges up and down, and the moving air that surrounds it does likewise, following it as it rushes off to the far parts of the earth and as it returns from these parts; and just as when people breathe their breath is exhaled and inhaled, flowing back and forth, so it is with the moving air there under the earth – oscillating in concert with the liquid, it creates unimaginably terrible winds as it goes in and out. Well, when the water retreats to the region we call "down", it flows through the earth into the streams there, filling them as if they were irrigation channels; and when in turn it leaves those parts and moves "up" again, rushing back in our direction, it fills the streams on this side, which then flow through underground channels and, arriving in the regions to which each has access, create seas, lakes, rivers and springs. From there they sink again beneath the earth, some of them travelling around more extended and more numerous regions, others fewer and smaller, until they discharge again into Tartarus, some of them much lower down than where they were channelled off, others only a little; but all flow in below the point of their outflow, some of them having poured out and down from the side opposite to their entry-point, others on the same side, while others still go round completely in a circle, coiling round the earth either just once or more than once, like snakes, discharging back into Tartarus after having gone down as far as possible – which is as far as the middle, on either side, and no further, since the opposite side, for each set of streams, will be uphill.

'There are, then, many great streams, of all different kinds; but among these many are a particular quartet, of which the greatest, and the one flowing furthest out, in a circle, is the river we call Oceanus. Opposite this, and flowing in the contrary direction, is Acheron,[201] which flows through desert 113a places, and most notably, when it goes underground, arrives at the Acherusian lake. There it is that the souls of most of those who have died go, and after they have stayed there for certain appointed periods of time, some longer, others shorter, they are sent back again to provide for the coming-into-being of new living creatures.[202] The third river of the four issues[203] between the first two: close to its point of issue, it discharges into a great region ablaze with intense fire, creating a lake that is greater than our sea, boiling with water and mud. From there it proceeds on a circular course, turbid and muddy; among the places 113b it comes to, as it winds around under the earth, are the margins of the Acherusian lake, but it does not mix with its water,[204] instead discharging lower down into Tartarus after coiling round many times under the surface of the earth. This river is the one people call Pyriphlegethon, whose lava-streams it is that blast up fragments at various points from the earth. Across from this river there issues the fourth, first into a wild and terrible region, as it is said, all of the darkest colour imaginable – 113c the one they call Stygian, as they give the name Styx to the lake the river creates. Discharging there, and taking up terrible powers in its waters, the river then sinks beneath the earth, coiling round and proceeding in the opposite direction to that of Pyriphlegethon, which it meets at the Acherusian lake, but from the opposite side, nor will its own water mix with any other; it too goes round in a circle and discharges into Tartarus, opposite Pyriphlegethon. This river's name, the poets tell us, is Cocytus.[205]

'This, then, is the nature of the regions under the earth. Now 113d when the dead come to the place to which each is conveyed by his divine guide,[206] they first submit themselves to judgement, both those who have lived fine and pious lives and those who have not. Those judged to have lived a middling kind of life[207] journey to the river Acheron, where they board the vessels

available to them and use these to journey to the lake; there
they reside and undergo purification, each as he deserves, paying
113e penalties to absolve him from any crimes committed and re-
ceiving honours for any benefits bestowed.[208] As for those
judged incurable because of the enormity of their errors –
whether they have repeatedly stolen large sums from temples,
persistently killed people contrary to justice and the law or
committed other such crimes as there may be, the fate of these,
fittingly, is to be cast into Tartarus and never to emerge again.
Another category fated to be thrown into Tartarus consists of
those judged to have committed errors that are curable but
114a serious, for example people who have committed an act of violence towards a father or a mother but live out the rest of their
lives regretting it, or who have become killers under some other
similar circumstances; but when these have been in Tartarus for
a year, the surge of the great river disgorges them, the killers by
way of Cocytus and the father- and mother-beaters by way of
Pyriphlegethon, and as they are carried along beside the Acherusian lake they scream and call out, the first sort to those they
killed, the second to those they assaulted; their calls are fol-
114b lowed by supplication, as they beg their victims to permit their
exit from their river to the lake, and to admit them there; if
they succeed in persuading them, they get out, and cease from
their suffering,[209] but if not, then they are carried off again into
Tartarus, and from there back again into the rivers, and that
will go on happening to them until they do persuade those they
wronged; because that is the penalty imposed upon them by the
judges. But those judged to have done exceptionally well
towards living piously are the ones who are freed from these
114c regions here, within the earth, and are released as if from prisons,
moving to that pure place of residence above and dwelling on
the surface of the earth.[210] And from among these very people,
those who have purified themselves sufficiently well by means
of philosophy dwell entirely without bodies for the time there-
after, and come to reside in places still more beautiful than
those, places that it is not easy to show you, and not in the time
we presently have. But it is for the sake of the things we have
described, Simmias, that one must do everything to ensure one's

share of goodness and wisdom in one's life; fine is the prize, and the hope great.

'Well, to insist that these things are as I have described them is   114d
not appropriate for a man of intelligence; but that this or something like it is true about our souls and the places in which they
dwell, given that the soul is clearly something immortal[211] –
this it does seem to me to be worth insisting on, and worth
risking, for someone who thinks it to be so; the risk, after all,
is a fine one.[212] Such are the charms, as it were, that one must
use on oneself, which is why I myself have long since been
spinning out my story.[213] In any case, these are reasons why a
man should have confidence about his soul – a man, that is,   114e
who in his life has waved goodbye to those other pleasures and
adornments, namely those of the body, treating these as alien
to him and doing more harm than good; who has instead occupied himself with the pleasures of learning, and adorning his
soul not with alien adornments but those that belong to it –
moderation, justice, courage, freedom, and truth – waits thus   115a
prepared for the journey to Hades, whenever fate should summon him.[214] So you,' said Socrates, 'Simmias and Cebes and all
you others, will all make your separate journeys there at some
future time; but for now it is I whom fate calls, as a tragic character might say, and I think it's about time for me to head for
the bath, because I think it'd be better to drink the poison
freshly bathed and not give the women the trouble of washing
a corpse.'

When he heard Socrates say this, Crito said, 'Very well, Soc-   115b
rates; and what are your instructions for these people or for
me, whether about your children or anything else? What can
we do to please you most?'

'Just what I'm always saying, Crito,' Socrates replied, 'nothing very new: if you care for your own selves, whatever you do
will be pleasing to me, and to mine, and to you yourselves too,
even if you don't presently agree with me about that;[215] whereas
if you neglect yourselves and prove unwilling to live along the
lines tracked, as it were, by our present discussions and those
we have had before, even after having vehemently agreed with

115c me, in the present circumstances, many times over,[216] you'll do no one any good at all.'

'Then we'll try our best to do as you say,' said Crito; 'but what kind of burial are we to give you?'

'Whatever you like,' said Socrates, 'that is, if you can catch me, and I don't get away from you.' Laughing quietly and looking at us, he said, 'Gentlemen, evidently I'm not persuading Crito that this Socrates person is me, the one who's talking with you and setting out the arguments one beside another; he thinks I'm

115d the other one, the one he'll shortly see as a corpse, and asks how he's to bury me! Everything I've been talking about all this time – about how, when I drink the poison, I'll no longer be with you but will be off and away to some happiness or other of the blest,[217] all of this I think he thinks I'm saying to no purpose, and just using it to comfort you at the same time as comforting myself. So please,' he said, 'stand surety for me with Crito, and give him the opposite of the guarantee he tried to offer the judges. What he guaranteed to them was that I would stay in prison; you must guarantee that I won't stay when I die,

115e but will be off and away, so that Crito may bear it more easily and won't be upset for me when he sees my body going up in flames or being buried, thinking that something terrible is happening to me, or say at my funeral that it's Socrates he's laying out or carrying to the grave or putting in the ground. Because, dearest Crito,' he said, 'you should know that speaking imprecisely doesn't just spoil what we're trying to say, it also damages our souls.[218] You should be more cheerful, and talk of

116a burying my body, which you can do in whichever way you like and think most in line with custom.'

With these words he got up and went into a room to bathe. Crito went after him, telling us to wait. And so we waited, talking to each other about the conversation and reviewing it; sometimes we went over the magnitude of the misfortune that had befallen us, simply thinking of it as if we'd be living the rest of our lives as

116b orphans deprived of a father. When he'd bathed, his children were brought in to him – he had two small sons and one big one – and those women from his household arrived too;[219] he talked to them, in the presence of Crito, instructing them about what he wanted

done, then told both women and children to leave and himself
came in to us. By now it was close to sunset, because he'd spent
a lot of time inside. He came and sat down, fresh from his bath,
and he'd said no more than a few words when the slave of the
Eleven[220] came in, went up to him and said 'Socrates, I won't   116c
be complaining about you as I complain about others, for getting angry with me and swearing at me when I pass on the
order from the authorities to take the poison. While you've
been here I've come to know you as the most gentlemanly and
mildest and best man that's ever come to this place, and especially now I'm sure you're not angry with me, because you
know who did this to you, and it's them you're angry with. So
now – because you know what I've come to tell you – goodbye,   116d
and try to bear what can't be undone, as easily as you can.' At
which he burst into tears, turned on his heels and left.

Socrates looked up in his direction and said, 'Farewell[221] to
you too, and we'll do just that!' Turning to us in the same
moment, he remarked, 'What a civil person! All the time I've
been here he's been coming in to see me and having a talk,
sometimes – he's been the best; and what a gentleman he is
now, weeping for me like that! So come on, Crito, let's do as he
tells us. Someone should bring the poison, if it's ready and
ground; if it isn't, let the man get on and grind it.'

Crito said, 'But Socrates, it seems to me the sun is still on the   116e
mountains, and isn't yet down. And anyway, I know of others
who've put off taking the poison after the order's been given;
they've had dinner and a lot to drink, and some of them have
even slept with people they happened to take a fancy to. Don't
be in a hurry; there's still time.'

Socrates replied, 'Yes, they have a reason for doing that, the
people you mention – they think they gain by it; and I have a
reason for not doing it, because I don't think there's anything   117a
to gain by drinking the poison that little bit later – unless it's an
opportunity to laugh at myself for clinging on to life and eking
things out when there's nothing left. Go on,' he said; 'do as I
tell you and don't delay.'

On hearing this, Crito nodded to his slave, who was standing near by. The slave went out and after some considerable

time came back with the man whose job it was to administer the poison; he was carrying it, ground and ready, in a cup. When he saw this person, Socrates said, 'So, my good man, since you're the expert in these things, what do I have to do?'

117b 'Nothing, except walk about after you've drunk it,' the man said, 'until there's a heaviness in your legs; then lie down, and it'll work by itself.' And with that he held out the cup to Socrates.

Socrates took it and quite unperturbed he was, Echecrates, without a tremor, or any change in his colour or his face. Fixing the man from under those eyebrows with the usual bull-like look, he asked, 'What do you say to using this drink to make a libation to someone? Is it allowed or not?'

'We only grind what we think is the right amount to drink,' the man replied.

117c 'I understand,' said Socrates; 'but I imagine we're permitted to say a prayer to the gods, and we should – that our removal from this to that other place may be attended by good fortune. Well, that *is* my prayer, and may things turn out like that.' And with these words he raised the cup to his lips and drained it dry, quite without flinching or distaste. Most of us, for a time, were able to hold back our tears fairly well, but when we saw him drinking, and then that the cup was drained, we could hold back no longer; in my own case, the flow of tears quite over-whelmed me, so that I covered my head and wept – for myself,

117d not for Socrates, and for my own ill fortune, such was the man whose friendship was now lost to me. Crito had reacted even before me, getting up and moving away when the tears started to come. Apollodorus, who hadn't stopped weeping even before this, now started bellowing and was in such patent distress that he caused every one of those present to break down, except of course for Socrates himself.

His response was to say 'What a display to make of your-selves! It was for just this reason, you realize, that I sent the

117e women away, to stop them making a noise like this, because I've heard that dying is something to be done in silence.[222] Keep your peace, and be strong.'

That made us ashamed, and we held back our weeping. He

walked about, and when he said his legs were getting heavy, he lay down on his back in accordance with the man's instructions; at the same time the man – this person who had given him the poison – took hold of him, and after a short time started examining his feet and his legs. Then he gave Socrates' foot a hard squeeze and asked if he could feel it; Socrates said no. After this he squeezed his shins and, by moving up the body in this way he showed us he was gradually becoming cold and numb. Keeping his hold on him, the man said that when it reached his heart he would be gone. 118a

Well, it was now pretty well the parts round the abdomen that were getting cold, when he uncovered his face – because he had it covered – and spoke – these were the last words he uttered: 'Crito,' he said, 'we owe a cock to Asclepius;[223] pay our debt, and no forgetting.'

'I'll do it,' said Crito; 'is there anything else?'

After Crito's question Socrates answered no further. After a little while there was a movement; the man uncovered Socrates' face again, and his eyes were fixed.[224] When he saw it, Crito closed the mouth and the eyes.

This was the end of our companion, Echecrates – a man, as we would assert, who was the best of that generation we'd ever encountered, the wisest, too, and the most just.

Notes

EUTHYPHRO

1. *your 'divinity' having intervened*: That is, an unnamed divinity, intervening in some unspecified (but unusual) way. 'Your "divinity"' (*to daimonion*): more literally, 'your "divine something"'. Euthyphro appears to take *daimonios* as indistinguishable from *theios*, the commoner term for 'divine' and the one used in the whole of the surrounding context. In the *Apology* Socrates himself is more informative: the *theion* and *daimonion* 'something' that happens to him, whenever it does, is 'a sort of voice' stopping him from doing what he is intending to do (*Apology* 31d).

2. *the Assembly*: The democratic Assembly, consisting of all adult male citizens, which had supreme legislative authority.

3. *resent him*: Sc. for his wisdom: this is Euthyphro's explanation, given that he's sure of his own expertise; Socrates, not in the least sure that he has any, will need a different account.

4. *has he already flown the coop?*: In the original Greek, Socrates says, 'Are you chasing/prosecuting something on the wing?'

5. *Exegetes*: The appropriate official experts, in Athens (Naxos being an Athenian colony).

6. *pious and impious behaviour*: Here is the first occurrence of the two key terms in the dialogue, 'pious', *hosios*, and 'impious', *anosios* (the corresponding nouns are *hosiotês* and *anosiotês*).

7. *divine matters*: Here *ta theia* (see note 1 above).

8. *impiety*: Here *asebeia* rather than *anosiotês* (see note 6 above), because *asebeia* is the technical legal term.

9. *the pious ... and the impious*: 'Pious' and 'impious' here are *eusebes* and *asebes*, the terms used in the context of the law and the case against Socrates; in the next sentence they are *hosion* and *anosion*, the terms favoured in the *Euthyphro* as a whole. The pairs seem to be entirely interchangeable, except in the legal context.

10. *type*: 'Type' is not explicit in the Greek, but must be what Socrates intends, insofar as his new question spells out an answer to his previous one. The question is: what is the common character that will be shared by all actions, i.e. actions in any context, if they're going to be pious actions (and similarly with impious ones)?

11. *some single character*: The Greek term translated here by 'character', *idea*, is one of the two Plato employs for those 'forms' about which he is supposed, famously, to have a theory (the other term is *eidos*: see 6d): forms like the form of the good, or the beautiful, in which particular good and beautiful things will 'share' or 'participate'. We may, but need not, suppose some or all of this to be lurking behind the use of the Greek term *idea* here. See General Introduction, §4.

12. *Of course, Socrates, absolutely*: Euthyphro's reply here presumably contains more than a tinge of irony; Socrates has suddenly gone all technical on him. But Socrates ploughs on regardless.

13. *the person committing ... any other crime of a similar sort*: I.e., acts typically regarded, and regarded by the law, as threatening our relations with the gods, and so as acts of impiety (Euthyphro will in a moment sum them all up specifically as 'acting impiously'). So actually the account he is presently giving of the pious and impious is incomplete even in his own terms, and this is a point that Socrates will shortly raise with him (6c–d, though only after raising a much larger issue, the nature of the gods themselves).

14. *what the law is*: Clearly not Athenian law, rather some larger rule or principle governing human and – as he'll now claim – divine behaviour alike.

15. *unjustly*: Euthyphro's language here ('not justly', *ouk en dikêi*) is evidently intended to echo his own first statement of his 'rule', at 4b ('the only thing to watch out for is whether the person who did the killing did so justly [*en dikêi*] or not'); but the idea it summons up, however fleetingly, that it might ever be *just* to eat one's children, is presumably meant – by Plato – to be as bizarre as it sounds.

16. *Yet they react angrily ... about me*: Here, in effect, Euthyphro responds to the second of his family's two arguments against him, i.e., that the real impiety is for a son to prosecute his own father; the first, that his father didn't actually kill the man in the ditch, remains unanswered, and the alleged parallel with the gory and obvious crimes of Uranus and Cronus (Zeus' father and

grandfather, if indeed gods can be criminals, which Socrates will dispute) makes the omission all the more important – Euthyphro, after all, is quite *certain* that he has right on his side.

17. *in the name of friendship*: Literally, 'in the name of Zeus Philios', i.e., Zeus as upholder of the institution (as it were) of friendship, *philia*.

18. *what you're doing now in proceeding*: Or 'what you're doing now, proceeding . . .' However Socrates' complaint is surely not so much that Euthyphro is identifying piety with a particular action, but rather that he is identifying it with a particular *type* of action. (See Euthyphro's speech at 5d–6a, which makes this especially clear.)

19. *that very character*: Cf. 5d, and note 11 above. Here the term is *eidos*, but in the very next sentence Socrates will revert to *idea*, again confirming that the two Greek terms are interchangeable.

20. *using it as a benchmark*: Or 'using it as a model'. The Greek term is *paradeigma*, typically used to describe an *original* from which, e.g., sculptors work, and a term that is itself of some importance in the context of Platonic 'form' theory. (Cf. General Introduction, §4.)

21. *thing or person*: 'Things' here (in the Greek, conveyed merely by neuters) are presumably actions; pious people will be those who act piously, i.e., do pious things.

22. *at odds over this sort of thing*: I.e., over things like 'punishing one's parents', as Zeus 'punished' his (Cronus), and Cronus his (Uranus), and as Hephaestus did his mother Hera for throwing him down from Olympus because of his lameness.

23. *that kind of person*: Once again, the reference is clearly to the *type* of action Euthyphro is undertaking, not the particular instance of the type in question.

24. *to be marked off*: The verb employed here (*horizesthai*) is or will become the standard verb for 'defining'; its more basic use is for marking boundaries, marking off territory.

25. *but you'd better look . . . promised*: I.e., that what he (Euthyphro) is doing to his father is the correct thing to do.

26. *I don't know what you're saying, Socrates*: A perfectly reasonable response. But Socrates' question is a crucial one: if a thing's piety is *only* a matter of its being loved by the gods, as Euthyphro has suggested, then – if he could have understood what was being asked – he would have had no choice but to go for Socrates' second option (pious, i.e., = god-loved, because loved by the gods); the first option, if pious = god-loved, would simply fail to

make sense, because it would involve saying that what is pious (i.e., = god-loved) is loved by the gods because it is god-loved (i.e., pious). This, in effect, is what Socrates proceeds to spell out in the following exchanges.

27. *It's not, then . . . because it's carried*: It is entirely in the style of the Platonic Socrates to give a series of examples issuing in a general rule of some kind (see the next-but-one sentence).

28. *something changes*: Or 'comes-to-be'; but this is probably to be understood as 'comes-to-be *something*' (so: 'changes').

29. *No: because it's pious*: Euthyphro now answers the question he failed to understand back in 10a.

30. *lovable*: I.e., as the Greek actually says, 'such as to be loved'. The 'one' is the god-loved, which is 'lovable' just to the extent that it is actually loved (by the gods); quite why or how 'the other', the pious, is lovable, and loved, remains to be established.

31. *feature*: Or 'attribute' – but the noun in question, *pathos*, belongs to the same family as the verb in the next clause translated as 'is affected' (for which see also 10c: 'if something . . . is affected in some way', etc.).

32. *Daedalus*: A legendary sculptor, whose statues were reputed to be so lifelike as to be able to move; Socrates calls him his 'ancestor' by way of reference to his father's trade as a stonemason.

33. *Not only to mine . . . but to others'*: So Socrates claims to be as hard on his own proposals as he is on those of others; he gives us no reason to doubt the seriousness of this claim.

34. *expert*: Or 'wise' (*sophos*). Given that wisdom and its absence are so central to Socrates' concerns, we should probably note that the word he uses here is the standard term for 'wise' (even if, in this context, its primary connotation is one of expertise).

35. *forms of words*: Or 'proposals', or 'hypotheses' (*logoi*); the most literal translation of the Greek is probably just 'things said'.

36. *But you're younger than me*: And therefore ought to be quicker; Socrates now behaves as if his lack of wisdom or understanding is because of his age.

37. *Zeus was the cause . . . Shame*: According to marginal comments in a manuscript, these verses (two hexameter lines in the Greek) came from the epic poet Stasinus' *Cypria*; the text is in part uncertain, but it will do no harm to suppose the context to be one in which Zeus has 'punished' another god for some sort of 'crime' – which would give the first sentence relevance, and so explain why Socrates might have quoted it as well as the second, which is all he actually needs for his present point.

38. *isoceles, and not scalene*: I.e., divisible by two ('isoceles' = 'has two equal legs') or not: a geometrical way of putting an arithmetical point. 'Scalene' numbers, then, will be the odd ones.

39. *so that I can tell Meletus, too*: The implication of the 'too' is apparently that dealing with Meletus' charge is a secondary consideration (the priority being to find out about piety).

40. *what's pious*: The Greek here and in Euthyphro's reply uses both of the two equivalent terms for 'pious', *eusebes* and *hosion* (for which see notes 6 and 8 above – the point, or the effect, is to continue to connect the discussion with Socrates' trial). Since English only has one term available, it seems less misleading, in the translation, to use that one by itself than to try to invent another.

41. *piety*: The Greek, again, uses two words (*hosiotês* and *eusebeia*: see preceding note).

42. *expertise*: There is no separate word in the Greek for 'expertise' here, or in the following exchanges, but, as Burnet says, 'the form of the word [sc. *huperetikê*] suggests an "art" [of serving]'.

43. *expert service to doctors*: I.e., 'service' given by doctors' slaves.

44. *the many fine things the gods bring about*: I.e., with our service.

45. *if you'd only answered ... piety*: Of course Euthyphro turned aside because he *couldn't* answer the question. So there is at least some irony here. The question is whether it extends any further – whether perhaps we are being given a signal that the real answer actually does lie around here. (See Introduction to *Euthyphro*, above.)

46. *because questioner must follow ... may lead*: Perhaps because, in the question-and-answer process of dialectic, any advance must depend on what is established between the parties – which in effect does make the questioner dependent on the respondent. The Greek text is in something of a mess here; an alternative reading would give 'because lover must follow beloved', but this would probably need to be understood in much the same way.

47. *expertise in*: Or 'knowledge of'; but 'expertise' makes the connections with earlier parts of the discussion slightly clearer.

48. *that's clear to anyone ... as a gift from them*: At the most basic level, it will be 'clear' to any ordinary pious person. For Socrates, it will be clear, and true, on condition that he understands wisdom as a 'gift of the gods' – which perhaps he may do, insofar as he holds that is is from wisdom that everything becomes good (see General Introduction, §2).

49. *Proteus*: A sea-god, proverbial for changing his shape; he is encountered by Menelaus in the *Odyssey* (4.349–570).
50. *expert*: I.e., 'wise' (*sophos* again): see note 34 above.
51. *live better for the rest of my life*: Thus at the very end of the dialogue Plato leaves us with the question: *could* Socrates have lived a better life?

APOLOGY

1. *where many of you have heard me*: That is, accidentally, while about their own (commercial) business.
2. *expert*: Or 'wise'. Socrates will, famously, go on to deny that he is wise in any respect at all (except insofar as he is aware of his lack of wisdom).
3. *one who dabbles ... stronger*: This is, as we shall see, a summary of the charges made against 'Socrates' in Aristophanes' comedy *Clouds*; 'making the weaker argument the stronger' is there a matter of enabling the unjust to overcome the just – but has rather more complex implications in the mouth of the relativist Protagoras, who evidently invented the phrase (and to whom both Aristophanes and Plato will undoubtedly have been alluding).
4. *a comic writer*: The primary reference, as would have been clear to the jury, is to Aristophanes; but he wasn't the only comic playwright to put Socrates on the stage (in the late 420s).
5. *some sort of success*: An important qualification: Socrates doesn't commit himself to saying that he wants to be acquitted (that will depend on what's best for the jury-members and himself).
6. *as it pleases the god*: Or 'the gods'; the singular 'god' often stands for the plural – unless Socrates is already thinking of Apollo, who will play an important role later on in the speech.
7. *conversation*: Or 'dialogue' (the verb is *dialegesthai*), the form Socratic talk typically takes; Plato's dialogues mimic this form.
8. *the same also holds good ... say about me*: I.e., that they're equally false.
9. *Gorgias of Leontini, or Prodicus of Ceos, or Hippias of Elis*: Famous teachers ('sophists'), of a variety of subjects; Socrates' endorsement of their possession of the ability in question is here ambiguous at least.
10. *five minas*: Not an inconsiderable sum in itself – as it happens, equal to the total value of Socrates' worldly goods, according to Xenophon, *Oeconomicus* 2.3; also one-sixth of the fine Soc-

rates' friends will propose as an alternative to the death penalty – and five hundred times the daily pay of a skilled workman. But some other teachers would evidently have charged much more.

11. *and teaches it at so low a price*: Because such teaching would be price*less*?

12. *the god at Delphi*: I.e., Apollo (the 'Pythia', just below, is his priestess and spokeswoman).

13. *who shared your recent exile . . . with you*: The reference is to the civil unrest surrounding the brief regime of the so-called Thirty Tyrants, at the end of the fifth century BCE.

14. *one of the political experts*: Anytus, perhaps? He is one of Socrates' actual prosecutors, and a democratic politician; he is pictured in the *Meno* as particularly dismissive of professional teachers (sophists) – and, in effect, claiming an educative role for people just like himself.

15. *by the Dog*: a favourite oath of Socrates', possibly referring to the Dog-star (though this is pure speculation).

16. *these labours*: Socrates here compares himself with Heracles (or Theseus).

17. *I went on to the poets . . . which they weren't*: The last few lines give what is virtually a summary of Plato's *Ion*, with the difference that Socrates is there confronted by a performer of (epic) poetry rather than a poet.

18. *I'd outdone the political experts*: See 21d above.

19. *wiser than me*: Here as before 'wisdom' is treated as interchangeable with expertise or skill.

20. *the good craftsmen*: I.e., excellent, expert ones.

21. *That's why I . . . still go around . . . service to the god*: Compare the *Euthyphro*'s attempted definition of piety as service to the gods: here in the *Apology* Socrates seems to succeed, as he and Euthyphro didn't, in identifying something that might count as an outcome of service to the gods (*Euthyphro* 13d–14b) – that is, an increase in the distribution of wisdom, understood as an increase in awareness of ignorance.

22. *Meletus has now joined . . . orators*: Meletus may have been the son of a poet; Anytus may have owned a tannery as well as being a politician; having Lycon, another democratic politician, represent the orators might be little more than a way of getting this latter group (who figure prominently in Plato's dialogues) into the list of the 'experts' Socrates has examined. In any case the main point here is to treat Socrates' actual prosecutors as just

three more in a long line of 'accusers', stretching way back. Not only are they not telling the truth; they aren't even saying anything the jury hasn't heard many times before.

23. *divinities*: The Greek here just has the neuter plural of the adjective for 'divine', i.e., (other new) *daimonia*: 'divine [things, unspecified]'. This will be of some importance later on. For those who have read the *Euthyphro*, the primary reference will be to the 'divinity' – in the Greek, 'the divine [thing]' – that Socrates (according to Euthyphro: *Euthyphro* 3b) reports as intervening with him.

24. *never meant anything to him up till now*: I.e., *ouden [Melêtôi] pôpote emelêsen* ... The Greek puns, here and several times more in the next few pages, on Meletus' name: the root *mel-* connotes caring for, showing concern for, taking seriously.

25. *Here, Meletus ... 'It is'*: In the exchange that now begins, Socrates' 'conversational' techniques transfer easily into the cross-examination of a prosecutor.

26. *corrupting them*: I.e., making them 'worse' – presumably, in relation to excellence 'of the human, citizen sort' (see 20b above). Exactly what this is, we have not been told, but it is hard not to suppose that for Socrates, at least, it will have something to do with knowledge, and knowledge about 'the most important things' (22d) – whatever these may be.

27. *every single Athenian*: Because every adult male Athenian in principle had the right to sit in the Assembly.

28. *aren't a meaningful subject for you*: There is the same untranslatable pun on Meletus' name here – see note 24.

29. *fellow citizens who are good or those who are vicious*: If we stick to the terms of the argument, 'goodness' here will be whatever excellence of a 'human, citizen sort' (20b) Socrates is imagining might be taught by a human trainer as opposed to a trainer of horses; and the signs are that he thinks this will be some sort of expertise or wisdom. Meletus, for his part, and any ordinary person who might be listening (or reading the dialogue), would probably identify the goodness in question more specifically with *justice*. 'Vicious' (*ponêros*) is one of two synonyms Socrates uses in this context for 'bad' (*kakos*), the other being *mochthêros* ('depraved').

30. *damage*: Or 'harm' – in any case whatever is the opposite of 'benefit' (so not 'wrong').

31. *depraved*: I.e., *mochthêros* (see note 29 above).

32. *something that bad*: I.e., by the logic of the argument, bad *for* Socrates.

33. *I don't think you'll convince anyone else in the world, either*:

That is, presumably, so long as they see the full force of Socrates' argument, which may include treating 'making people bad/ worse' as a matter of making them *ignorant/less wise*. (Make others less wise, and you run the risk of their damaging you – and especially in respect to your own wisdom.)

34. *concerned himself*: That well-worn pun comes in yet again.

35. *Anaxagoras*: An Athenian natural philosopher whom Socrates might well have heard in his youth, and whose ideas will play an important part in the *Phaedo*.

36. *the orchestra*: Either a part of the theatre stage, mainly occupied by the chorus, or – according to a late source, not necessarily to be trusted – a part of the agora, which seems a more likely location for the sale of scrolls (here translated 'books'), if we suppose that that's what Socrates is referring to.

37. *especially when they're so strange*: This last clause is (deliberately?) two-edged, since usually it's *Socrates* who's described, in the dialogues, as 'strange'.

38. *if I express myself in my habitual style*: See 17c–d.

39. *one protest after another*: Like: 'What a stupid question! Where's it leading?' Socrates' own question here is an immediate, and splendid, example of the way he 'habitually' talks (certainly, in the Platonic dialogues).

40. *whether these are new ones or old ones ... I don't mind*: See 24b–c and 27b–c, with note 23.

41. *divinities*: Socrates here takes advantage of the fact that the Greek word here translated as 'divinity' (*daimôn*, the origin of our 'demon') can either be used as a synonym for *theos*, 'god', or to refer to different sorts of beings located somewhere between gods and men – including, as we'll see, 'heroes' or demigods.

42. *good men too*: Socrates carefully avoids the implication that *he's* 'good'; which is just as well, given his tendency to associate goodness with wisdom, and his denial that he possesses wisdom about anything much.

43. *poor creatures*: I.e., for having made the wrong calculation.

44. *the son of Thetis*: I.e., Achilles.

45. *the poet*: I.e., Homer (the text gives a version of part of *Iliad* 18.98; Achilles' response, below, derives from the next lines in the poem – though actually only the first few words and the last few bear any close relation to the text of Homer we have).

46. *Potidaea or Amphipolis or Delium*: Famous battles during the long war with Sparta and her allies, in at least two of which Socrates actually fought, as a heavy-armed infantryman.

47. *someone better than me*: Once again, degrees of 'goodness' are plainly associated, above all, with degrees of wisdom. Of course, whether any human is actually 'better' than Socrates, even his commanders as chosen by the Athenians, will be an open question. (At least one might hope they knew something about strategy and tactics.)

48. *may even be good*: I.e., good for him, or for anyone.

49. *declaring myself*: Or, alternatively, 'giving my demonstrations', i.e. of people's lack of wisdom (23b).

50. *What I do*: And what Socrates actually does, after all, is what his imagined objector asked him to tell the court (28b).

51. *It's not from money . . . public life*: Some have claimed that the sentence must mean 'It's not from money that excellence comes, but from excellence come money and the other good things, all of them, for human beings . . .' The translation offered here has Socrates *seeming* – teasingly – to be about to say that, but ultimately saying something quite different (and something rather more in line with the rest of what he has been saying, and will say). What makes the things normally counted as goods into real goods is 'excellence' or virtue (or, more specifically, wisdom, knowledge of how to *use* the things in question: cf., e.g., *Euthydemus* 281d).

52. *I'd say to you*: I.e., if the jury said they'd acquit him if he stopped doing philosophy (29d).

53. *not permitted*: The same kind of expression as used here (*ou themiton*) was used at 21b to rule out the possibility that the god should lie. Socrates seems in this context to be supposing that the only way of doing damage to someone is to corrupt him, i.e., according to his previous arguments, by making him less wise. According to his own account, he himself is wiser than anyone (just by virtue of being aware of his ignorance), and so will be wiser, better, than Meletus. It will then actually be impossible for Meletus to damage, or harm, Socrates (especially if, as Socrates has repeatedly said, he has no interest in such matters at all); and it will be no more possible for anyone who isn't wise to harm anyone who is.

54. *excellence*: I.e., 'virtue': that quality, or those qualities, that make for a better human being and citizen – which will include the standard virtues ('excellences') of justice, courage, and so on, as well as wisdom.

55. *you yourselves have often heard me talking about*: How many of the jury would actually have heard anything of the sort is surely

open to question. The real audience here may be the *reader* – who will already be familiar with this feature of Socrates from a passage like *Euthyphro* 3b. 'Some god or "divinity" intervenes with me' in the translation is intended to evoke that passage, which may be partly mimicked in the Greek (but with a reference to 'god', in the light of Socrates' clarification in *Apology* 27b–28a that, when he talks about a 'divine' intervention, he really does mean intervention by a god/gods).

56. *the sea-battle*: I.e., the battle of Arginusae in 406 BCE. 'My tribe . . . held the presidency': see following note.

57. *the Thirty . . . the Roundhouse*: For the 'Thirty', see note 13 above, with 21a; they had evidently taken over the use of the 'Roundhouse' (Tholos), normally the 'Prytaneum', the home of the 'presidents' (*prutaneis*) of the Council and Assembly, who dined there daily at public expense (see 36d).

58. *those they slanderously call my pupils*: A prize exhibit for the prosecutors here would undoubtedly have been the brilliant but traitorous Alcibiades. Plato's *Symposium* includes what purports to be an account, from Alcibiades' side, of the real nature of his relationship with Socrates.

59. *whether he communicates . . . human beings*: Is Socrates here telling us not to take the story about the oracle's response to Chaerephon too seriously? One thing he *is* surely saying is that to have been given a task by the god is no different in kind from similar claims made by other people – e.g., by the poets and seers, who claim to be 'inspired'. (On prophets and prophecy, see further note 71 below.)

60. *Crito . . . Apollodorus*: Crito is Socrates' interlocutor in the dialogue named after him; he was, as the *Phaedo* shows, very close to him and his family. Some of the others in the list are better known to us than others: Aeschines was himself a writer of Socratic dialogues; Adimantus, apart from being Plato's brother, is one of the two main interlocutors in the *Republic*; and Apollodorus appears in the role of narrator in the *Symposium*. Aeschines, Apollodorus and Critobulus are among those who will be present, along with Crito, at Socrates' death (*Phaedo* 59b–c).

61. *There are many reasons . . . fifth of the votes*: The jury consisted of either 500 or 501 citizens; according to what Socrates has just said, he will have lost either by 60 votes or by 59. In either case, there were 280 votes against him – which would 'obviously' leave fewer than 100 to be attributed to Meletus, if the total were to be divided about evenly between the three prosecutors.

But even that, according to the first part of the sentence, would be generous; Socrates claims, in effect, to have offered a complete refutation of Meletus' arguments, presumably in the cross-examination.

62. *apply the same rule . . . in caring for everything else*: I.e., presumably, by giving priority to the promotion of 'goodness and wisdom'.

63. *the Prytaneum*: See note 57 above.

64. *because someone like that makes you seem happy*: Insofar as Athenians generally would enjoy the reflected glory of Olympic success by one of their own.

65. *am I to choose one of the things I know . . . to be bad . . . as my penalty*: Socrates perhaps here anticipates a tetchy response from a juryman ('so what about others things you surely *do* know to be bad?'). Whether he really does regard the options he goes on to raise as bad, and if so exactly why, he chooses not to make clear.

66. *the Eleven*: The prison authorities, appointed annually by lot.

67. *about goodness and the other subjects you hear me talking . . . about*: 'Goodness': or 'excellence' ('virtue', *aretê*). 'Hear me talking . . .': i.e., engaging in dialectic (*dialegesthai*).

68. *I'm not used . . . anything bad at all*: As he's said before (37b).

69. *viciousness*: I.e., the opposite of 'excellence' or 'virtue'. The adjective corresponding to the noun in question, *ponêria*, was used earlier as a synonym of the ordinary word for 'bad' – similarly with the adjective corresponding to the noun translated as 'depravity' (*mochthêria*) a few lines below: see text to notes 29–31 above. Here as in the earlier context the question will be what exactly it is that human excellence, and its opposite, consist in; there is little doubt that both Socrates and his audience would include injustice, or, more generally, 'viciousness' (or 'depravity'), under the heading of human 'badness', but the audience would be unlikely to share Socrates' tendency – not so visible here, but clear enough in the *Apology* as a whole – to treat *ignorance* as the source of such 'badness'.

70. *'jurymen' is the correct name to give you*: I.e., you, as opposed to those who voted against me – and who by implication failed to live up to their oath (see 35c), and have behaved unjustly, *adikôs*, so belying their status as *dikastai*, 'jurymen' or 'dispensers of justice'.

71. *that accustomed prophetic ability of mine*: Greek 'prophets' or seers, it should be noted, are able to see into the present and

the past as well as the future. For this 'seership' of Socrates', see 31c–d.

72. *the Great King himself*: I.e., the king of Persia – the ultimate exemplar of power and wealth, and of the kind of person who could (supposedly) have anything he wanted.

73. *Minos, Rhadamanthus, Aeacus and Triptolemus*: Minos, Rhadamanthus and Aeacus are the more traditional judges of the dead; Triptolemus is connected with the mysteries of Eleusis, which promised largely unspecified benefits to initiates after death.

74. *Orpheus, or Musaeus, or Hesiod, or Homer*: Orpheus is a mythical singer, and putative author of a range of texts connected with a shadowy set of beliefs and practices labelled as 'Orphic', themselves probably forming part of the background to the *Phaedo* (see notes 20 and 51 to *Phaedo* in this volume); Musaeus is another singer, one especially connected with Eleusis (see preceding note). Hesiod is the other great epic poet typically paired with Homer.

75. *Palamedes, or Ajax son of Telamon*: Palamedes, a traditionally clever hero, was falsely denounced to Agamemnon by Odysseus for plotting to betray the Greeks at Troy (see below); Ajax killed himself after losing the great prize of the arms of Achilles to Odysseus.

76. *the man who led that great army against Troy, or Odysseus, or Sisyphus*: 'The man who led that great army against Troy' is Agamemnon. The great Agamemnon, in Book XI of Homer's *Odyssey*, is among the shades or souls of the dead that Odysseus is allowed to encounter and question on his brief visit to Hades during his journey home; Socrates envisages himself as going one better, and questioning Odysseus as well. Sisyphus was a trickster who managed to persuade the gods of the underworld to let him return to the world above, but then refused to go back down again; his punishment was to push a large boulder up a hill only to have it roll back to the bottom every time, and for all time. Socrates' interest in *him*, to judge from the *Phaedo*, might have been his feat in coming back to the land of the living (one of the themes of the *Phaedo* being the 'rebirth' of souls, but without the disastrous consequences of Sisyphus').

77. *examine them*: Presumably while continuing to examine himself (see 28e and 38a).

78. *to be rid of life's ordinary business altogether*: Even, it seems, if death is no more than a dreamless sleep. But Socrates will argue at length against this possibility in the *Phaedo*.

79. *that's what they deserve to be blamed for*: That is, for their lack of *understanding* of what they were really doing?

CRITO

1. *I've been struck . . . pleasant way possible*: See *Apology* 40c–e, on the pleasure of dreamless sleep.
2. *the easy and relaxed way . . . facing you*: Crito himself, then, is immediately presented as someone who wasn't persuaded by Socrates' arguments in his defence speech about death, and about the proper attitude towards it (Crito was of course there: his was the first of the names Socrates listed at *Apology* 33d–34a; he was one of those who would have contributed to the proposed fine at 38b, and he actually refers, at *Crito* 45b, to what Socrates said at his trial).
3. *the arrival of the ship from Delos*: The background to this is mainly given by the *Phaedo*, where it has to be supplied for the benefit of a non-Athenian audience (58a–c). Athens had once been in thrall to King Minos of Crete; each year the Athenians sent seven boys and seven girls as tribute, to be fed to the Minotaur. Finally, the great Theseus managed to kill the Minotaur and save the last set of intended victims. 'The story goes,' says Phaedo, 'that the Athenians had made a vow to Apollo that if they did get back safe, they'd offer an annual mission to Delos in return, and they've gone on sending it to the god every year since.' Executions, as Phaedo also says, could not take place while the ship was away.
4. *'to the fertile land . . . shall you come'*: The woman here more or less quotes the *Iliad* (IX.363), where the context is the homecoming Achilles might have had if he hadn't stood firm and avenged Patroclus. Cf. *Apology* 28c–d.
5. *once they've been taken in by slander about someone*: Cf. *Apology* 18d.
6. *the greatest of evils . . . the greatest of goods too*: As Socrates is about to suggest, the worst evil is ignorance, the greatest good wisdom; and if wisdom is knowing certain things, then making someone ignorant would involve knowing what to make him ignorant *of*. But in that case, those wanting to create ignorance would be wise, and no one wise would want to make other people ignorant.
7. *Simmias of Thebes . . . Cebes*: The Thebans Simmias and Cebes will be Socrates' main interlocutors in the *Phaedo*.

8. *guest-friends*: I.e., friends bound to him by the rules of hospitality; they will have been *his* guests while in Athens and so owe him hospitality in Thessaly.

9. *It doesn't seem to me ... destroy you*: Crito here plays on a notion of justice that Socrates criticizes elsewhere (*Republic* I, 332d), i.e., that justice consists in doing good to one's friends and harm to one's enemies. (The sense in which Socrates' enemies have 'actively' promoted his present situation is of course by their having taken him to court and had him condemned to death. Is Plato here hinting that there were, after all, purely personal motives behind the trial?)

10. *this other sort of thing I used to say*: Socrates here begins a new stage in his argument, the conclusion of which will be reached in 47e–48a.

11. *the part that is improved by justice and destroyed by injustice*: 'Destruction' here is merely an alternative term for 'corruption'; Socrates shows no indication of supposing that injustice causes a soul actually to perish (and the fact that it doesn't is actually a premise in another argument for the immortality of the soul, at *Republic* X, 608c–610e). The 'part' in question is, presumably, what Socrates is elsewhere quite happy to call the 'soul' (see General Introduction, §6).

12. *As for those points ... we've been talking about*: It isn't so much that Socrates doesn't care about such things as spending money (i.e., others spending it), or caring about his children (see 45a, 54a), as that he thinks they shouldn't be the points of departure for the argument (the right line of inquiry starts, not with these, but with the question about *justice*).

13. *Do we say that we should never intentionally ... sometimes not?*: There may at first sight appear to be something odd about Socrates' proposal here, because Plato regularly represents him as claiming that no one does wrong intentionally in any case: if anyone does, or goes, wrong it is only out of ignorance. Or, in other words, if we really know how bad wrong/unjust actions are for us, we will realize that those actions were really not what we wanted to do, and won't do them. (No one sets out deliberately to harm himself or herself, and, as Socrates will claim in the very next sentence here in the *Crito*, 'acting unjustly [is] never, by its very nature ... good [sc. for the agent]'.) But at the same time people will *appear*, even to themselves, to intend injustice (or to do harm, or damage: see 49c); they will set out to injure others, or fail to draw back from an action they know will do harm. In

such cases, and for such people, 'never intentionally do what's unjust' will be a useful and important piece of advice – 'don't do any damage to others that you can avoid!' ('Do we say that we should never . . . or sometimes . . .': 'never' and 'sometimes' translate Greek phrases that might more naturally be rendered as 'in no way'/'in some way'. However the issue here and in the following lines is clearly whether *circumstances* make any difference.)

14. *or gentler*: Because, for Socrates, his impending execution isn't in fact so harsh a thing for him to suffer.

15. *do harm*: Or 'do damage' or 'do wrong' (*kakourgein*).

16. *It's never just*: See note 13 above.

17. *doing harm to people . . . unjustly*: I.e., doing harm, or damage, to people intentionally is no different from doing them injustice intentionally; for 'intentional injustice', see 49a, with note 13.

18. *running away*: Previously it was just a neutral 'getting out'; that, by Socrates' argument, is a misdescription (it would be no mere 'getting out', like leaving one's house in the morning).

19. *the laws, the common foundation of the city*: Literally 'the laws and the common/shared [aspect]of the city' (*to koinon tês poleôs*). The latter phrase ('the common . . .') is frequently taken as referring to 'the state'; but in what follows Socrates pictures himself as confronted by the laws alone (not by the laws *and* the city – hardly distinguishable, if at all, from 'the state' in the present context). Additionally, as the laws themselves suggest, to destroy the laws *is* to destroy the city. The 'and' in 'the laws and the common/shared [aspect]of the city' will then be explanatory rather than connecting two distinct entities (law and city/state).

20. *There's plenty that could be said, especially by an expert orator . . . to be observed*: The way in which Socrates begins the sentence ('There's plenty that could be said . . .') probably indicates – given his usually low opinion of orators – that he isn't himself interested in this particular line of defence; and after all, if there ever was an actual law of the kind in question ('judgements made are to be observed'), it might appear doubly superfluous to spend a lot of energy defending it. In fact, he will concentrate on the idea that his 'running away' from prison would constitute an act of injustice against the laws, because tending to undermine them, and therefore the city herself.

21. *literature and music*: These together constituted Greek 'music' (*mousikê*, the art or sphere of the Muses). Question: would

Socrates in fact have been happy with an education that limited itself to literature and music (and gymnastics) – and excluded philosophy?

22. *for gods*: The idea is not that the gods revere their fatherland more (they hardly have a 'fatherland', even if they have parents), but that they take – even – more notice of humans who fail to pay proper respect to their country than they do of those who offend against parents.

23. *a fine impression of not being upset at having to die*: See *Apology* 36a.

24. *either of the places you claim ... to be well governed, Sparta or Crete*: It might well be consistent with Socrates' position as described in the *Apology* to praise the Spartans and the Cretans for paying systematic attention to 'virtue' or excellence in at least one respect: Spartan institutions, and the Cretan ones that followed the Spartan example, were particularly concerned with imbuing the young with the sorts of qualities required for fighting. Their commitment to the other virtues or excellences, however, was less clear, as the main speaker in Plato's late dialogue *Laws* – who, as it happens, is not Socrates – points out (*Laws* I, 632d–635e). The Athenian laws are here, somewhat huffily, suggesting a general approval on Socrates' part for Sparta and Cretan cities (so echoing the sorts of accusations made by Aristophanes, probably himself reproducing popular opinions: see e.g. Aristophanes, *Birds* 1281); and by doing so they betray themselves for what they are – not the spokesmen of a neutral law somehow transcending particular perspectives and interests, but the laws of (democratic) Athens.

25. *since both of these are well governed*: Not in Socrates' terms (see preceding note) so much as in the sense that they are properly law-governed cities, who will worry about his undermining their laws as he will allegedly have undermined Athens'.

26. *to have a destructive effect on people*: I.e., to be the sort of person who 'corrupts' them.

27. *guest-friends*: See 45c.

28. *changing your appearance*: Particularly difficult for Socrates, whose appearance was distinctive (he was notoriously ugly, with a snub nose and protruding lips).

29. *a Thessalian dinner*: The Athenian laws propose that Thessaly is short on culture but long on hospitality; there is some evidence that this was a typical Athenian view.

30. *if you go off to Hades*: I.e., if you're dead.

31. *those who control things down there*: I.e., the judges of the dead; see *Apology* 41a.

32. *doing harm to those you should have hurt the least*: Cf. 50a.

33. *the Corybants*: Devotees of Dionysus, who dance in a trance-like state induced by his music.

34. *if you try saying anything . . . speak out*: See 48d–e.

35. *that's the way the god is leading us*: A somewhat mysterious remark, insofar as 'the god' has not figured at all in the *Crito* (unless the reference is simply to the dream Socrates reported at 44a–b, and 'the god' stands for the god or gods who sent it). But cf., e.g., *Apology* 40b.

PHAEDO

1. *It's the one . . . back safe*: See note 3 to *Crito*.

2. *do your best to give us*: Echecrates is evidently there with a number of philosophically minded friends (see 'us all' at 102a).

3. *when he arrived there, too, his lot if anyone's would be a good one*: As Socrates will himself go on to claim, and provide arguments for claiming.

4. *Critobulus was there with his father*: The father is Crito. Of the others mentioned, Hermogenes is one of Socrates' interlocutors in the dialogue *Cratylus*; Epigenes is mentioned as a young member of Socrates' circle at *Apology* 33e; Aeschines, like Phaedo (and Plato), wrote Socratic dialogues; Antisthenes founded the Cynic school of philosophy; Ctesippus makes an appearance in the *Lysis* and in the *Euthydemus*; Menexenus is an interlocutor in a dialogue named after him as well as in the *Lysis*; Simmias and Cebes have already turned up in the *Crito* (45b); Euclides founded another philosophical school (the 'Megarians'), and also appears, along with Terpsion, in the *Theaetetus*; Aristippus, from Cyrene, founded the Cyrenaic school. It is altogether a significant group of people. (In the third century, Callimachus wrote an epigram about a Cleombrotus who committed suicide after reading the *Phaedo* – perhaps on seeing himself permanently recorded as having missed the great man's death.)

5. *as we left the prison in the evening . . . the ship had arrived from Delos*: So, if Socrates and not Crito was right about when the ship would arrive (*Crito* 43d–44a), the dramatic date of the *Crito* should be two days before that of the *Phaedo*.

6.   *The Eleven*: See *Apology* 37c and note 66. The prison guard, and
      the person in charge of the poison (63d–e, 117a–118a), would
      both have been slaves (see 116b), answering to the citizens mak-
      ing up the Eleven.

7.   *the gods*: the Greek has the singular 'the god' – apparently here,
      as elsewhere, used collectively (see, e.g., *Apology* 19a).

8.   *Evenus*: See *Apology* 20a–c.

9.   *'music'*: See note 21 to *Crito*.

10.   *the god*: Here Apollo, who is also god of music.

11.   *I thought it safer not to go off*: Sc. to Hades.

12.   *that's not permitted*: Socrates uses the same expression (*ou
      themiton*) at *Apology* 30d, with note 53; see also *Phaedo* 82c
      with note 94.

13.   *conversation*: Plato here uses his favourite word for *philosoph-
      ical* conversation or 'dialogue' (*dialegesthai*). See *Apology* 19d
      with note 7.

14.   *Philolaus*: See Introduction to *Phaedo* above.

15.   *between now and sunset*: I.e., between now and when the execu-
      tion will take place.

16.   *perhaps you may hear one*: Does Socrates mean now, from him,
      or just sooner or later?

17.   *Probably it will appear . . . than to live*: Socrates expresses him-
      self in this convoluted way perhaps because Cebes hasn't yet
      accepted that *philosophers*, in particular, will be better off
      dead.

18.   *the right thing*: Or 'the pious thing'; but the reference is still to
      what is 'permitted' (see 61c, e, and note 12 above).

19.   *in his own dialect*: I.e., Boeotian Greek (Thebes being part of
      Boeotia, a region to the north of Attica).

20.   *a deep saying*: The 'saying' also seems curiously reminiscent of
      the argument of the *Crito* (now transposed to a quite different
      context); the *Crito* – as a written document – would be a thor-
      oughly 'secret' doctrine from Socrates' point of view. But com-
      mentators are probably right in seeing the primary reference as
      being to 'Orpheus and his crew', who are credited at *Cratylus*
      with the idea that the body is a kind of prison for the soul. (See
      also note 74 to the *Apology* in this volume.) If so, it will be useful
      to recall, later on in the *Phaedo*, that Socrates appears, here at
      least, to be less than wholly enthusiastic about the idea – or else,
      perhaps, it is merely 'deep and difficult to penetrate' because its
      elements, e.g., the special notion of 'soul' involved, have yet to
      be introduced in the *Phaedo*.

21. *we human beings count, for them, among their possessions*: So
    that 'we' will be the gods' slaves (and slaves have no business
    running away from their masters; Socrates will spell out the
    point). In *Euthyphro* and *Apology*, Socrates has presented him-
    self as a rather special servant of, or slave to, the gods.

22. *the gods*: See note 7 above – Socrates is again using the singular;
    but the reference appears to be precisely the same as that of 'the
    gods' (he used the plural) in 62b.

23. *it's not unreasonable ... find myself*: If Socrates is suggesting
    that *he* is killing himself, or about to do so, that is perhaps less
    because he will administer the lethal dose of hemlock to himself
    than because, as we understand from the *Crito*, he could actually
    have avoided execution. The gods have made it 'necessary' for
    him to die both because there are overwhelming reasons – the
    ones he has rehearsed in the *Crito* – against his running away,
    and also because, evidently, his 'divinity' hasn't intervened (see
    Euthyphro 3b, *Apology* 40a–b, *Crito* 54e; its absence, in the
    Apology passage, he takes as an indication of approval for his
    actions, and no doubt he will be doing so here – so that they will
    actually, in his case, be signalling their wish for him to die).

24. *this kind of service*: Yet another echo of Socrates' way of describ-
    ing his own situation (his own 'service', or slavery, to the gods).

25. *let me try to make ... at the trial*: That is, on the specific 'charge'
    in question now, of being too ready to abandon his friends, and
    his masters, the gods. The effect of this sentence of Socrates' is to
    make a direct and specific connection between the argument or
    arguments he is about to put forward and the concluding page or
    so of the *Apology*, where he mused on what might lie in store
    for him after his death.

26. *dead men better than those to be found up here*: The remark
    might be aimed especially at the jury at his trial. In any case Soc-
    rates will immediately soften his claim about the quality of the
    humans he'll meet even in Hades.

27. *if I insist on anything of this sort*: I.e., presumably, anything to
    do with what happens to humans after death.

28. *so it's long been said, at any rate*: If anything of the sort had
    'long' been said, it would have been in the context of mystery
    religion; but there, in place of the opposition between 'good' and
    'bad', we would be more likely to find one between those who
    had and those who had not been initiated into the relevant rites
    (see *Phaedo* 69c–d). What the present passage represents is a mix
    that will become altogether familiar in later parts of the *Phaedo*,

between distinctively Socratic-Platonic ideas (see, e.g, *Apology* 41d: 'there is nothing bad that can happen to a good man whether in life or after he has died, nor are his affairs neglected by the gods') and ideas drawn from religious practices. See General Introduction, §2, and Introduction to *Phaedo* above.

29. *our countrymen*: I.e., in Thebes, or Boeotia generally, a region generally thought of by Athenians as uncultured (and by Simmias, evidently, as a philosophical desert).

30. *we think of it*: 'We' here can be understood quite generally; even 'ordinary people' would have been likely to think the same. The question which will be raised later will be the different one, about what happens to the soul *after* its separation from the body. See General Introduction, §6.

31. *cloaks*: A 'cloak' here (*himation*) is a large, single piece of cloth thrown over the shoulder, wrapped around the body and reaching to the ground.

32. *the actual business of acquiring wisdom*: I.e., the thing that is the philosopher's real business.

33. *any aspect of things*: Or 'any of the things that are' (*ti tôn ontôn*). The reference of the phrase 'the things that are' (*ta onta*) in Plato will frequently be to the special set of entities called 'forms', each of which is, roughly speaking, the *essence* of whatever it may be: goodness, say, or justice (see General Introduction, §4). But it would probably be misleading actually to translate the phrase in this way in the present context. For the moment, Socrates is in the process of arguing for the more general point that in order to understand anything – goodness, justice, or whatever it may be – we have to understand it 'by itself', rather than as we see it, or think we see it, exemplified in the world around us; and, for now, 'the things that are' may reasonably be taken as 'the things that exist', which will include ordinary things as well as 'forms'. But later on (beginning at 75d) such phrases will be recognized as having a more specialized, semi-technical use; see note 70 below.

34. *what things really are*: Or 'what is' (*to on*; see preceding note).

35. *something that's just and nothing but just*: I.e., the sort of thing we are talking about when we talk about justice 'in the abstract' – though for Plato things like justice will be anything but abstract entities.

36. *without ... dragging in any of the other senses to accompany his reasoning*: As we shall discover later on, this is evidently not intended to rule out some different kind of role for the senses in the search for truth (i.e., other than 'in the company of' reason).

37. *each aspect of things*: Or 'each of the things that are'. See note 33 above.

38. *how things really are*: Or 'what is' (*to on*, as in 65c).

39. *those who are genuinely philosophers*: I.e., those who are genuinely *philo-sophoi*, 'lovers of wisdom (*sophia*)' (see 66e).

40. *not letting it infect us with the kind of thing it is*: For a more complete working-out of this idea, see 83c–e.

41. *everything unalloyed*: I.e., all things as understood or grasped 'by themselves' (66e). For the idea of grasping 'everything unalloyed' or pure, see further 109a–111c.

42. *a freeing and parting of soul from body*: Contrast Socrates' earlier definition of death at 64c (merely as a neutral *separation* of the two things, soul and body).

43. *human darlings*: I.e., beloved boys (*paidika*).

44. *a lover of wisdom*: I.e., *philosophos*, (a) philosopher (see note 39 above).

45. *the same person will also be a lover of money and a lover of honour*: In the *Republic* too (see especially 580d–581c) Plato has Socrates divide the whole of humanity into lovers of wisdom, honour and money; in the *Phaedo* itself, those who 'love the body' have already been identified, implicitly, with lovers of money (66c–d), but 'honour', if identified with power and office, will be hardly less a distraction from the life of the mind than money is.

46. *those in the state we've described*: I.e., 'lovers of wisdom'.

47. *moderation*: The Greek term (*sôphrosunê*) has traditionally been rendered as 'temperance', because of its connection with self-control, i.e., control of one's desires and passions. However 'temperance' has now largely fallen out of ordinary English usage – and also fails to convey the further, and fundamental, connection of *sôphrosunê* with 'sound-mindedness'. 'Moderation' fares better than 'temperance', at least on the former of these two grounds, 'self-control' being ruled out by the fact that in *Socrates*' 'philosophical' version of *sôphrosunê* there will actually be no 'self' – no desires, at any rate – to be controlled.

48. *one's desires*: I.e., plainly, in this context, the desires 'of the body'.

49. *loving wisdom*: Or 'in philosophy'.

50. *virtue*: Or 'excellence' (*aretê*) – but it is some of the traditional 'virtues' that Socrates and Simmias have just been discussing.

51. *when they said ... using riddles to hint at the truth*: The reference here is to what generally goes under the heading of 'Orphic' teaching.

Plato's Socrates is noticeably dismissive of such teaching in its original context (see *Republic* 363d). Towards the end of the *Phaedo*
Socrates will expand on his interpretation here of Orphic 'truth', in
his description of the geography of Hades: see 109a–114c.

52. *the thyrsus*: The emblem of Dionysiac worshippers (the 'Bacchoi':
the Greek has 'few that are Bacchoi', i.e. genuine followers of
Bacchus/Dionysus).

53. *dispersed like breath or smoke*: Cebes here refers to the kind of
view reflected in Homer: see especially *Iliad* 23.100–101, with
16.856 and 22.362.

54. *and that it has some capacity for wisdom*: It is another essential
feature of the insubstantial 'soul' that survives the body in Homer
that it is mindless; see *Iliad* 23.103–4. In case there is any doubt that
Plato had these lines in mind (and the ones referred to in the previous note), he has Socrates quote them verbatim at *Republic* III,
386d–387a.

55. *talk these things through*: Or 'go through the story' (*diamuthol-
ogein*) – an expression that Plato can use even to describe
stretches of argument.

56. *I certainly don't think . . . don't concern me*: See *Apology* 19b–d,
on Aristophanes' lies about Socrates.

57. *there's an ancient doctrine . . . out of the dead*: The 'ancient doctrine' in question is usually associated with Pythagoras and his
followers, and with Empedocles (himself a 'Pythagorean', in a
broad sense, though hardly a 'follower' of anybody).

58. *even if we don't always have names for them*: I.e., presumably,
names for the processes.

59. *it must indeed be like that*: Whatever we may conclude about the
strength of Socrates' argument here for the survival of the soul,
the theory of change on which it is based is in itself an interesting
one; Socrates goes out of his way to stress that it is intended as a
quite general theory (70d–e).

60. *Endymion*: Endymion was loved by Selene, the moon, and
granted eternal sleep as an alternative to death.

61. *what Anaxagoras describes . . . 'All things together'*: For Anaxagoras, see *Apology* 26d. 'All things together' is Anaxagoras'
description of the state of things in the cosmos before Mind
started the process of the creation of the present order.

62. *recollecting*: Or 'being reminded' (*anamimnêiskesthai*, the Greek
term here, in fact, combines both meanings). What Cebes is
introducing is what has come to be known as Plato's 'theory of
recollection'.

63. *deathless*: Or 'immortal' (*athanatos*). The two English terms are essentially synonymous; but 'immortality' perhaps carries more connotations than 'deathless', and more than the argument in the *Phaedo* may have justified at this point (or at various other points later on, where 'deathless' will be preferred to 'immortal').

64. *There's one quite beautiful argument ... how things are*: Cebes has here given what looks much like a summary of the 'demonstration' of the true nature of learning (i.e., as 'recollection') in the *Meno*: see *Meno* 81e–86b.

65. *if, on seeing something ... came to have in mind*: So 'recollection', in this context, will always be a matter of being reminded of something by something else (see note 62 above); the 'theory of (learning as) recollection' might itself more helpfully be labelled the 'theory of being-reminded'.

66. *deficient at all in respect of its likeness to the thing he's recollected*: At least, perhaps, to the extent of seeing that the first thing *isn't* the second one, because it's there while the second one isn't.

67. *are we to say that something of the sort exists?*: Or 'are we to say that this is something?' The question is whether there is such a thing as equality, over and above or besides things like sticks and stones that are equal (have the property of being equal). This is the kind of entity to which Socrates will shortly attach the title of 'form' – but which he is introducing gradually, and in a series of steps, no doubt because of the metaphysical commitments that it involves.

68. *the equals by themselves*: These, here, are (any) two equal things thought of just as equal and nothing else. That carries no implications for the way he proposes to understand 'equality' (see the preceding note); it is merely a way of introducing his real question, about the difference between equality itself and equal sticks, stones, etc., and making it more transparent.

69. *those other equals*: I.e., equal things like sticks or stones.

70. *what is*: I.e., presumably (given how we have got to this point) 'what is beautiful (sc. and only beautiful), good (and only good)', and so on. 'What is', expressed as a noun, will be *to on* (plural *ta onta*) – a phrase which was first introduced, in the *Phaedo*, back at 65c, but which now acquires a more specialized sense (cf. note 33 above). (The expression *to on* is actually juxtaposed with *ho esti* at 78d, perhaps for the very purpose of indicating the interchangeable nature of the two phrases.)

71. *those pieces of knowledge*: Literally, 'those knowledges' – the plural taking us back to things like lyres, cloaks, and the owners, our knowledge of each of which, it was established, would be distinct (73d; cf. Simmias at 76d). The kind of knowledge involved in these more ordinary cases will presumably need to be distinguished from the kind that Socrates will shortly introduce in relation to the beautiful, the good, and so on: knowledge that implies the ability to *give an account of* the thing known (76b).

72. *all the things of that kind that there are*: More literally, 'all such being'.

73. *So this is where we end up . . . hold either*: So now significant metaphysical commitments *are* being made: there must be things like the beautiful itself, the good itself, and the equal itself, to which we can 'refer' – and so compare – good things, beautiful things, equal things, and so on; the kinds of thing that we will find these ordinary good, beautiful, and equal things 'falling short of' (as particular equals 'fall short of' equality: 74c). They must also exist in such a way as to be accessible to souls before they are born into the bodies they are in now. Quite how souls came to have knowledge of them, Socrates does not say and will not say; however, in the next part of the discussion he will give us some further general characteristics of the entities in question ('forms', as he will call them).

74. *my own view is that our proof is good enough*: Socrates' own position was more cautious, insofar as he treated the conclusion about the soul as dependent on the existence of the beautiful, the good, etc., and treated *that* as a hypothesis – as he will continue to do (see, e.g., 107b).

75. *after it dies*: Here 'dying' will emphatically not imply perishing; we need to recall here the definition of death as the separation of soul from body (64c).

76. *perhaps there's a child in us, all the same, that has fears like that*: Cebes perhaps responds here with a joke of his own: if our souls are to be reborn, into new bodies, won't there be a potential baby in all of us?

77. *to be sung to . . . charming it out of him*: The sort of 'incantation' that Socrates is likely to have in mind here is of a strange sort, i.e., rational argument (as illustrated in the surrounding context, here in the *Phaedo*); for the idea, see especially *Charmides* 157a.

78. *there's nothing you could better spend your money on*: If the reference here is to paying money to professional teachers (like Evenus: 60d), the suggestion is hardly serious; hence Socrates' next proposal.

79. *to do what's needed*: I.e., finding the 'charms' required. 'You' presumably refers not just to Cebes and Simmias but to Socrates' friends in general.

80. *that set of things ... our answers*: 'That set of things': or 'that being'; but 'being' (*ousia*) is probably here a collective noun, as at 76d. 'Of whose essence': or 'of whose being' (*tou einai*). 'As we question each other and offer our answers': i.e., in the kind of 'dialectical' exchange Socrates has with Euthyphro in the *Euthyphro* on the nature of piety – or, better, the kind he might have on the same subject with someone like Cebes, more philosophically adept than Euthyphro.

81. *each 'what is' by itself, which just is whatever it is*: See 75d. In fact, what is offered here in the translation is a considerable over-translation: Socrates himself merely juxtaposes the two phrases he uses for 'what is' (*ho esti* and *to on*). On this juxtaposition, see note 70 above.

82. *in contact with things that are themselves unchanging*: The 'contact' in this case will be metaphorical.

83. *resembles the divine*: I.e., resembles the immortal (since the gods are 'the immortals').

84. *the sort of thing that is naturally subject and slave*: As, e.g., Socrates is himself the 'slave' of the god or gods?

85. *mindless*: Also 'not the object of intellect' (*anoêtos*).

86. *when a person dies ... age that that implies*: One might perhaps have expected an older, already decrepit body to decay more quickly than a young one; Plato either doesn't know that this isn't in fact the case, or else he is choosing to pretend – to have Socrates to pretend – ignorance (perhaps as a light way of drawing attention back to his own case: old, ugly . . .?).

87. *to the true place of Hades*: There is a pun in the Greek on *aidês*, 'unseen', and *Haidês*, 'Hades', in the form of the phrase *eis Haidou*, i.e., 'to (the place of) Hades' – where 'Hades' is now the god who lives in the place often itself called by the same name; hence 'to the presence of the good, wise god', given that Socrates has already expressed his conviction that on death he himself will go to join 'wise and good gods' (63b). This (place) Hades will itself be 'unseen' ('a second place of the same sort') just because it is '*Ha(i)dês*' (i.e., *aidês*); the *first* such place will have been the one that the soul 'takes itself off to' in life, which itself was populated with those special items, themselves unseen, such as the beautiful itself, the good itself, and so on. But that first place was purely a metaphorical one, as the 'taking off' was itself

metaphorical; hence the fact that Socrates calls the second place the 'true' (place of) Hades. We should probably notice that he doesn't quite say here, as he has every opportunity to say, that those same special objects – what he will later call the 'forms' – are actually in the 'true' Hades (as well as in the imaginary one); death, it seems, won't automatically take our souls to where the 'forms' are. This is consistent with what Socrates typically says about such things, outside the context of myth, namely that they are not actually the sort of thing to *have* a location in the first place; at the same time he is clearly more than flirting with the general idea that getting away from ('out of') the body will increase our chances of accessing the truth – and who would not want the *truth* about things?

88. *out of fear of Hades and the unseen*: That pun again on *Ha(i)dês/ aidês* (see preceding note).

89. *weren't on their guard . . . a similar sort*: 'Weren't on their guard': i.e., against such behaviour becoming a habit. 'The kinds': or 'the species' (*genê*, 'families').

90. *where every other type of soul will go . . . resemble*: Will there then be a question whether any particular soul is actually still that of a human, or rather that of some kind of animal, even in life?

91. *the common, civic virtue*: See 68c–69c.

92. *decent men are born from them*: It would surely be out of tune with Socrates' general message if some people were actually born 'decent' or respectable, since that would suggest that they would be born already with some kind of 'virtue', even without 'habit and practice'. Should we suppose a the presence of another pun – with a covert reference to Herodotus, *Histories* 2.32, where men 'of a decent size' (*metrioi*, as here) are contrasted with pygmies?

93. *to arrive at that destination*: I.e., by becoming pure soul, without admixture of body (see 114c). Socrates is presumably not seriously suggesting that humans (human souls) may become gods; they will rather belong to a kind which, like the gods, consists of free-floating souls – just as tyrants become wolves *or* hawks *or . . .*

94. *not permitted*: See 61c, with note 12.

95. *it's forced to investigate things*: E.g., equality, beauty, goodness (*ta onta* again: see notes 33 and 70 above).

96. *apprehends . . . what each thing . . . is*: Or 'apprehends . . . whichever it may be of the things that are (*ta onta*) . . .' (see preceding note).

97. *what the soul sees . . . is . . . unseen*: The paradox in effect takes us back to that recurrent pun on the name 'Hades': see notes 87 and 88 above.

98. *causes it to be of the same kind as the body*: Or 'makes it bodily', i.e., corporeal; but this is, presumably, no more to be taken literally than is the idea that the body 'says', or believes, anything.

99. *the divine, the pure, and the uniform*: With which, as Socrates has said, it is naturally akin, despite what it has become.

100. *not for the reasons ordinary people are*: See 82a–c, with 68c–69c – to which both 82a–c and the present passage have now given a specific spin. Philosophers will be truly 'orderly' ('moderate'), courageous, and so on as a by-product of their philosophical quest, and of their understanding of where true value lies (i.e., in finding the truth).

101. *Penelope*: Wife of Odysseus, who promised her suitors – who, like her, supposed that her husband was dead – that she would choose between them when she had finished her weaving. She then managed to delay having to make the choice by unpicking by night what she had woven during the day.

102. *not merely the subject of belief*: I.e., not merely believed to be true; the contrast is with the state of non-philosophers, who think true 'whatever the body . . . says is so' (83d).

103. *Surely you don't think . . . what we said?*: As the next sentence surely confirms, Socrates is here being ironic; and in fact he has himself presented his last argument as anything but conclusive. Note especially 80b '[soul is] absolutely indissoluble, *or something close to that*', and the curiously roundabout, and qualified, manner in which he expressed himself in 84b: 'there's no danger that *[the truly philosophical] sort of soul will be afraid*' that it'll be blown apart – that is, one that has been brought up, and has behaved, as Socrates has suggested such a soul will. In other words, its convictions about 'Hades', which themselves remain more than a little murky, will be dependent on a soul's way of life, and its view of how the world is constituted; and a non-philosopher, or someone still to make a choice between doing philosophy or not, might well need more argument before going down the philosophical route and giving up his 'childish' fears about death, especially if that also means giving up the pleasures – or what 'ordinary people' call the pleasures – of life.

104. *and more loudly*: I retain here the manuscript reading *malista*; the editors of the new Oxford text prefer an emendation which would give us 'more *beautifully*'. The key issue is, perhaps, about

how Socrates would here want to describe his own performance, insofar as he is here describing that as much as the swans'. (Would he want to describe his own performance as 'beautiful'? Perhaps; perhaps not.)

105. *nightingale . . . swallow . . . hoopoe*: A reference to the story of Philomela, Procne and Tereus, who turned into birds after a series of violent events.

106. *sacred to the same god*: See 60c–61b, together with Socrates' description of his service or slavery to Apollo, god of Delphi, in the *Apology*.

107. *eleven Athenian men*: See 59e and note 6 above ('the Eleven').

108. *we*: 'We' is either Simmias on his own or Simmias and other members of Socrates' circle or, as some interpreters have held, 'we Pythagoreans'. But against the third option, see Introduction to *Phaedo* above.

109. *in what we call death*: Even on Simmias' account, 'perishing' will be different from 'death' – that is, for the body.

110. *the person hasn't actually perished but exists intact somewhere*: I.e., the whole person, consisting of both body and soul.

111. *the weaver will have worn out . . . less robust than a cloak*: That is, a person can still be *more* robust than a cloak even if, like cloaks, a person actually perishes.

112. *to a person putting forward the case you're proposing*: Omitting a word (*ê*) from the transmitted text, as proposed by some editors (but not those of the Oxford text). Cebes is still trying – and presumably failing – to be tactful, by not attacking Socrates too directly.

113. *you'll be cutting off this beautiful hair of yours*: I.e., in grief, according to custom.

114. *the Argives*: The oath of the men of Argos related to a particularly heavy defeat by, and loss of territory to, the Spartans.

115. *not even Heracles could fight alone against two . . . so long as the light lasts*: The 'two' are the monstrous Hydra and a giant crab; Heracles called on Iolaus' help to defeat them. 'So long as the light lasts': darkness would mean fighting had to be suspended – and nightfall will also bring Socrates' death.

116. *arguments aren't like human beings in that respect*: The idea that really bad human beings are quite a rare phenomenon is consistent with Socratic intellectualism (see General Introduction, §2). People go wrong not because they are *naturally* bad, but because their reasoning is faulty; and Socrates seems generally unwilling to give up reasoning with anyone.

117. *spent all his time on constructing opposing arguments*: I.e., on the special art of 'antilogic', the essence of which consisted in the ability to lead a respondent who starts with one position, on anything whatever, into asserting the opposite of that position, the result being – since the second position would be as vulnerable to counter-argument as the first – to make everything (whatever) equally uncertain. Socrates is not just talking here about expert practitioners of 'antilogic', but also – and perhaps particularly – about those who have been drawn into studying it.

118. *Everything there is . . . period of time*: The chief reference here is to the 'flux' theory of Heraclitus, but Protagoras' relativism is also in the frame (see *Theaetetus* 152–60). The Euripus is the narrow strait between the island of Euboea and mainland Greece.

119. *I'm presently in danger . . . attitude towards it*: See *Theaetetus* 167e–168a. Socrates may well particularly have in mind here the 'eristics' – people like the brothers Euthydemus and Dionysodorus, as portrayed in the *Euthydemus*, whose only concern is to appear to the audience to win the argument, by any means available. There is a clear overlap between 'eristics' and 'antilogicians' (for which see note 117 above), but the former are perhaps mere opportunists, while the latter are genuine theorists, or provide material that serious theorists like Protagoras can use.

120. *see how determined I am to get the advantage*: I.e., because either way he will actually 'win'.

121. *the set of things*: Or 'that being' (= 'those beings': *ousia*), as, e.g., at 78d. 'The name "what is"' was originally introduced in 75d.

122. That *hypothesis*: I.e., presumably, 'that the set of things that bears the name "what is" exists by itself'.

123. *if it's been tuned more . . . a lesser one*: It is not clear that Socrates has in mind more than one set of circumstances here, namely when a (multi-)stringed instrument is tuned more or less successfully; but just possibly 'tuned more' may refer to the tuning of particular strings, 'tuned to a greater extent' to the tuning of a larger number of strings.

124. *bodily events*: Or, perhaps, 'the bodily passions' (*pathê*); but since Socrates immediately goes on to mention 'heat' (i.e. getting too hot?), he is evidently casting his net more widely.

125. *He struck his chest . . . you have endured*: Homer, *Odyssey* 20.17–18.

126. *we wouldn't be in agreement . . . or with ourselves*: The second consideration – 'agreement with ourselves' – is presumably the more important for Socrates (he and Simmias have agreed that

the attunement theory is incompatible with a number of other things they both accept).

127. *Cadmus*: 'Attunement' in the preceding argument translated the Greek *harmonia* (for which 'harmony' would be an inappropriate translation); Harmonia was the wife of Cadmus, mythical founder of Simmias' and Cebes' home city of Thebes.

128. *labours its way*: I.e., because it is perpetually 'weaving' new bodies.

129. *the reason behind coming-into-being and perishing in general*: Socrates will be talking about more than mere *causes*; the subject will be explanation in a rather broader sense.

130. *the next step . . . your own position*: I.e., in so far as Cebes' own position includes an implicit account of coming-to-be and ceasing-to-be in the world? The main point of Socrates' account, however, will be that the world somehow *makes sense* – whereas Cebes' implicates even soul and mind itself in a purely mechanical process of change.

131. *as some people used to say*: The reference may be to Archelaus of Athens.

132. *Is it blood that we think with, or air, or fire?*: That we think with our blood was Empedocles' idea; air and fire were central to the accounts of the cosmos, and of its animal inhabitants, given respectively by Diogenes of Apollonia and by Heraclitus.

133. *Or is it none of these . . . knowledge comes about?*: Contrast the rather different account of the source of knowledge that Socrates has offered, which gives a much reduced role to the senses.

134. *whenever flesh was added to flesh . . . big one*: All of this looks remarkably like the kind of thing that might have been got from Anaxagoras' book – which Socrates will actually only introduce in 97b–c. But then he was already quoting from Anaxagoras back in 72c.

135. *one and the same knowledge*: I.e., knowledge of what's good must bring with it knowledge of its opposite. Socrates perhaps introduces this point to correct the impression, which he might otherwise be giving, that he thinks that mind actually succeeds in ordering *everything* for the best. We know, for example, that he thinks there are bad, that is, misguided, people in the world: see 90a–b, with note 116 above.

136. *the other stars*: The sun, the moon and the other planets (apart from earth in the centre) are themselves 'stars', even if 'wandering' ones (*planêtai*).

137. *grabbing the books . . . what was worse*: For Anaxagoras' books, see already *Apology* 26d–e.

138. *makes no use of his mind ... bizarre things instead*: 'Makes no use of his mind': i.e., either his own mind or his cosmic Mind. 'And doesn't charge it with any part ... citing ...': there is a further pun in the Greek here, on *aitia* = 'reason' and *epaitiasthai* (*aitian*) = 'charge' (before a court).

139. *by the Dog ... what appeared best to them*: For the oath, see *Apology* 22a. 'Well, I think they would': if his bones and sinews were operating independently of his mind, he mightn't know what they were up to. 'Carried along by an appearance of what was best': i.e., that it would be best for them to save their own skin.

140. *ordinary people ... grope around in the dark*: 'Ordinary people' are, as usual, non-philosophers. By implication Anaxagoras (it's his book or books, after all, from which the present discussion started) is no different from the non-philosophical many – nor are whichever other students of 'natural philosophy' are about to be alluded to. 'As they grope around in the dark': apparently we're to imagine a game of blind man's buff, where the participants have to guess the name of the person they catch.

141. *they'll discover an Atlas ... hold everything together*: The implication presumably is that these people will still need to add in an Atlas (the Titan in myth who holds up the heavens on his shoulders), to supplement their mechanical account; by contrast, Socrates claims, his own preferred 'Atlas', i.e., his preferred kind of explanation, already has all the power needed to 'hold things together'.

142. *that wasn't offered to me*: I.e., by Anaxagoras or any of the other materialists referred to.

143. *'second sailing'*: The sense of this phrase has been much discussed: either, as in the translation given, it is a metaphor for second best (as when a ship's captain resorts to using oars in place of sails – an ancient explanation), or else it indicates little more than a second attempt, perhaps by a different route.

144. *I feared my soul could be completely blinded*: See 96c.

145. *What I decided ... world in them*: Back in 85c–d, Simmias described what looked like a similar position, but there is rather more behind Socrates' version (e.g., his disappointing encounter with Anaxagoras); and in fact Simmias went on to admit, at 92c–d, that the kind of statement he himself was relying on, i.e., soul as attunement, wasn't so plausible after all. 'Reasoned accounts' is something of an over-translation of the plain Greek term *logoi* here; other possibilities might be a plain 'statements'

('things said'), or else 'theories'. But, as will become clear, whatever it is that Socrates has in mind has close connections with his typical methods, which are above all concerned with reasoning things out – and in particular, giving 'reasoned accounts' of them (which neither just 'statements' nor 'theories' will succeed in bringing out).

146. *someone who examines things . . . in front of us*: There is probably an implicit reference here to one of the possible ways of describing the relationship between 'things in themselves' ('forms') and the particulars that 'share' in them, i.e., as a relationship between original and image. This is not included in the short list of such descriptions Socrates will soon give (in 100d), but see, e.g., *Phaedrus* 250b, *Republic* 520c, *Timaeus* 48e–49a.

147. *I posit . . . as untrue whatever is not in tune with it*: As Simmias singularly failed to do with his soul-as-attunement hypothesis (see especially 92c).

148. *in the preceding discussion*: That is, since 65d.

149. *show you the reason for things and establish that the soul is something immortal*: The immediate connection between the two subjects (the 'reason' for things, and the immortality of the soul) presumably lies in Socrates' original promise (95e–96a) of an 'investigation of the reason behind coming-into-being *and perishing* in general'.

150. *all those other 'reasons' . . . added to it*: 'All those other "reasons" confuse me': see 96a–97b. 'That other beautiful thing': i.e., the beautiful itself, (what will soon be labelled) the 'form'. 'Or in whatever way or manner it has come to be added to it': reading *prosgenomenou* instead of *proagoreuomenê* (as printed in the Oxford text), for the reasons given in my 1993 commentary. The idea that 'the beautiful' has come to be 'added' to particular beautiful things may come as something of a surprise, given the way Socrates has hitherto emphasized that such things exist 'alone and by themselves'; but if the beautiful can be 'present' in beautiful things, or 'in association' with them, then it is already clear that it must be *both* an independently existing entity *and* – somehow – in the many beautiful particulars. The question is also raised, but by no means definitively answered, in the *Parmenides*. But meanwhile things like 'bigness in us', and 'smallness in us', will play an important role in the argument that Socrates is now launching: an argument that he hopes will assure us of the permanent survival of the soul.

151. *by virtue of his head*: See 96e.

152. *Cebes laughed and said, 'Yes it would!'*: Cebes is probably laughing at Socrates' joking evocation of monsters rather than laughing off the objections; Socrates is clearly serious about these, for
reasons that will become apparent.

153. *having come to share in the appropriate essence . . . share in*: For
this talk of 'essence', see 65d, 78d.

154. *As for you . . . answer accordingly*: The present sentence begins
one of the most controversial and difficult short passages in the
Phaedo (even if Simmias and Cebes, and Echecrates, claim to
understand it at once: 102a), and considerable annotation seems
to be required – not least to place the various parts of the passage
in the context of the exchanges that have preceded it. In order to
avoid undue disturbance to the flow of the text, the notes – which
amount to a mini-commentary – are gathered together at the end
of the passage, at 102a.

155. *As for you . . . the way I describe*: 'The safety that's to be found
in the hypothesis': i.e., the particular hypothesis that Socrates
introduced as 'safest' at 100d–e. 'If someone held on to the
hypothesis itself': i.e., on the interpretation adopted here, if
someone picked up the hypothesis and treated it as something
other than a hypothesis (as Simmias himself did with the soul-as-
harmony theory?). The person 'holding on' to the hypothesis in
this case might perhaps be an opponent or sceptic as much as a
supporter; in any case, as the next sentence shows, it will be
someone who is asking questions prematurely. 'To see if they
were in tune with each other, or out of tune': as were the 'consequences' of the natural scientists' theories in 96a–97b; Simmias'
theory was 'discordant' in a different way. 'Whichever appeared
best of those above the first one': 'above', because more explanatory? A possible example might be the sort of account of the
relationship between 'forms' and particulars that Socrates
declined to give in 100d. 'Until you arrived at something sufficient for the purpose': i.e., presumably, something that provided
the kind of reasoned account that was being asked for. 'The
antilogicians': on these see note 117 above. 'By talking about
your starting-point and its consequences as if there were no
difference between them': whatever it is, exactly, that Socrates
has in mind here, it will be true in any case that the 'antilogicians' have no stable starting-points – and certainly no 'safe'
ones like his own. 'To stir everything together': there is an echo
here of that phrase of Anaxagoras' quoted by Socrates back
in 72c, a phrase with which Anaxagoras' cosmology evidently

began (*homou panta chrêmata ên*: '[in the beginning] all things were together'). This can hardly be accidental; it is in any case part of Socrates' point that the consequences of materialist science, and of 'antilogic', as Socrates has described them, are hard to tell apart.

156. *extraordinary clarity*: There is not the slightest sign of irony on Echecrates' part here (any more than there is in Simmias' and Cebes' response); evidently Plato did not think the preceding passage as difficult as his modern interpreters have found it.

157. *each of the forms exists*: This is the first time that the term 'form' has been used in the *Phaedo*, even if the things it is being used to refer to – those special 'things in themselves', representing the 'essence' of each kind of thing – have long since been at or near the centre of attention.

158. *talking like a handbook*: I.e., using the dry, technical language of a handbook (though actually his own language will turn out to be slightly more colourful, and metaphorical, than most handbook-writers would allow themselves to be).

159. *too much for bigness, being what it is*: This bigness will, it seems, just be a kind of miniature replica of 'bigness itself', which is something that's big and nothing else (not something that's big by way of extension, just what bigness is, the 'essence' of bigness).

160. *its counterpart in nature*: I.e., clearly, the 'form', as it exists independently (of 'us' or anything else).

161. *three*: Either the form, threeness, or something 'sharing in' it, i.e., a particular group of three things viewed just as such; or, more probably, both (cf. note 163 below).

162. *whichever form it is*: Here the Greek term is *idea*, Plato's second semi-technical term for 'form', the other being *eidos*.

163. *the opposite forms*: 'Forms' here – Socrates switches back to the term *eidos* – are evidently the Platonic forms as they are *in* things; a form itself, Socrates has said, is that by virtue of which a particular thing comes to have the corresponding property, or 'character' (*idea, morphê*: see immediately below) – which, however, can also be thought of as the form 'in us', as, e.g., bigness is in Phaedo.

164. *whatever occupies them*: I.e., whatever form (Socrates continues with his military metaphor).

165. *whatever the character of three . . . odd as well*: 'Whatever': i.e., whatever group of things. 'The character of three': or 'the form (*idea*) of three', i.e., 'in us'; but this *is* 'the character of three' (see note 163 above).

166. *the character opposite . . . will never come to belong to the sort of thing in question*: I.e., to something 'occupied by' three, and so by oddness too. 'The one that has this effect': in the case in question, as Socrates will immediately confirm, this will be the odd – which is, after all, that 'by virtue of which' anything odd will be odd. ('The character opposite to the [character] . . .': Socrates uses first *idea*, then *morphê*. See note 163 above.)

167. *will never come to belong to the three*: I.e., it will never be 'let in to', 'admitted to', the three.

168. *any more than the half-as-much-again . . . character of the whole*: I here borrow David Gallop's interpretation of a puzzling and perhaps corrupt part of the text (more literally: 'Nor again will one-and-a-half, and the rest of that series, the halves . . .').

169. *don't answer me by giving me back whatever it is I'm asking you about*: That is, 'if I ask why something is beautiful, don't say "by virtue of the beautiful, of course!"' – as Socrates had previously insisted, and would no doubt still be insisting if he didn't need a rather different kind of account of things for the purposes of the present argument. He is very careful to avoid even suggesting that the new kind of answers will be *explanatory*, as well he might be, since they look dangerously like the sorts of explanations ('reasons') he castigated Anaxagoras and others for giving.

170. *a cleverer answer*: It is at the least extremely rare for Socrates to use the adjective he employs here ('clever': *kompsos*) in a genuinely positive sense; and the present context appears to be no exception to this general rule. See the preceding note.

171. *oneness*: I.e., in the presence of the extra unit that will distinguish an odd from an even number.

172. *deathless*: I.e., 'un-dead', 'immortal' (*a-thanatos*, where the *a-* is alpha privative, the equivalent of English 'un-', and *thanatos* is 'death' or, in the present context, the property of being dead – 'deadness'). See note 63 above.

173. *if the immortal is also imperishable*: Only living things can die – or not die; and what other way will living things have of perishing, except dying? Socrates is not here justifying the move from 'immortal' to 'imperishable' so much as presupposing it (for the moment; his next step will be to check with Cebes that he's happy about it), and spelling out what the immortality/imperishability of soul entails for any soul when death 'advances on' it.

174. *won't let death in*: I.e., won't let in deadness.

175. *at the onset of the even*: As when an odd number is doubled (see 105a).

176. *the gods*: Socrates uses the singular; Cebes' response has the plural 'gods'; both are talking about the same thing – the gods (plural). See also 61c, 62c, *Apology* 19a and elsewhere.

177. *immortal*: I.e., again, in terms of the preceding argument, 'un-dead', or deathless.

178. *there in Hades after all*: About this Hades, Socrates will shortly have a great deal more to say.

179. *if you analyse them*: The primary reference here will presumably be to what Socrates said in 99d–101e; see especially 101d–e, and his recommendations there about what one should do if required to 'give an account' of a hypothesis.

180. *except by becoming as good and wise as possible*: The implication plainly is that all of us will suffer, unless we become as wise and good as we can; since according to Socrates most of us don't pay much attention to such things, there will on his account be a lot of (unnecessary) suffering in the world. That squares with the fact that, on his account, most souls will go after death to the dismal shores of Lake Acheron, to undergo 'purification' before entering bodies again (113a–e).

181. *taking nothing with it . . . person who has died*: See 81d. 'The person who has died' is now represented, of course, only by his or her soul.

182. *What they say . . . on their journey from here to there*: While the idea of a judgement of the dead is at least as old as Homer, the details of the picture Socrates will paint certainly owe as much to Plato as they do to tradition. See General Introduction, §§2 and 3. 'Each person's own divinity': i.e., his or her own *daimôn*. It is hard not to think, here, of Socrates' talk about the 'divinity' – his 'divine something' – that intervenes with him (*Apology* 31c–d, with *Euthyphro* 3b); evidently the divinities in charge of others are less effective – or else these others are just less receptive than he is. 'Tries to bring him': and evidently, in some cases, it takes some doing (108a–b; cf. 81c–e). 'With the guide whose job it is to lead them on their journey from here to there': traditionally this would have been Hermes Psychagogos, Leader of Souls; the vagueness of Socrates' phrasing reflects the fact that he is actually transferring the job from Hermes to each person's 'divinity'.

183. *Aeschylus' hero Telephus*: Few of Aeschylus' tragedies survived; Socrates here refers to one of the many lost.

184. *a simple road to Hades*: The 'road to Hades' here probably

includes both the one to the initial place of judgement and the one that leads – or the ones that lead – on from there.

185. *there would be no need of guides*: I.e., like Hermes – or Socrates' new leaders of souls (see note 182 above).

186. *When it has arrived . . . turns aside from it*: 'The common destination for all souls' is the first destination, the place of judgement, where they will be assigned new, and very different, further destinations. 'Other such acts that are in fact akin to these and belong to kindred souls': Socrates' somewhat mysterious phrasing here may hint at a non-standard view of what the most serious offences are. Just how radical Plato's Socrates is capable of being may be judged from the extraordinary proposal, in the *Republic*, that it is 'a lesser mistake involuntarily to become someone's killer than (sc. involuntarily) to deceive decent people in relation to things just and lawful' (*Republic* 451a5–7). Alternatively, and less interestingly (or additionally), Socrates is just delaying a longer description – which he will give in 113e–114a.

187. *the skill of a Glaucus*: Beautifully explained by David Sedley, following Konrad Gaiser, as a reference to the Glaucus identified by Herodotus (I.25) as the inventor of welding. Accepting this explanation means also accepting Sedley's extremely attractive interpretation of the description that follows here, according to which Socrates is providing a sketch of the sort of explanation he earlier said he was looking for but couldn't find: one that would show how 'what is good and binding truly does bind and hold things together' (99c).

188. *doesn't need either air or any other such physical necessity to stop it from falling*: See 99b–c.

189. *the complete uniformity, everywhere, of the heavens . . . where it is*: So the earth stays where it is as part of an ordered system, in which (so, perhaps, the subtext runs), everything is 'as it is best for it to be': see note 187 above.

190. *the next thing*: I.e., the next thing he's been convinced about. None of what follows, right to the end of his story, is his; he owes it all to 'someone' (108c, and then, for later parts, to what 'is said': 110b).

191. *the Phasis river and the Pillars of Heracles*: 'The Phasis river' is the modern Rion, flowing into the eastern Black Sea. 'The Pillars of Heracles' are the rocks marking either side of the Straits of Gibraltar.

192. *those other things*: I.e., water, mist and air.

193. *its stones*: I.e., even its harder parts; but Socrates will soon be talking specifically about 'precious' stones.

194. *on islands, close to the mainland*: Presumably Socrates' (or rather his source's) version of the Isles of the Blest.

195. *Their seasons are of a blend*: Perhaps of hot, cold, dry and wet.

196. *to see better . . . ether surpasses air*: The (relatively) greater wisdom of these blessed folk seems to be connected directly with the fact that they see better, hear better and so on, both because they are equipped with superior senses and because the mediums through which they see and hear are superior; presumably the superior quality of what they see and hear around them also has something to do with it. All of this may perhaps help to put Socrates' earlier criticisms of the reliability of the senses into perspective: it is not so much that there is something unreliable in principle with sense-perception as a source of understanding of the world around us; the problem lies rather with the senses we happen to have, the mediums through which we happen to have to use them, the quality of the objects which we happen to have available to us.

197. *just as they also see sun, moon and stars for what they are*: See *Apology* 26d–e.

198. *and this oscillation occurs . . . the following kind*: In the second half of this last sentence Socrates finally gives up telling his story in indirect speech ('[it's said] that . . .'), but in fact he must still be telling his 'story', on someone else's authority rather than his own.

199. *'Far, far away . . . under the earth'*: Iliad 8.14.

200. *each river*: I.e., each kind of river, whether of water, fire, or mud (or of a particular kind of mud: 111d).

201. *Opposite this, and flowing in the contrary direction, is Acheron*: Acheron, after all, is the river of the dead, while Oceanus traditionally encircles the world of the living.

202. *they are sent back again . . . new living creatures*: See 81e–82b.

203. *issues*: I.e., from Tartarus.

204. *it does not mix with its water*: Thus it is associated with Acheron, but distinct from it; it will be the destination of a special category of the dead.

205. *Cocytus*: I.e., the River of Wailing; Pyriphlegethon is the River of Blazing Fire.

206. *conveyed by his divine guide*: See 107d.

207. *those judged to have lived a middling kind of life*: Or, just possibly, 'those thought to have . . .' – but there is no other indication

that the judges in the underworld are capable of getting things wrong in the way that their human counterparts do.

208. *there they reside . . . benefits bestowed*: All, in any case, seem to require 'purification' (from their excessive attachment to the body?).

209. *cease from their suffering*: I.e., what they were suffering in Cocytus and Pyriphlegethon; hardly from suffering altogether, since Acheron itself is not at all a pleasant place to be. In Athenian law, it seems, killers at least were not subject to legal action if their victims forgave them before dying.

210. *But those judged . . . surface of the earth*: Presumably Socrates himself might expect to be judged one of these; and his language suggests that he at least hopes he might qualify for the even greater prize that he is about to describe, albeit rather sketchily. 'Freed from these regions here, within the earth': either from Acheron, etc., or from 'worlds' like ours within the hollows (which will, after all, themselves be 'within the earth'); or from both.

211. *given that the soul is clearly something immortal*: This might appear to suggest rather more confidence than the phrase he used at 107c ('if the soul really is immortal').

212. *the risk, after all, is a fine one*: I.e., because the possible consequences are so fine.

213. *Such are the charms . . . spinning out my story*: It is hard, here, not to think back to Socrates' previous reference to 'charms', or incantations (*epôidai*) at 77e–78a. At first sight, it looks as if what he was calling a kind of incantation here is just the 'myth' or story he has just related – in which case, as his death approaches, he will apparently no longer be quite so whole-hearted about his endorsement of the healing powers of reasoning: *arguments* were what he had in mind in the earlier context, and now he is recommending the use of mere *stories*. However his use of the expression 'long since' ('I've long since been spinning out my story') at least suggests the possibility that he intends here to include much more under 'my story' than the myth itself, perhaps the whole conversation of the *Phaedo*, or at least his whole 'defence', of which the myth is the final instalment. And after all, this 'myth' as he tells it is in most important respects continuous with earlier parts of the dialogue (nor in fact is it particularly long or 'spun out', at any rate by comparison with several other Platonic 'myths').

214. *waits thus prepared for the journey to Hades, whenever fate should summon him*: See the prohibition of suicide at 61d–62c.

215. *even if you don't presently agree with me about that*: I.e., because of your (misplaced) grief at my death. What exactly he expects them not to agree about, at least for now, is presumably that making themselves better and wiser people will please him, this being one of the things he himself has been trying to do, as well as pleasing them – because they're the ones directly benefited (as Socrates' children will benefit indirectly).

216. *even after having vehemently agreed with me ... many times over*: It's true – Simmias and Cebes, at least, have gone on assenting to Socrates' proposals about the importance of caring for themselves and their souls; but the question is whether they will actually do anything about it.

217. *some happiness or other of the blest*: A striking phrase in the Greek, derived from the more standard 'Isles of the Blest' (for which see 111a).

218. *speaking imprecisely ... also damages our souls*: I.e., presumably, by encouraging us to think in imprecise ways too.

219. *those women from his household arrived too*: This must refer primarily to Xanthippe (60a); the plural perhaps shows that she is accompanied by one or more female slaves (lamenting like Xanthippe?).

220. *the slave of the Eleven*: I.e., presumably, the prison guard of 59d–e.

221. *Farewell*: We should probably bear in mind the more literal meaning of the Greek (and of the English) here – 'be happy'.

222. *dying is something to be done in silence*: Usually it would be exactly the reverse, with plenty of noisy lamentation (of the sort provided, until Socrates cut it off, by 'the women of the household'). But Socrates, as we should know well enough by now, thinks death is no cause for lamentation – and hopes to be going off to join the company of gods, in which context 'words of good omen' (= saying nothing) might be rather more appropriate.

223. *Asclepius*: The god of healing.

224. *uncovered Socrates' face again, and his eyes were fixed*: According to Socrates, they will actually no longer be *his* eyes, if he is already dead. But the narrator Phaedo's point of view is not the same as Socrates', as his concluding remark to Echecrates will now confirm: 'This was the end of our companion.' (Were Socrates still there to respond, he might well have complained that Phaedo hadn't, after all, been listening.)

PENGUIN CLASSICS

HOMERIC HYMNS

'It is of you the poet sings ...
at the beginning and at the end
it is always of you'

Written by unknown poets in the sixth and seventh centuries BC, the thirty-three
Homeric Hymns were recited at festivals to honour the Olympian goddesses and
gods and to pray for divine favour or for victory in singing contests. They stand
now as works of great poetic force, full of grace and lyricism, and ranging in tone
from irony to solemnity, ebullience to grandeur. Recounting significant episodes
from mythology, such as the abduction of Persephone by Hades and Hermes' theft
of Apollo's cattle, the *Hymns* also provide fascinating insights into cults, rituals
and holy sanctuaries, giving us an intriguing view of the ancient Greek relationship
between humans and the divine.

This translation of the *Homeric Hymns* is new to Penguin Classics, providing a key text
for understanding ancient Greek mythology and religion. The introduction explores
their authorship, performance, literary qualities and influence on later writers.

'The purest expressions of ancient Greek religion we possess ... Jules Cashford is
attuned to the poetry of the Hymns' Nigel Spivey, University of Cambridge

A new translation by Jules Cashford with an introduction by Nicholas Richardson

PENGUIN CLASSICS

MEDEA AND OTHER PLAYS
EURIPIDES

Medea/Alcestis/The Children of Heracles/Hippolytus

'That proud, impassioned soul,
so ungovernable now that she has felt the sting of injustice'

Medea, in which a spurned woman takes revenge upon her lover by killing her
children, is one of the most shocking and horrific of all the Greek tragedies.
Dominating the play is Medea herself, a towering and powerful figure who
demonstrates Euripides' unusual willingness to give voice to a woman's case.
Alcestis, a tragicomedy, is based on a magical myth in which Death is overcome,
and *The Children of Heracles* examines the conflict between might and right,
while *Hippolytus* deals with self-destructive integrity and moral dilemmas. These
plays show Euripides transforming the awesome figures of Greek mythology into
recognizable, fallible human beings.

John Davie's accessible prose translation is accompanied by a general introduction
and individual prefaces to each play.

'John Davie's translations are outstanding … the tone throughout is refreshingly
modern yet dignified' William Allan, *Classical Review*

Previously published as *Alcestis and Other Plays*.

Translated by John Davie, with an introduction and notes by Richard Rutherford

PENGUIN CLASSICS

CONVERSATIONS OF SOCRATES
XENOPHON

Socrates' Defence/Memoirs of Socrates/The Estate-Manager/The Dinner-Party

'He seemed to me to be the perfect example of goodness and happiness'

After the execution of Socrates in 399 BC, a number of his followers wrote dialogues featuring him as the protagonist and, in so doing, transformed the great philosopher into a legendary figure. Xenophon's portrait is the only one other than Plato's to survive, and while it offers a very personal interpretation of Socratic thought, it also reveals much about the man and his philosophical views. In 'Socrates' Defence' Xenophon defends his mentor against charges of arrogance made at his trial, while the 'Memoirs of Socrates' also starts with an impassioned plea for the rehabilitation of a wronged reputation. Along with 'The Estate-Manager', a practical economic treatise, and 'The Dinner-Party', a sparkling exploration of love, Xenophon's dialogues offer fascinating insights into the Socratic world and into the intellectual atmosphere and daily life of ancient Greece.

Xenophon's complete Socratic works are translated in this volume. In his introduction, Robin Waterfield illuminates the significance of these four books, showing how perfectly they embody the founding principles of Socratic thought.

Translated by Hugh Tredennick and Robin Waterfield and edited with new material by Robin Waterfield

Penguin Classics

THE GREEK SOPHISTS

'In the case of wisdom, those who sell it to anyone who wants it are called sophists'

By mid-fifth century BC, Athens was governed by democratic rule and power turned upon the ability of the individual to command the attention of the other citizens, and to sway the crowds of the assembly. It was the Sophists who understood the art of rhetoric and the importance of being able to transform effective reasoning into persuasive public speaking. Their inquiries – into the gods, the origins of religion and whether virtue can be taught – laid the groundwork for the next generation of thinkers such as Plato and Aristotle.

Each chapter of *The Greek Sophists* is based around the work of one character: Gorgias, Prodicus, Protagoras and Antiphon among others, and a linking commentary, chronological table and bibliography are provided for each one. In his introduction, John Dillon discusses the historical background and the sources of the text.

Translated by John Dillon and Tania Gergel with an introduction by John Dillon

---

PENGUIN CLASSICS

THE ODYSSEY
HOMER

'I long to reach my home and see the day of my return. It is my never-failing wish'

The epic tale of Odysseus and his ten-year journey home after the Trojan War forms one of the earliest and greatest works of Western literature. Confronted by natural and supernatural threats – shipwrecks, battles, monsters and the implacable enmity of the sea-god Poseidon – Odysseus must test his bravery and native cunning to the full if he is to reach his homeland safely and overcome the obstacles that, even there, await him.

E. V. Rieu's translation of *The Odyssey* was the very first Penguin Classic to be published, and has itself achieved classic status. For this edition, his text has been sensitively revised and a new introduction added to complement E. V. Rieu's original introduction.

'One of the world's most vital tales. *The Odyssey* remains central to literature'
Malcolm Bradbury.

Translated by E. V. Rieu
Revised translation by D. C. H. Rieu, with an introduction by Peter Jones

---

PENGUIN CLASSICS

THE RISE OF THE ROMAN EMPIRE
POLYBIUS

> 'If history is deprived of the truth,
> we are left with nothing but an idle, unprofitable tale'

In writing his account of the relentless growth of the Roman Empire, the Greek statesman Polybius (c. 200–118 BC) set out to help his fellow-countrymen understand how their world came to be dominated by Rome. Opening with the Punic War in 264 BC, he vividly records the critical stages of Roman expansion: its campaigns throughout the Mediterranean, the temporary setbacks inflicted by Hannibal and the final destruction of Carthage in 146 BC. An active participant in contemporary politics, as well as a friend of many prominent Roman citizens, Polybius was able to draw on a range of eyewitness accounts and on his own experiences of many of the central events, giving his work immediacy and authority.

Ian Scott-Kilvert's translation fully preserves the clarity of Polybius' narrative. This substantial selection of the surviving volumes is accompanied by an introduction by F. W. Walbank, which examines Polybius' life and times, and the sources and technique he employed in writing his history.

Translated by Ian Scott-Kilvert
Selected with an introduction by F. W. Walbank

PENGUIN CLASSICS

THE POLITICS
ARISTOTLE

'Man is by nature a political animal'

In *The Politics* Aristotle addresses the questions that lie at the heart of political science. How should society be ordered to ensure the happiness of the individual? Which forms of government are best and how should they be maintained? By analysing a range of city constitutions – oligarchies, democracies and tyrannies – he seeks to establish the strengths and weaknesses of each system to decide which are the most effective, in theory and in practice. A hugely significant work, which has influenced thinkers as diverse as Aquinas and Machiavelli, *The Politics* remains an outstanding commentary on fundamental political issues and concerns, and provides fascinating insights into the workings and attitudes of the Greek city-state.

The introductions by T. A. Sinclair and Trevor J. Saunders discuss the influence of *The Politics* on philosophers, its modern relevance and Aristotle's political beliefs. This edition contains Greek and English glossaries, and a bibliography for further reading.

Translated by T. A. Sinclair
Revised and re-presented by Trevor J. Saunders

PENGUIN CLASSICS

THE BIRDS AND OTHER PLAYS
ARISTOPHANES

The Knights/Peace/The Birds/The Assemblywomen/Wealth

'Oh wings are splendid things, make no mistake:
they really help you rise in the world'

The plays collected in this volume, written at different times in Aristophanes'
forty-year career as a dramatist, all contain his trademark bawdy comedy and
dazzling verbal agility. In *The Birds*, two frustrated Athenians join with the birds to
build the utopian city of 'Much Cuckoo in the Clouds'. *The Knights* is a venomous
satire on Cleon, the prominent Athenian demagogue, while *The Assemblywomen*
considers the war of the sexes, as the women of Athens infiltrate the all-male
Assembly in disguise. The lengthy conflict with Sparta is the subject of *Peace*,
inspired by the hope of a settlement in 421 BC, and *Wealth* reflects the economic
catastrophe that hit Athens after the war, as the god of riches is depicted as a
ragged, blind old man.

The lively translations by David Barrett and Alan H. Sommerstein capture the full
humour of the plays. The introduction examines Aristophanes' life and times, and
the comedy and poetry of his works. This volume also includes an introductory
note for each play.

Translated with an introduction by David Barrett and Alan H. Sommerstein

PENGUIN CLASSICS

THE REPUBLIC
PLATO

> 'We are concerned with the most important of issues,
> the choice between a good and an evil life'

Plato's *Republic* is widely acknowledged as the cornerstone of Western philosophy. Presented in the form of a dialogue between Socrates and three different interlocutors, it is an inquiry into the notion of a perfect community and the ideal individual within it. During the conversation other questions are raised: what is goodness; what is reality; what is knowledge? *The Republic* also addresses the purpose of education and the roles of both women and men as 'guardians' of the people. With remarkable lucidity and deft use of allegory, Plato arrives at a depiction of a state bound by harmony and ruled by 'philosopher kings'.

Desmond Lee's translation of *The Republic* has come to be regarded as a classic in its own right. His introduction discusses contextual themes such as Plato's disillusionment with Athenian politics and the trial of Socrates. This new edition also features a revised bibliography.

Translated with an introduction by Desmond Lee